Etching techniques

Etching Techniques

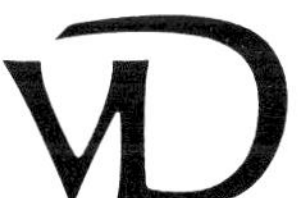

van Dobbenburgh Amsterdam/Kidderminster

Etching techniques
Original titel. Etstechnieken
Editors: Robert Klaster, Jaap Krijff
Translation from the Dutch
The Old Rectory, Pyworthy,
Holsworthy, Devon. Ex 22 6LA, England

English Edition distributed by
Ruskin Book services Ltd.
15 Comberton Hill, Kidderminster
Worcestershire DY 10 1QG U.K.
Telephone 0562 515151 and 68014
Telex RBS 335672
Printed in Spain by I.G. Domingo, S.A. San Joan Despí

ISBN 9-06-557036-4

Contents

Introduction

Etching is a method of printing in depth in which the hollowed out parts of the etching medium (copper or zinc plate) are filled in with printing ink which is transferred to paper when the paper is pressed against it in a printing press.

The hollowed out areas are created through the action of acid applied in particular places, i.e., 'etching'.

This technique was used in the Middle Ages, mainly by Arab weaponsmiths in Damascus, to decorate the metal of weapons; the hollowed out areas were then filled with pigment or soot. In some cases prints were made on parchment or paper to check the engraving that had been made.

This method was first adopted in Europe during the fifteenth century, and at the beginning of the sixteenth century it was first used by artists including Urs Graf (1513), Albrecht Dürer (1515) in Germany, Lucas van Leiden, Hendrik Goltzius and Breughel the Elder in the Netherlands.

These used the technique for making prints.

Since then, etching has continued to be an important graphic technique and it is still widely used by artists.

Preparing a zinc plate for a zinc etching

The lines or planes which form the picture are hollowed into the metal by the action of acids or salts; they are then filled with ink. The derivation of the term 'etching', as this technique is called, refers to the corrosive effect of acids on metal. It is based on a word meaning to make something eat or bite.
The so-called 'dry needle' technique and engraving are also included under the heading of etching techniques, although no acids are used and the lines are scratched or cut into the metal by hand.
When the prepared plate had been inked, it is passed through an etching press, a type of rolling press, which presses the ink from the grooves onto dampened paper.
Before starting the etching the metal plate should first be cut to size and the edges should be filed at an angle or rounded. You can also buy the zinc plates ready-made and polished – they have a protected back. However, it is more economical to buy the plates from a plumber or ironmonger's shop.
A zinc plate of 14 or 16 mm is thick enough for etching, When you have cut the plate to size, polish it with waterproof polishing paper (no. 400-1200).
To sand or polish the plate, start with the coarsest polishing paper and rub with circular movements, then use increasingly fine papers and repeat the process until the plate is polished quite smooth.
While you are polishing use water to keep the plate quite wet. Finally, finish the polishing with a metal polish (Brasso or Sidol).
Unpolished plates produce a light grey tone on the prints. Instructions are given below on how to cut the plates to size and prepare them for making an etching. You will need the following materials:
files, emery paper suitable for metal, zinc, a steel rule, a pen, clamps, a hammer, nails, engraving needles, a steel scraper, metal polish, some steel wool, a piece of wood and a table.

1

Lay out the tools and materials required which are listed above.

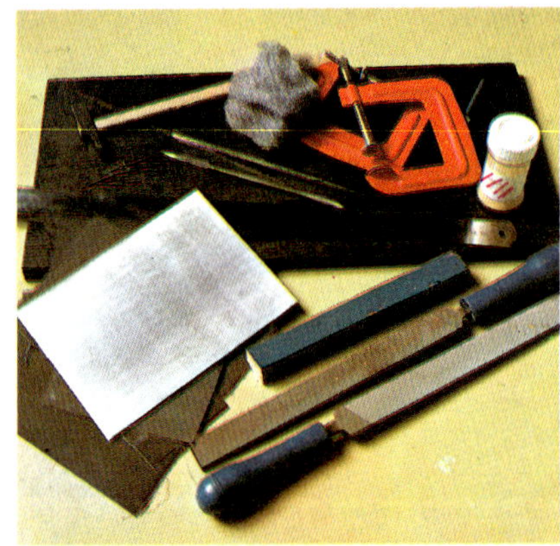

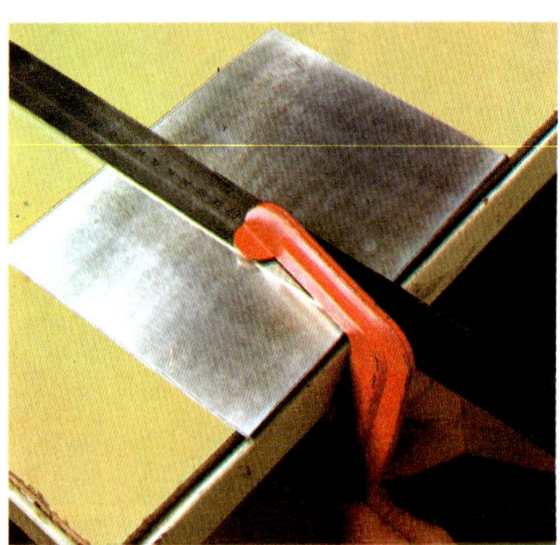

2

Clamp the zinc plate and the ruler onto the table at the required size.

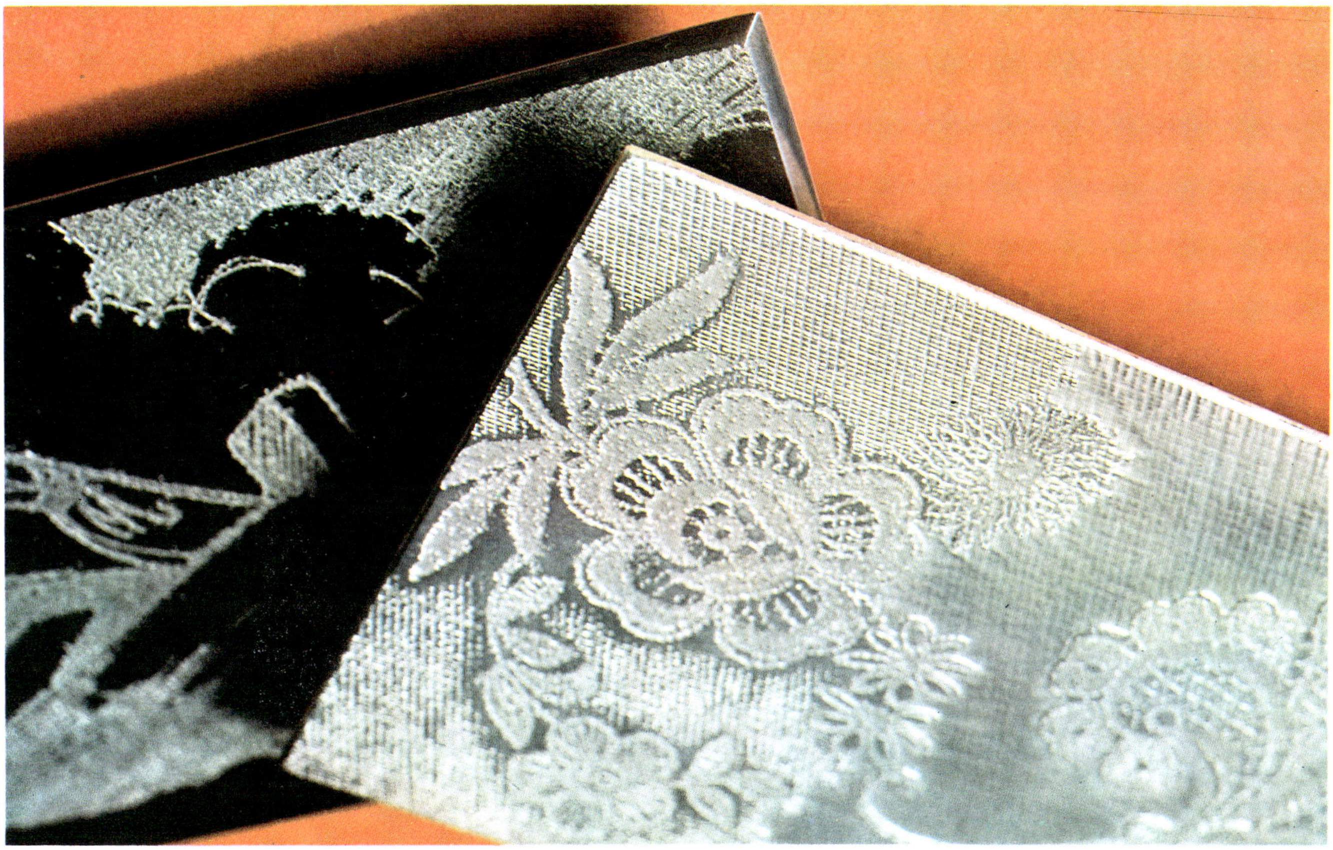

3

Score into the plate along the ruler with a steel pen or zinc cutter until there is a deep groove.

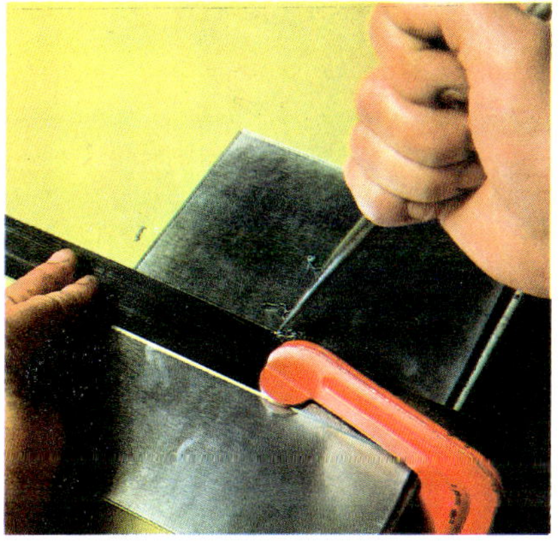

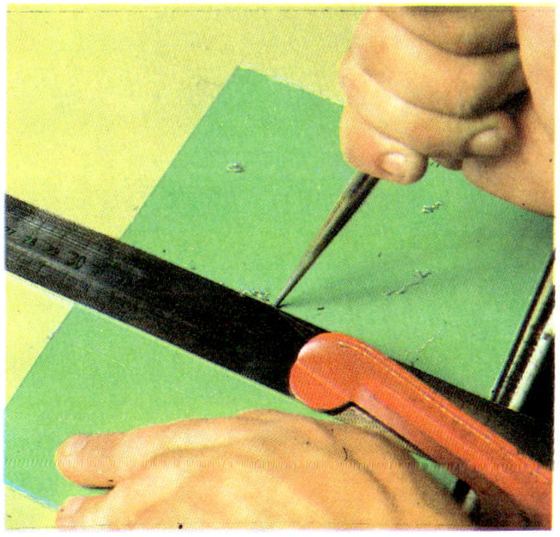

4

Turn the plate over and score it with the pen on the other side in the same place. The green colour on the back of the plate is an acid-proof layer.

5

Lay the plate on the edge of the table and carefully press down along the groove.

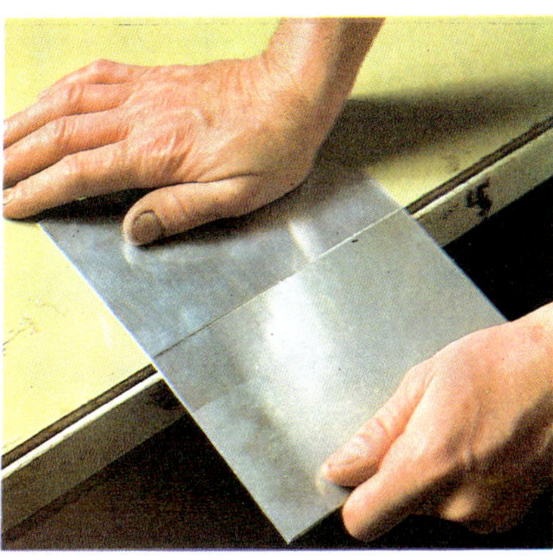

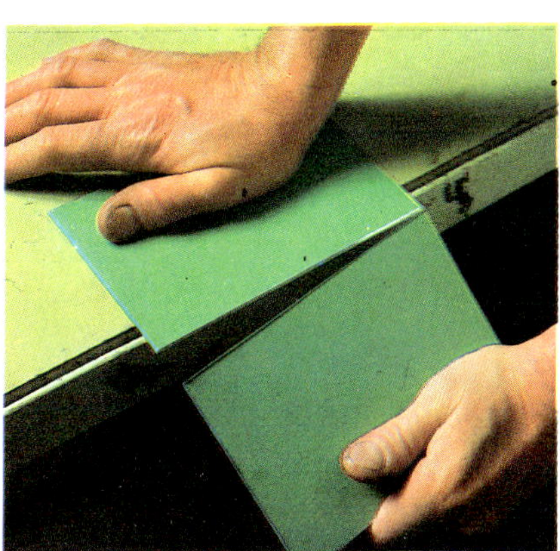

6

If the plate was carefully scored, it will break exactly along the groove.

7

With a steel scraper remove any burrs which may have been formed when the plate was cut.

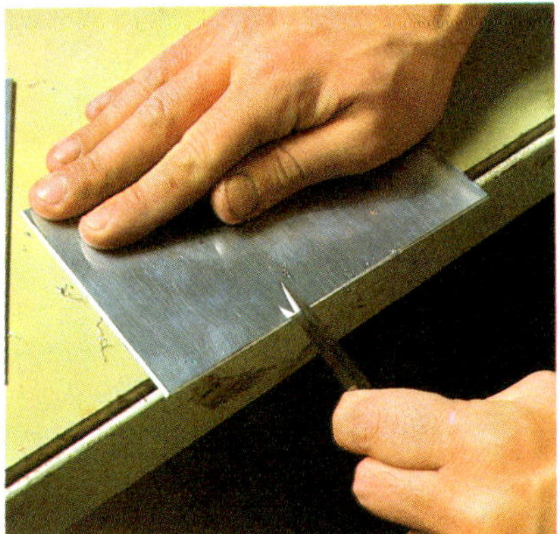

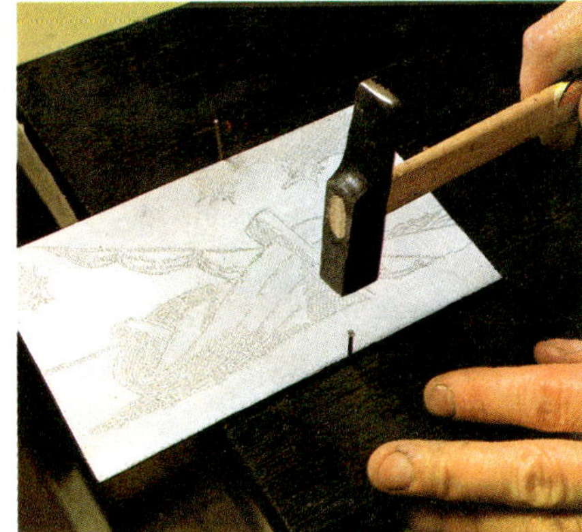

8

Fix the plate to the table with a few nails at the edges so that it cannot move about. In the example the plate has already been etched.

9

With a coarse file, file the four sides of the plate at an angle.

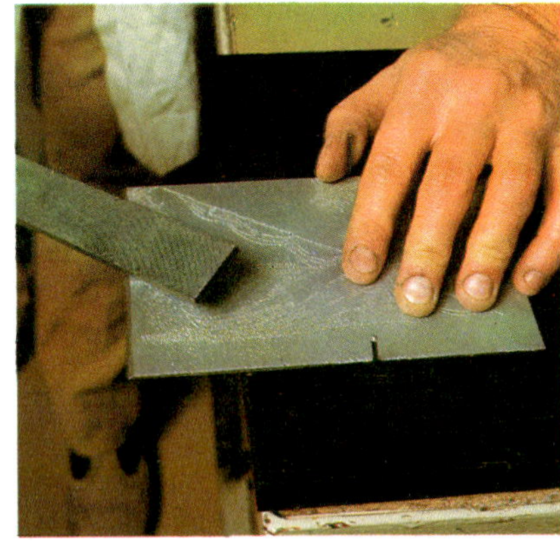

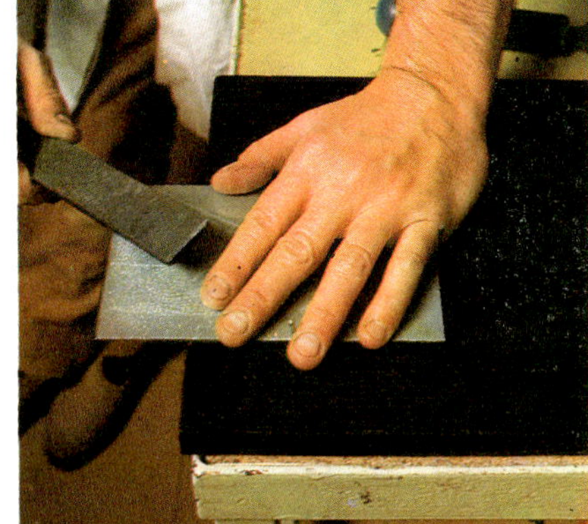

10

Remove the burrs along the edges with a fine file.

11

Wrap the piece of wood with waterproof sandpaper and wet it with water. Then sand the edge as smooth as possible.

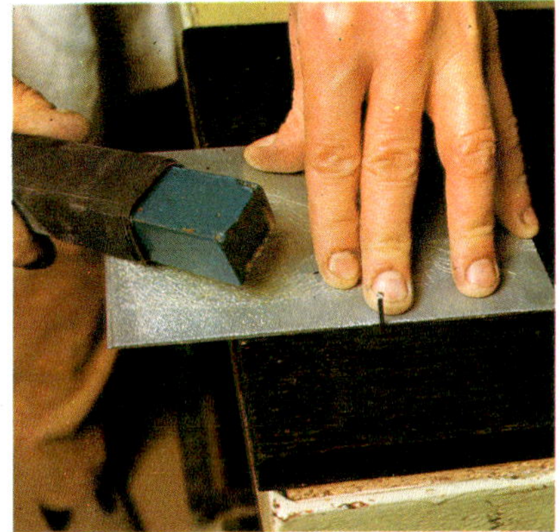

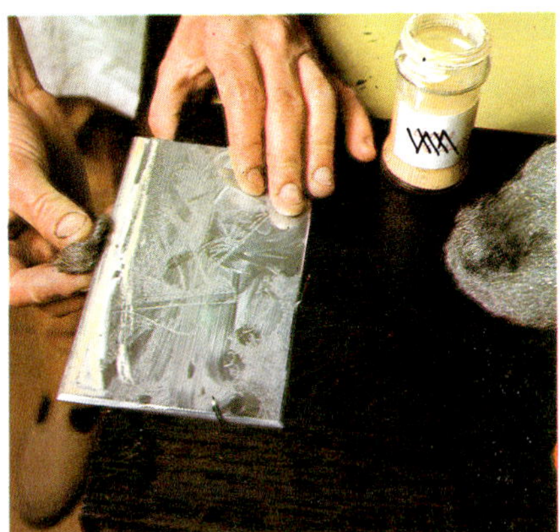

12

Remove all unevennesses from the edges with metal polish and steel wool so that they look quite shiny.

13

Cut and etched zinc plates may have two sorts of edges, bevelled or rounded, as shown in photographs 12 and 13.

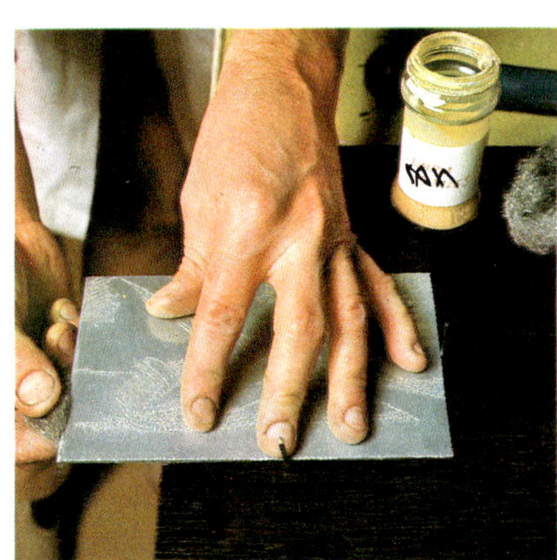

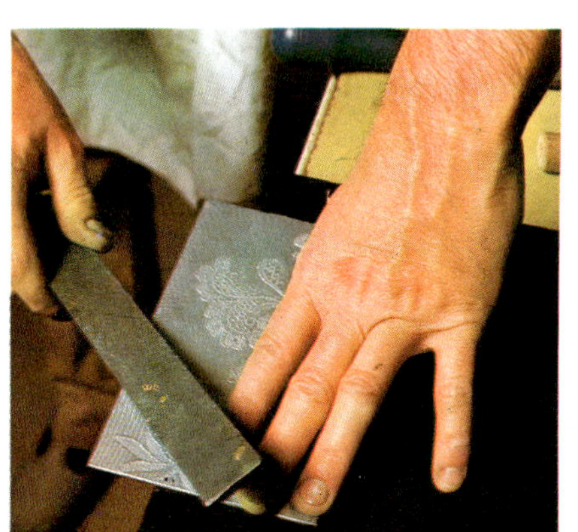

14

Using a file, completely smooth the edges.

Dry needle etching

The dry needle technique is the technique in which a solid and sharp needle is used to scratch onto the metal plate, without the necessity of using an acid solution. Although it is normally described as a 'dry needle etching', this is not strictly correct, as no acid is used. Unlike the burin, which is used to engrave deep grooves, the grooves cut using the dry needle technique are shallow, leaving burrs on one or both sides of the line which are very characteristic of this technique.

The burrs retain a lot of ink, and this produces a typically velvety finish. However, the numer of prints that can be made is very small compared with the number that can be produced with the burin technique. This is

This seascape is a print of a zinc plate which has been worked with the dry needle technique, without the use of an acid bath.

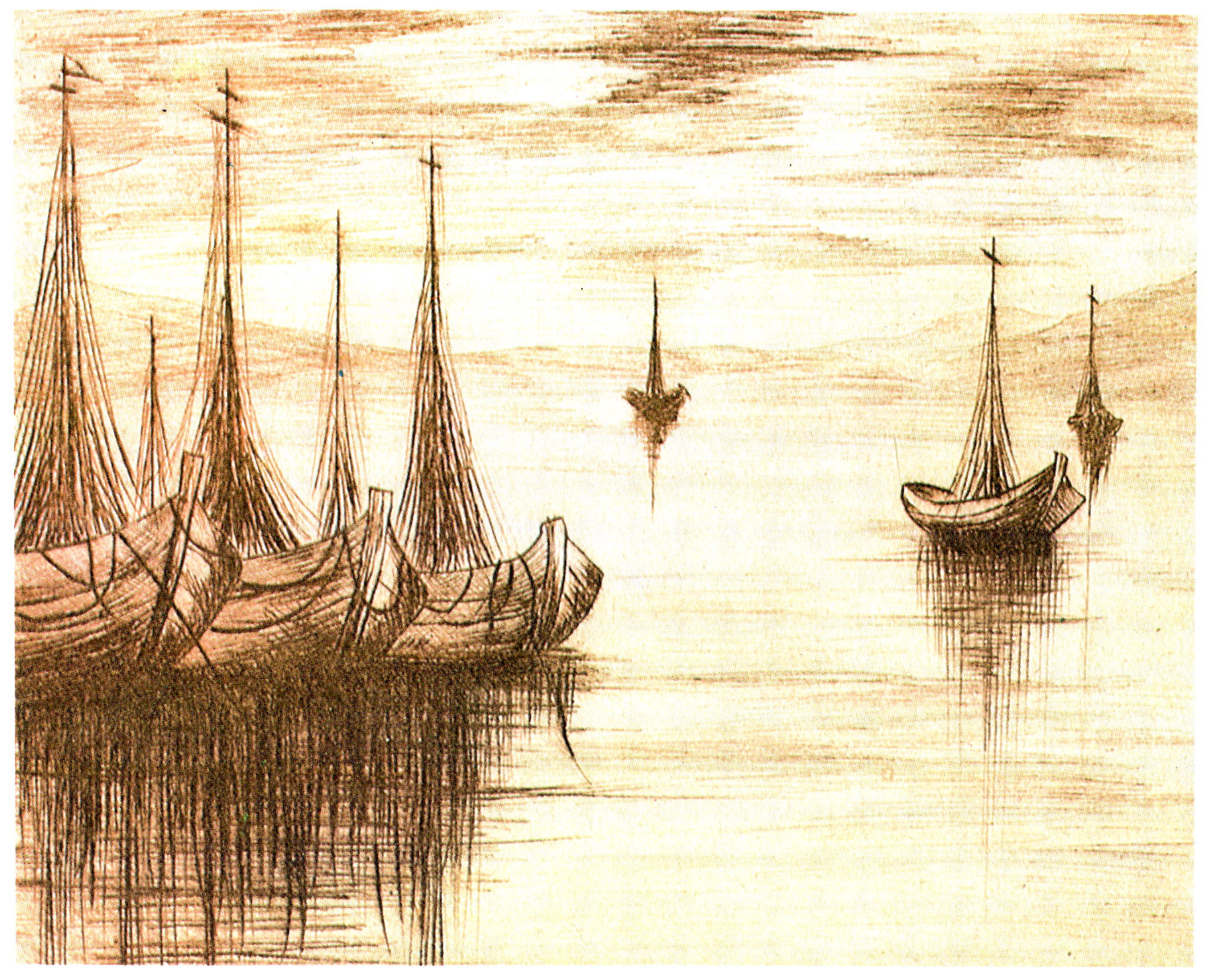

because the burrs gradually disappear during printing. If desired, the burrs can also be partly removed. It depends on the artist's creativity whether the burrs should be removed, either partially or totally, according to the subject matter. The materials and tools required are: a press, a design, carbon paper, a zinc plate, blotting paper, printing paper, a tray, a bowl of water, sandpaper, fine steel wool, a spatula, a steel scraper, a steel polisher, a steel dry needle, ink, methylated spirits (meths), alcohol and metal polish.

1

All the tools and materials required (see above).

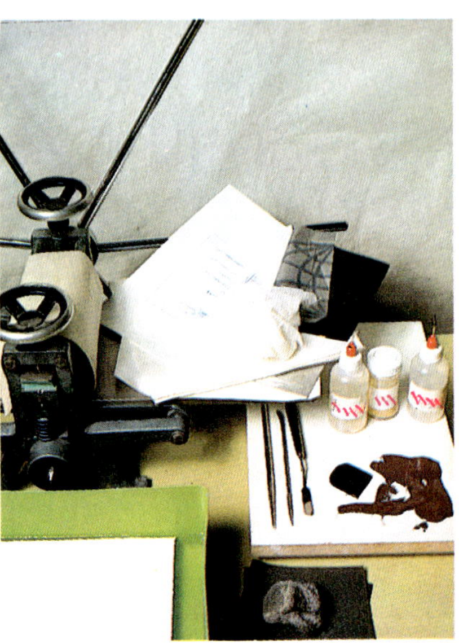

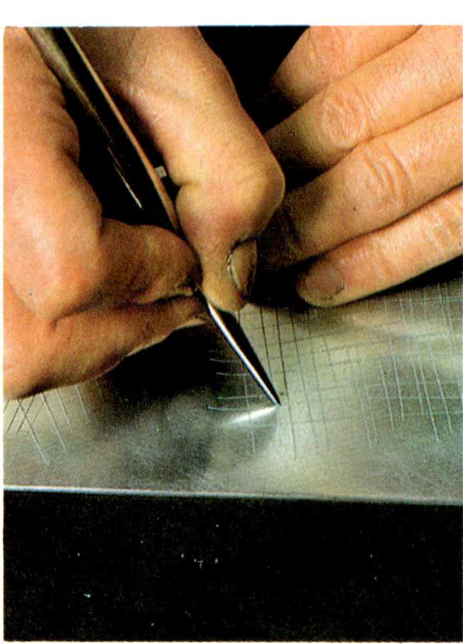

2

Make a few scratches with the steel dry needle producing some burrs.

3

These burrs can also be removed.

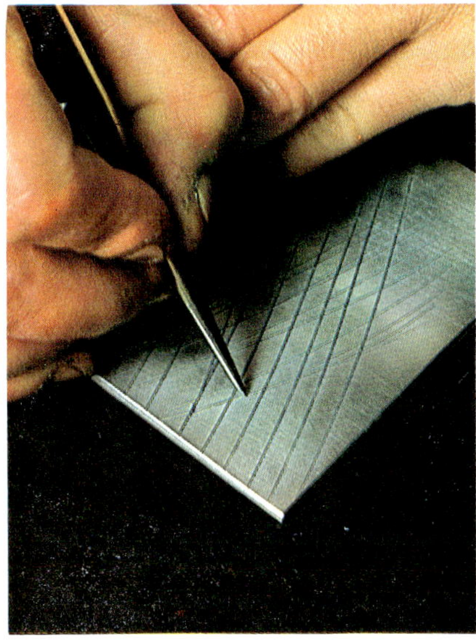

4

Using a steel scraper, the burrs are removed from part of the lines.

5

Now treat these lines with a steel polisher.

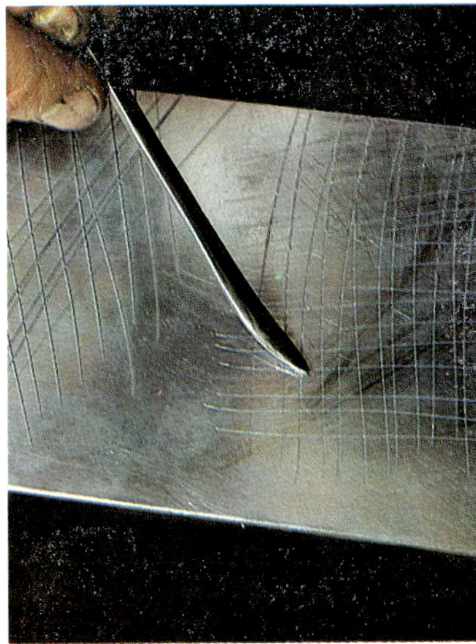

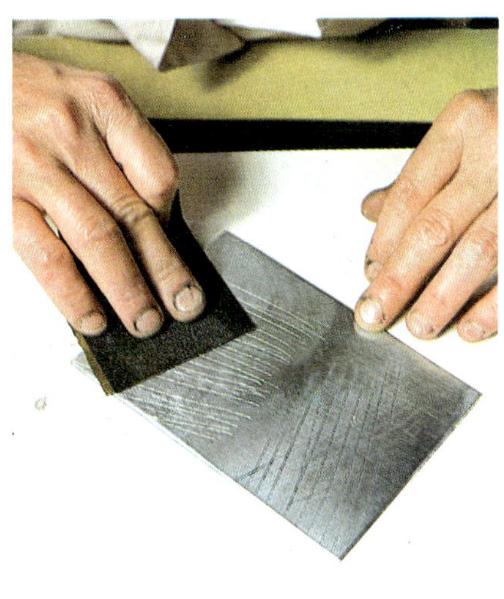

6

Remove any unevennesses with very fine sandpaper and some water.

7

The unevennesses are the result of using a steel scraper and steel polisher.

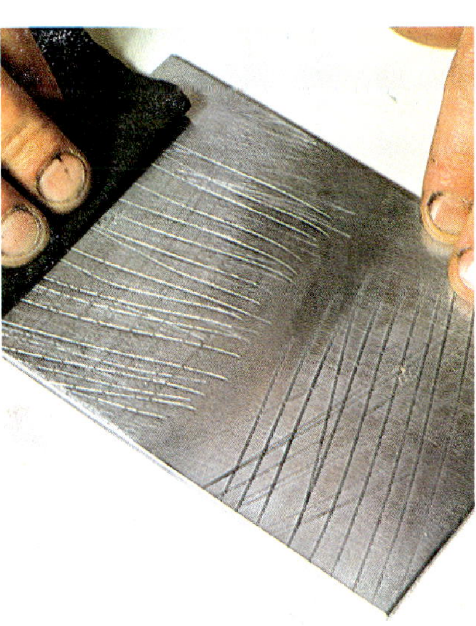

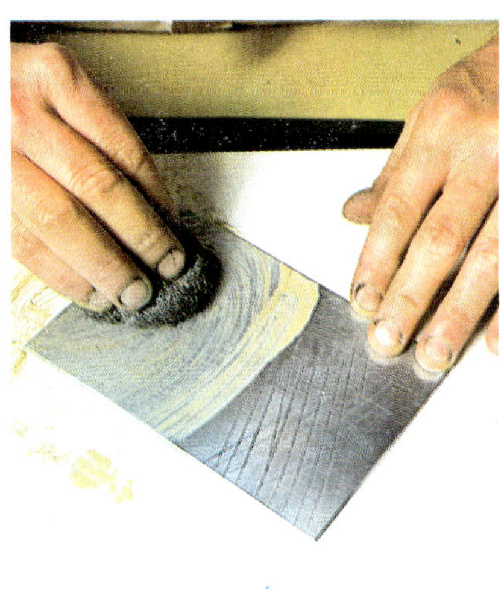

8

Go over the lines that have been sanded, using fine steel wool and metal polish.

9

Dry the metal plate and rub to a shine with a cloth.

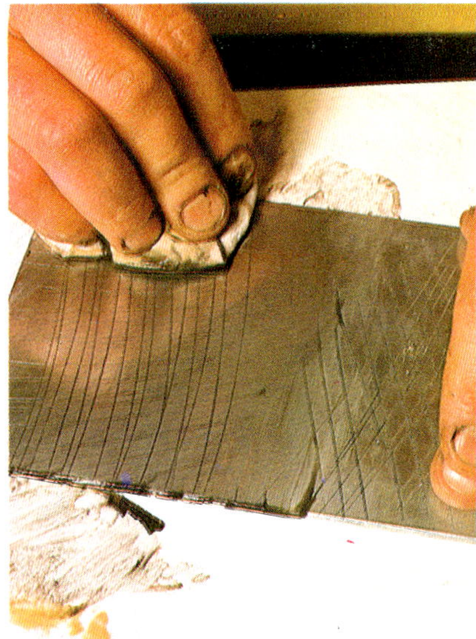

10

Make a print. The difference between the grooves with burrs and those without is clearly visible both on the plate and the paper.

11

Do a drawing and transfer it to the zinc plate with carbon paper.

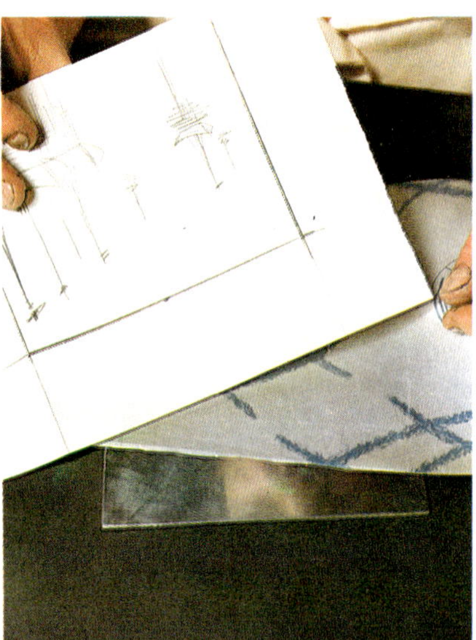

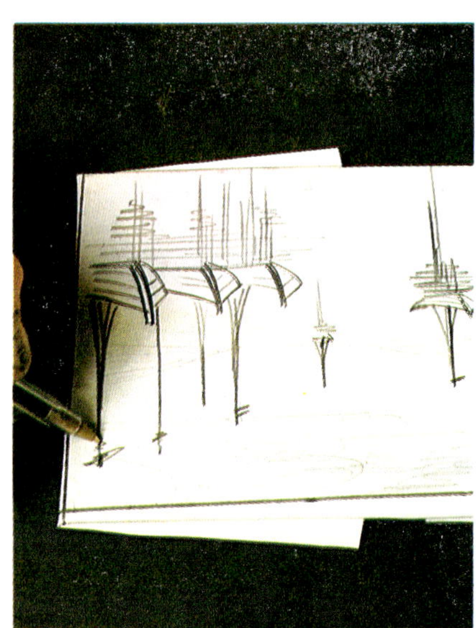

12

The drawing and the carbon paper should be securely placed on the plate.

13

Follow the lines on the plate with a dry needle.

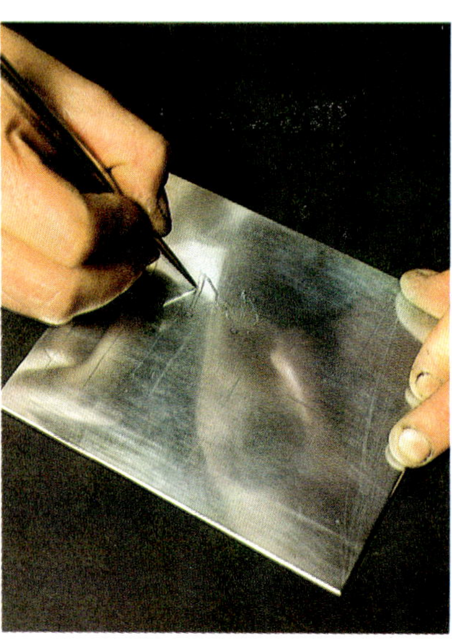

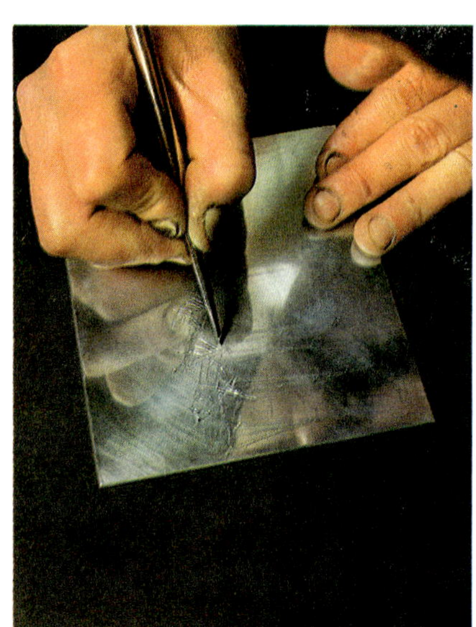

14

Do not press too hard, or there will be too many burrs.

15
Complete the drawing.

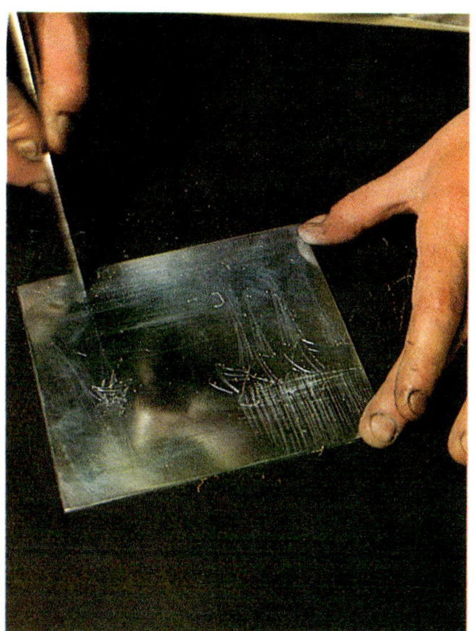

16
The drawing is finally ready.

17
Now apply ink to the plate with a rubber spatula.

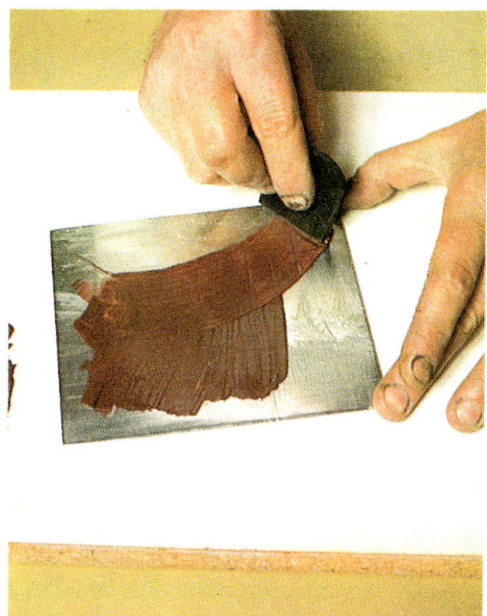

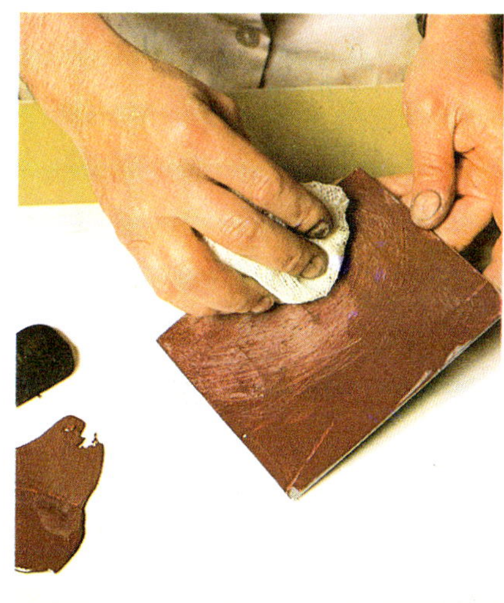

18
Rub the plate with a piece of cheesecloth so that the ink fills the lines and the rest is wiped off.

19
Clean the plate – especially those parts where there are fewer grooves – with a piece of cheesecloth.

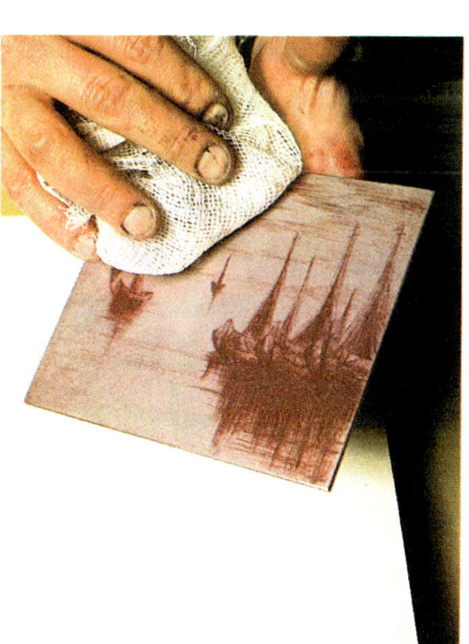

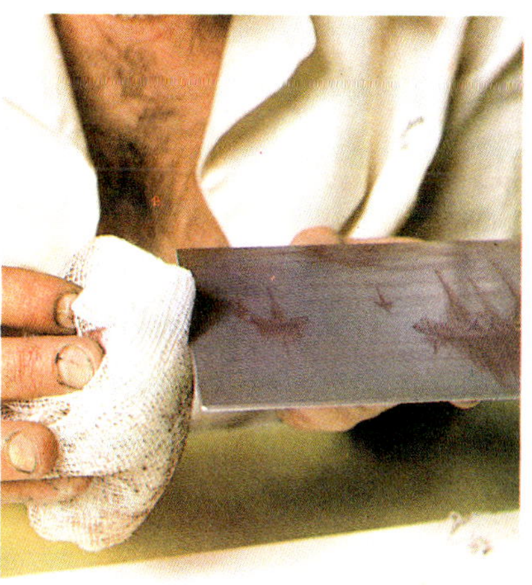

20
Make sure the edges are clean so that there are no marks on the prints.

21
Finally, remove the last traces of ink from the edges with a cloth.

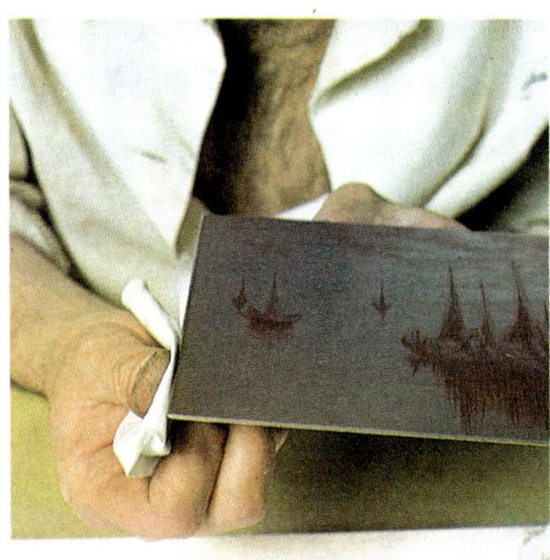

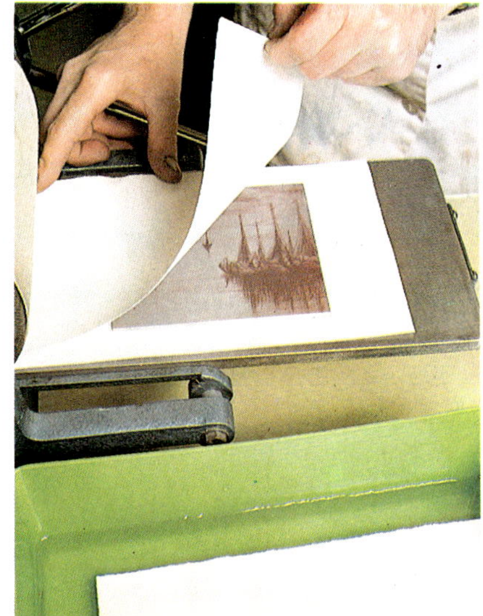

22
Lay the plate on the bed of the press and cover with printing paper.

23
Pass the plate through the press steadily. This is how the print is made.

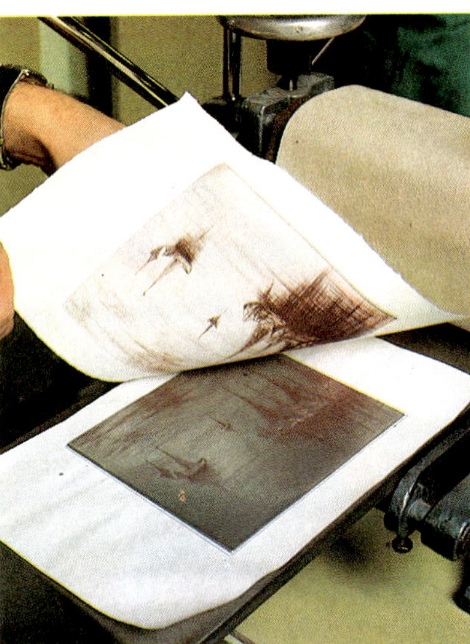

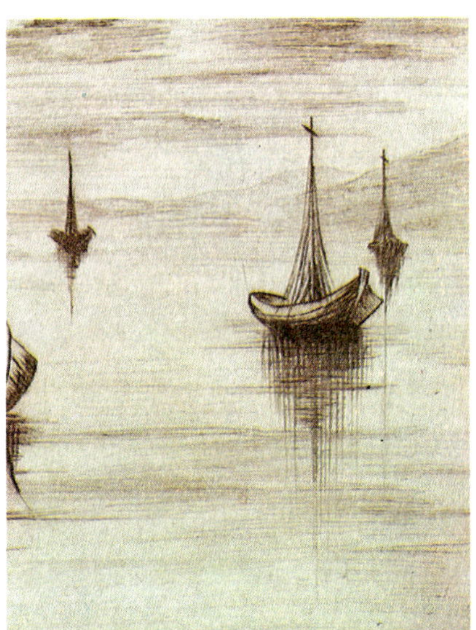

24
This example shows how the dry needle technique has been used successfully to depict the ships' sails.

Etching a zinc plate

Now that you know how to prepare a zinc plate before starting an etching, you can make a first attempt at etching based on the previous exercises. You could start, for example, with a church and a few trees in the distance, and a large tree in the foreground taking up most of the plate. It should therefore be etched with slightly deeper and broader lines.

When all traces of grease have been removed from the zinc plate and it has been covered with an acid resistant layer, the drawing can be scratched into this layer with an etching needle.

Use the etching needle like a pencil. If you want to draw different thicknesses, use needles with different diameters. It doesn't matter if there are mistakes in your drawing, as any unwanted lines can be erased by covering them with varnish.

It is not necessary to exert a lot of pressure in the drawing as long as you make sure that the metal is laid bare. Zinc plates are best for printing because zinc has an attractive light grey colour and is softer and more easy to etch on than copper, as well being cheaper. In addition, it reacts faster and better to acid than other metals do.

For this reason, zinc plates are used in the etchings in our examples.

Some advice for beginners in this technique follows below, but always remember: practice makes perfect.

The etching liquid is prepared in a plastic bath (photographic bath) or a bath made of a material that is not affected by acid.

The nitric acid that can be bought commercially is usually in a 50% concentration. It should be kept in a glass bottle with a glass stopper, or in a plastic bottle. You also need a larger bottle to store used etching fluid. Label all the bottles containing acid clearly and keep the bottles out of the reach of children or anyone who might mistake them for something else. Never throw the acid down the sink or the toilet as nitric acid will corrode the drainage system and is very harmful to the environment. Most council cleaning services make special provisions for the disposal of acidic fluids.

When you have finished with the liquid, immediately return it to the storage bottle using a funnel.

Never leave a bath of acid standing longer than is strictly necessary. The fumes of nitric acid are injurious to the health of people, animals and plants.

If possible, work in a well ventilated room or under an extractor fan. Make sure that the acid never splashes in your eyes, but if this does happen, immediately rinse the eyes thoroughly and for a long time under running water. It's always advisable to wear rubber or plastic gloves.

For etching a zinc plate the 50% nitric acid silution should be diluted to approximately 15%. Pour six or seven measuring beakers (small glass or porcelain cups) of water into the etching bath and then gradually mix in one beaker of nitric acid. This will slightly increase the temperature of the etching solution. When the liquid has cooled down, test it by immersing a strip of zinc in the liquid and if a little gas is produced after about 1 minute (hydrogen) this is the correct concentration for etching.

If the gas produced is too little, add a small quantity of acid; if there is too much gas, dilute the solution with water.

When the drawing on the zinc plate is finished, place it in the acid bath and remove the gas bubbles with a feather so that the acid can easily get into the lines that have been drawn.

The following tools are required: a press, a zinc plate, a sketch, white carbon paper, water, nitric acid, asphalt, alcohol, petroleum, etching ink, an engraving needle, a brush or spatula for varnishing, a small file, a ballpoint pen, and a bath for the acid solution.

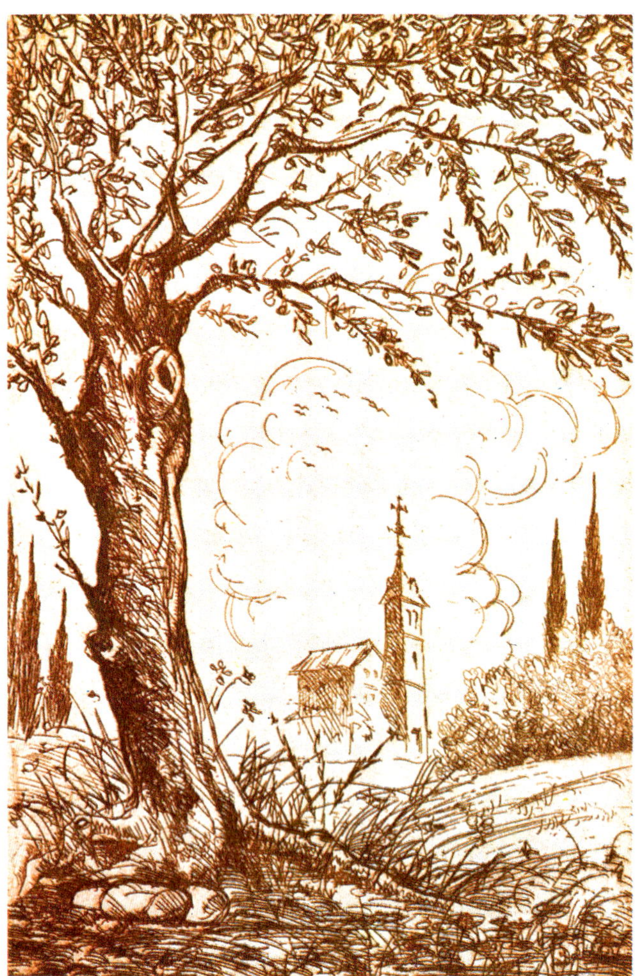

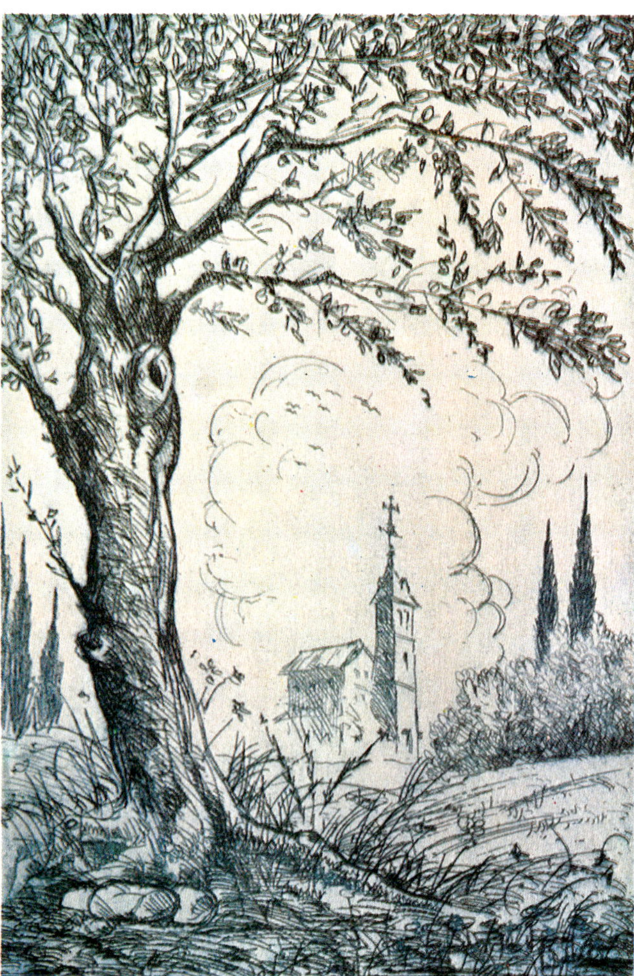

Two different coloured prints of the first etching.
This landscape printed on etching paper has been drawn on a zinc plate and immersed in nitric acid.
The types and colours of ink used in these prints are a question of personal preference.

1

All the tools and materials needed for etching (see previous page).

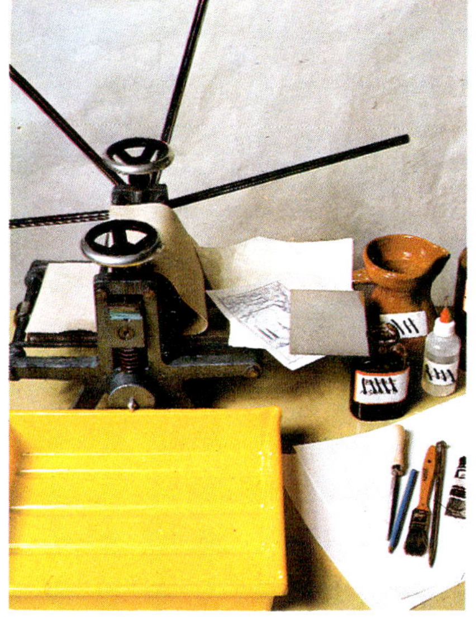

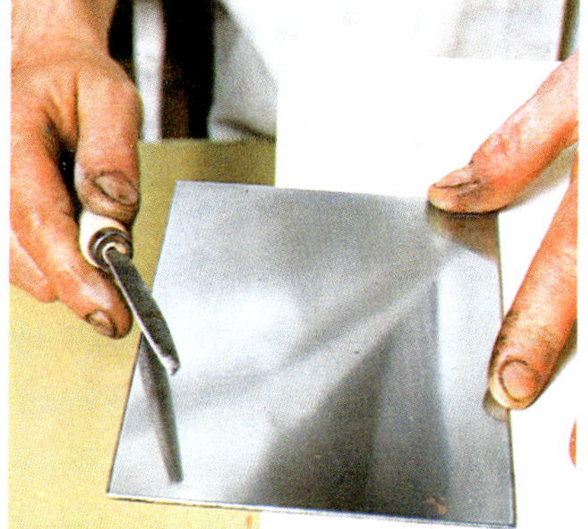

2

Now file the edges of the plate.

3

Cover the whole plate with liquid etching ground. If the back of the plate is not protected, first cover it with quick drying methylated spirit based varnish.

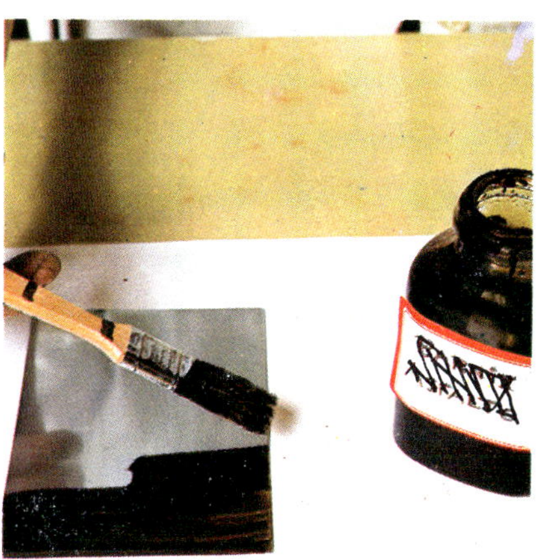

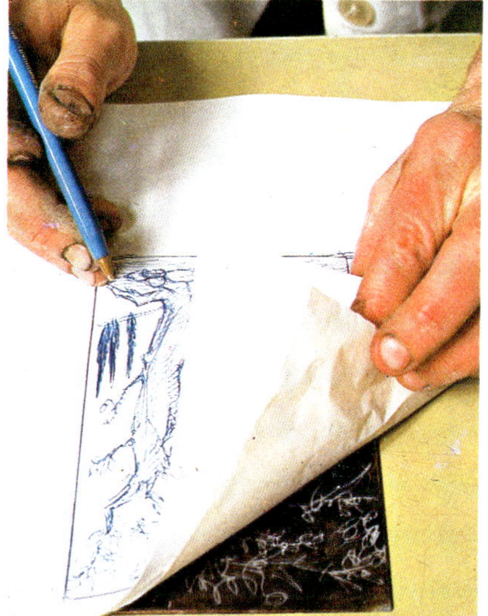

4

When the etching ground is dry, transfer the drawing to the plate with white carbon paper.

5

With an etching needle draw over the lines of the drawing into the etching foundation.

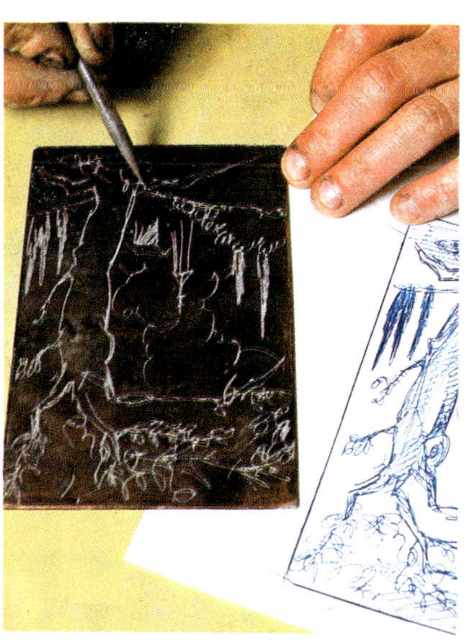

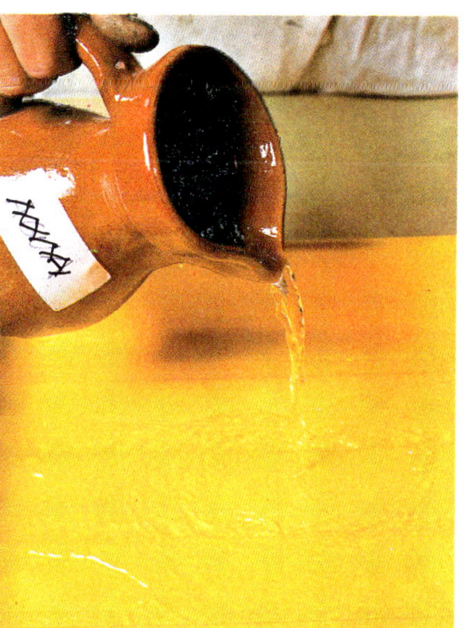

6

Pour water into the bath.

7

Add the nitric acid in the proportion of 1:6 in the correct order.

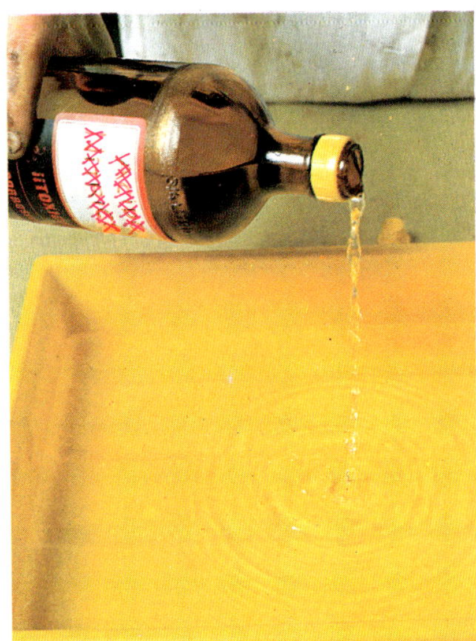

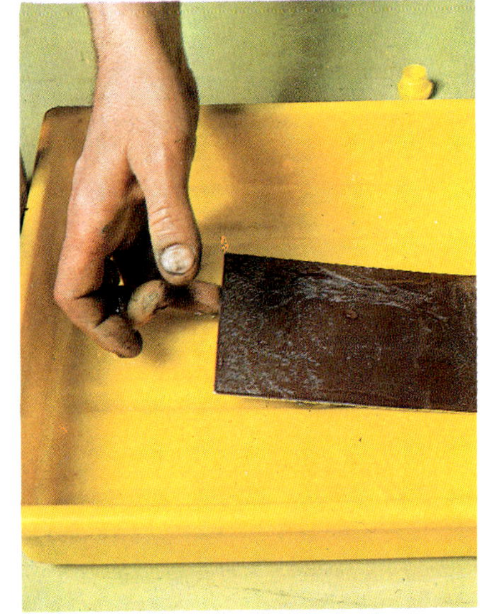

8

Lay the etched plate in the acid solution.

9

Leave the plate in the acid solution for between 45 minutes and 1 hour. Do not forget to brush the plate regularly with a feather to remove the bubbles of gas, and remember to wear gloves.

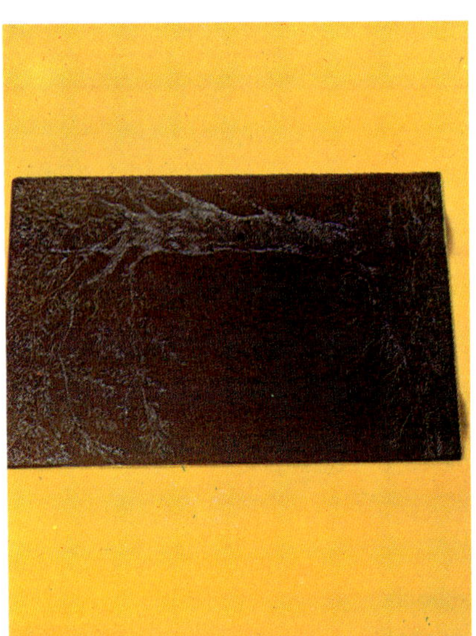

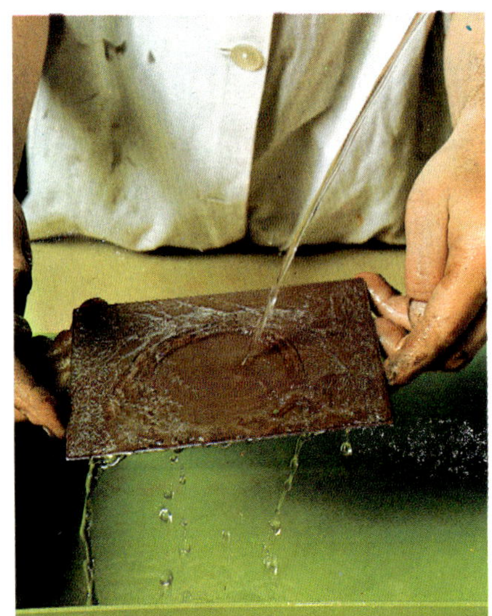

10

Take out the plate and rinse thoroughly in water.

11

Use a cloth soaked in turps to remove the ground from the plate and dissolve the methylated spirit based varnish on the back with methylated spirit, and clean.

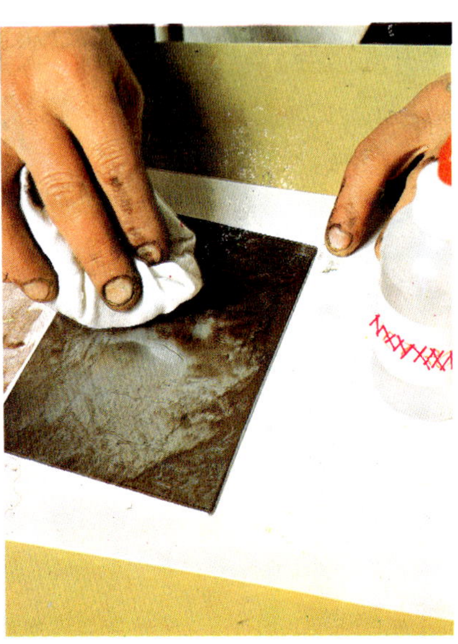

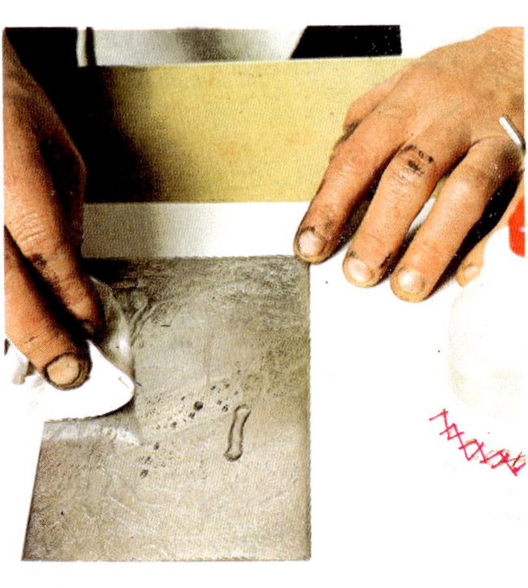

12

Immediately remove all traces of grease from the plate with a cloth soaked in meths.

13

Use a cheesecloth to spread ink over the plate.

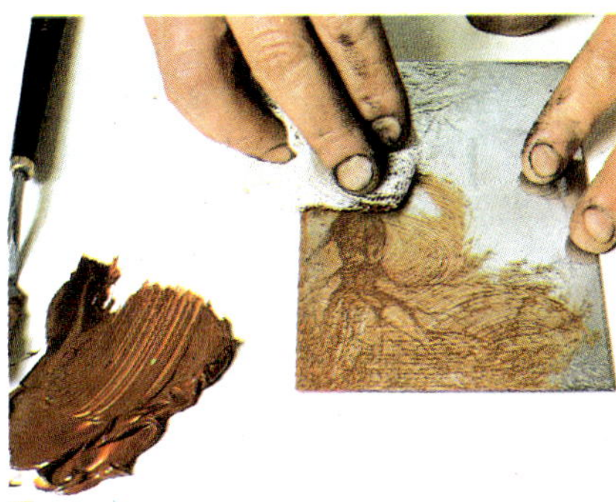

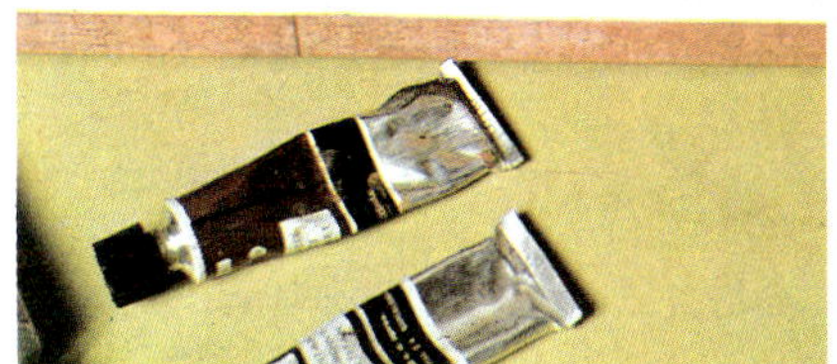

14

Carefully remove excess ink with a clean piece of cheesecloth.

15

Remove all the ink or leave a sheen. For a clear print you can strike the plate quickly with the palm of your hand.

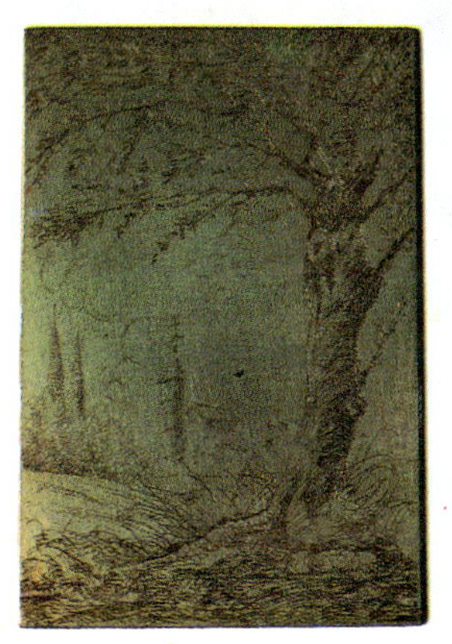

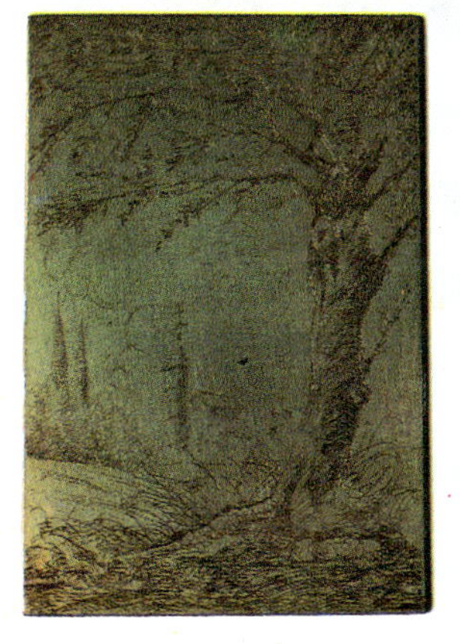

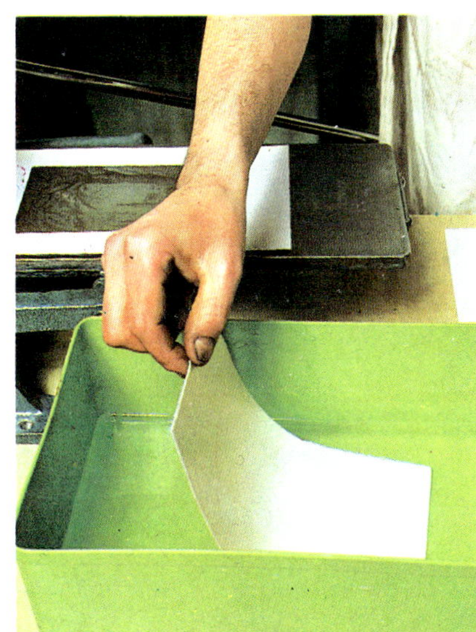

16

The paper used for printing should be soaked in water for an hour before use.

17

Take the paper out of the water and place between two sheets of blotting paper to absorb excess water.

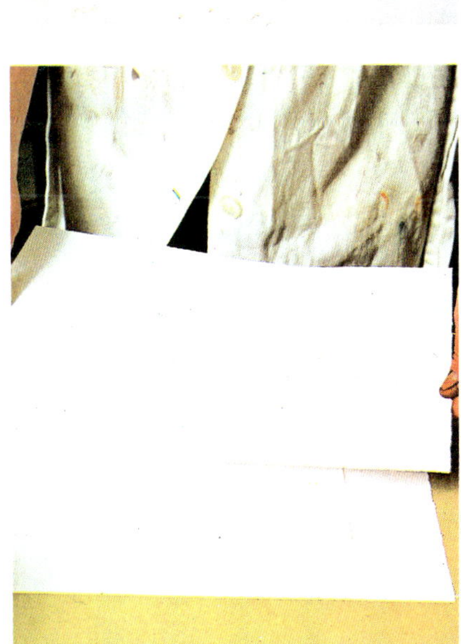

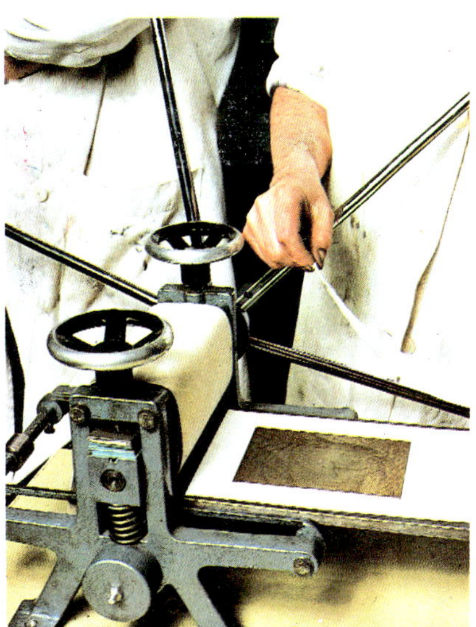

18

Place the plate in the press with the paper on top of it.

19

Now place the felt pad or cloths of the press on top of the paper and the plate.

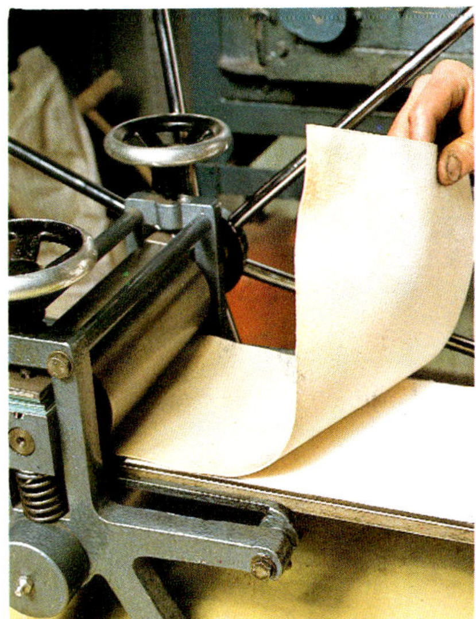

The lines used in etching
The lines etched into the zinc plate after it has been treated with acid can vary in width and depth, depending on the thickness of the engraving needle used and the pressure applied when drawing the lines.
When the print is made, the lines vary correspondingly in width.

20

Adjust the pressure on the press with the two adjustable screws. Push the plate between the rollers with the wheel.

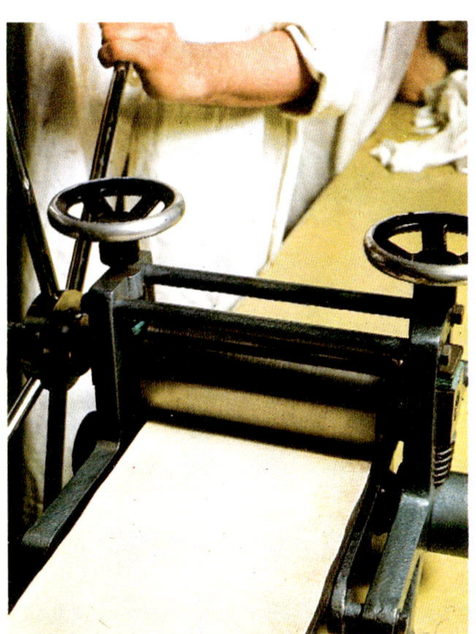

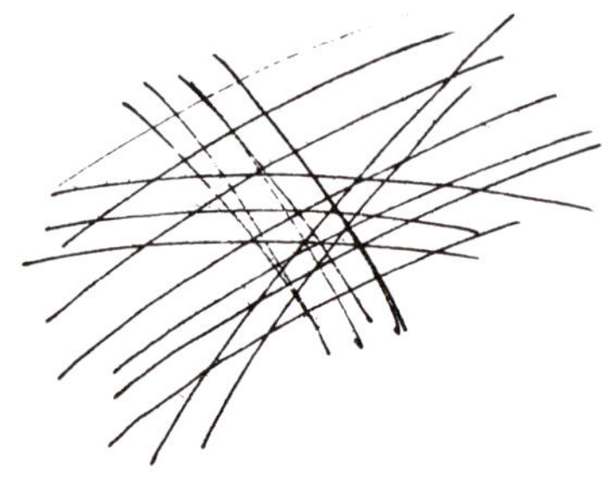

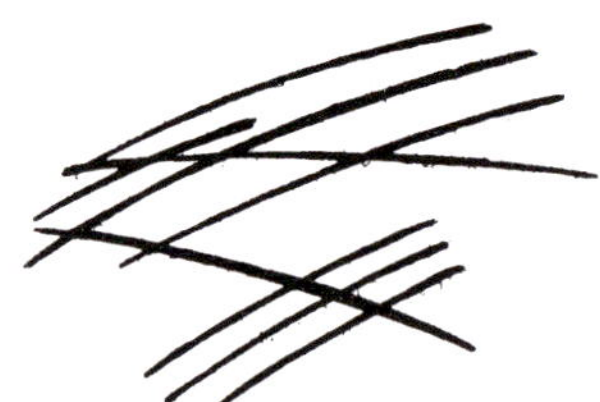

21

Lift off the pad and remove the paper with the printed drawing.

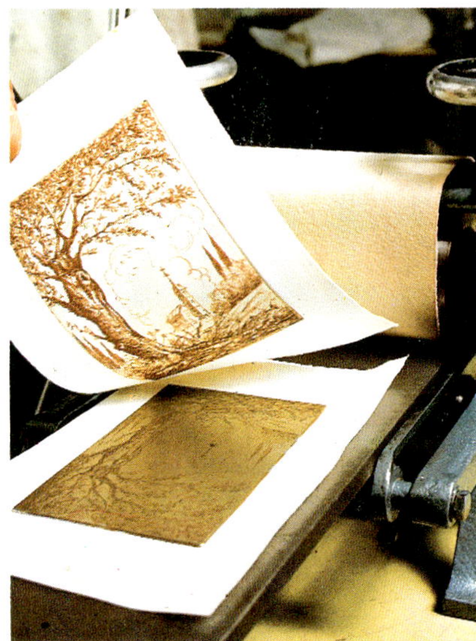

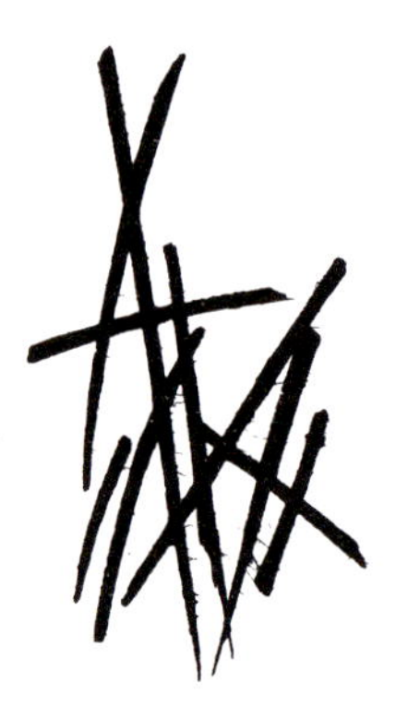

Correcting line etchings

When you are etching it is often necessary to erase lines which have been too deeply etched or which have been carelessly drawn. This is not very difficult but you must work patiently and precisely to avoid damaging the rest of the etching or removing too much of it. If you're not careful, you can do irreparable damage.
Before starting to correct the lines on the metal plate, examine a print from the plate very carefully to determine which parts and which lines need removing or correcting. This print should be used as the basis for the corrections and it should be compared with successive test prints. Use sharp steel scrapers to scrape out the lines and then use very fine steel wool to polish the corrected areas absolutely smooth.
This technique can be used to correct the etched lines on a plate which has already been etched.
You will need the following tools and materials to correct a line etching: a printing press, an etched plate, a print taken from this plate, blotting paper, metal polish, ink, meths, parafin, linseed oil, a whetstone, a spatula, a brush, a small spatula for applying the ink, a steel file, a steel scraper, an engraving pen, fine steel wool, tarlatan, tissue paper, various files and a rubber block to separate the ink.

1
All the tools and materials mentioned above.

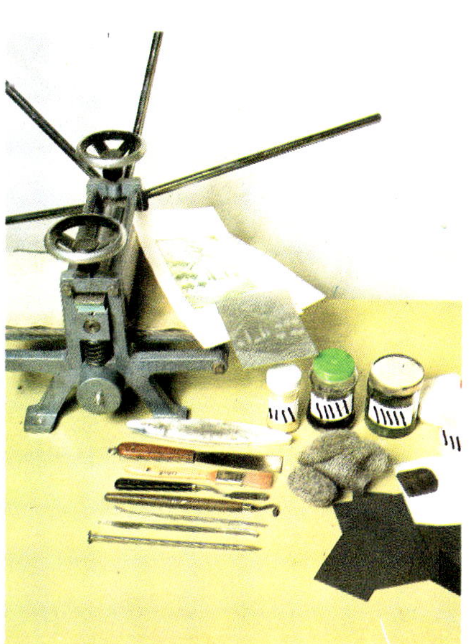

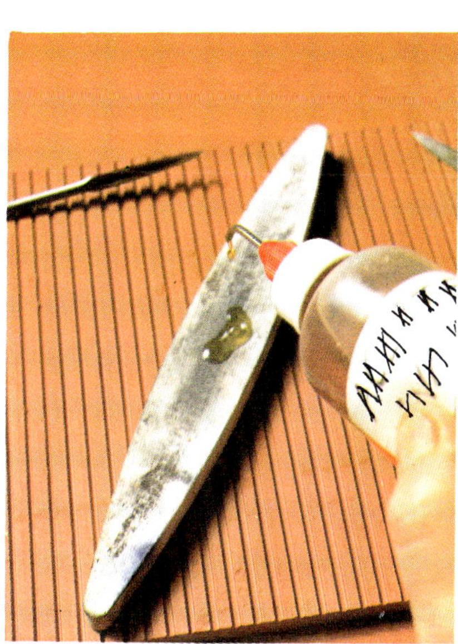

2
Drip a few drops of oil onto the whetstone to sharpen the steel file.

3
Add a drop of two of parafin to the oil before starting the sharpening.

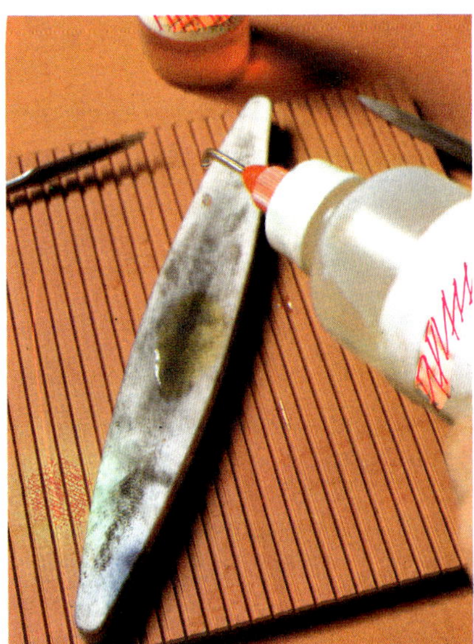

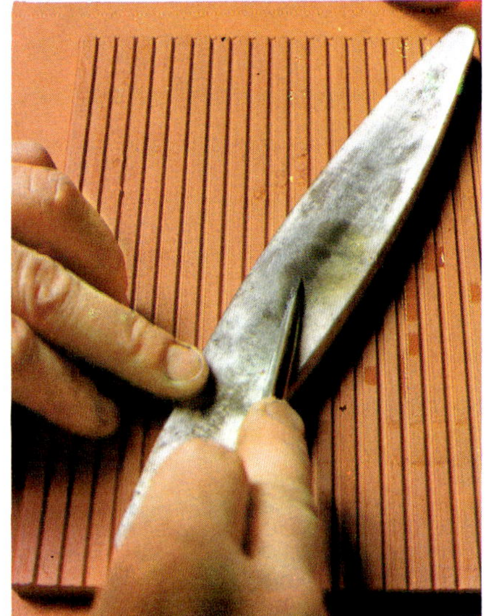

4
Sharpen the scraper by going over the whetstone with both flat sides.

5
Examine a print of the etching from which a few lines are to be removed.

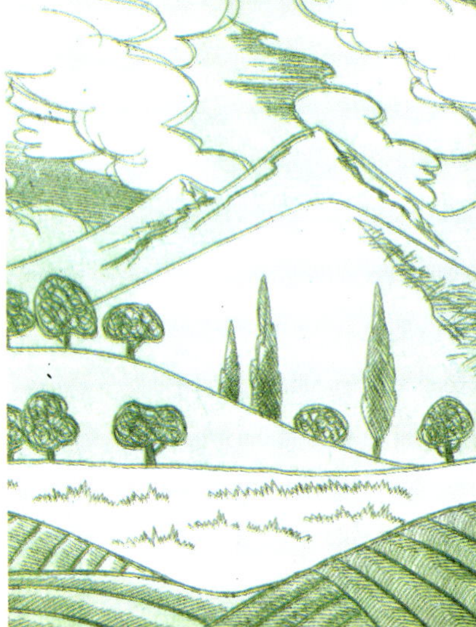

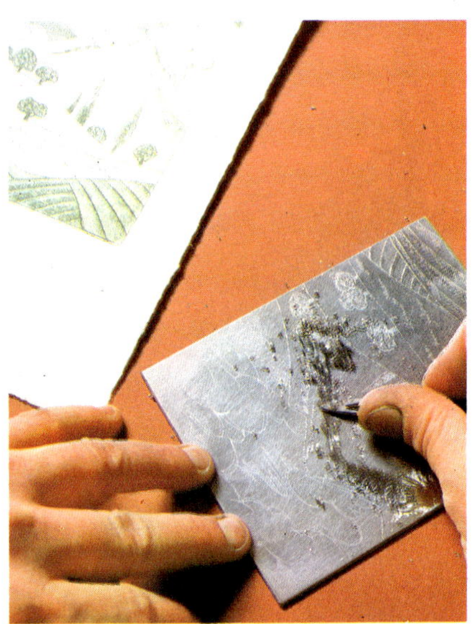

6
Remove these lines from the zinc plate with the steel scraper.

7
Remove not only the lines but also the area immediately surrounding them. Brush away the metal dust.

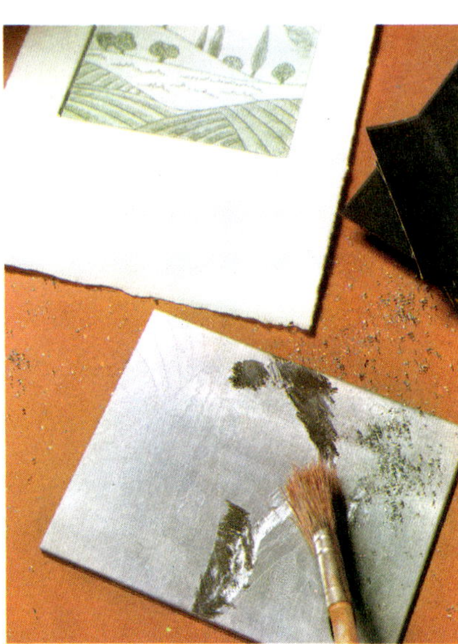

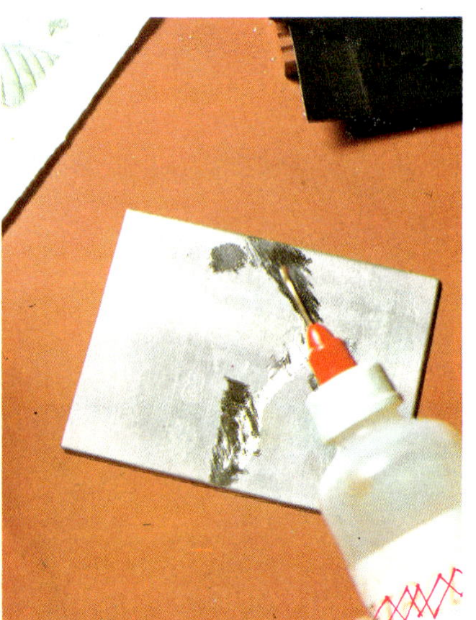

8
Before sanding, apply a few drops of parafin to the scraped areas; then sprinkle a little linseed oil onto the parafin.

9
Using sandpaper of various grades, sand the surface, removing the marks left by the scraper.

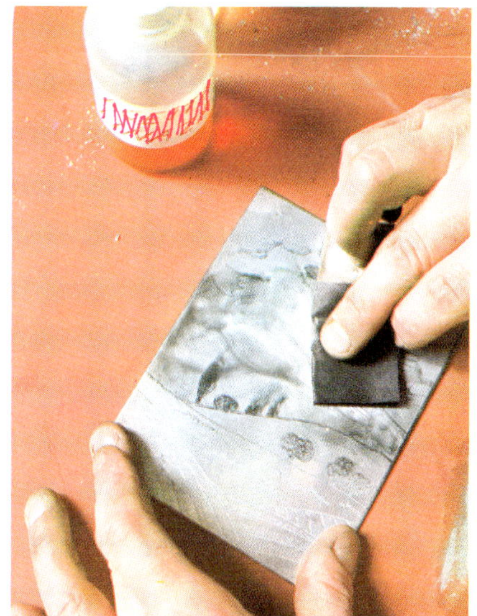

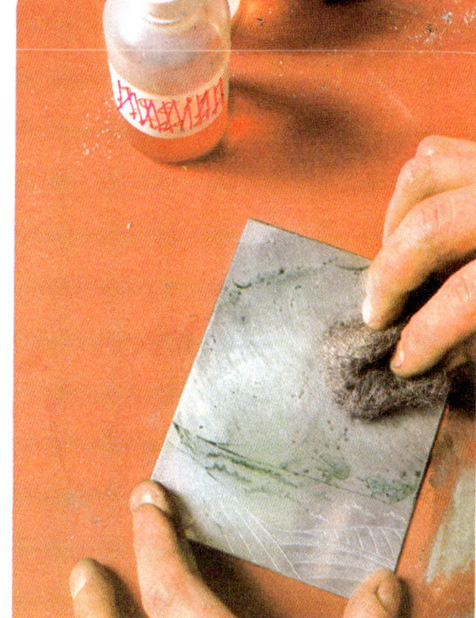

10
After using the finest grade of sandpaper, polish the plate absolutely smooth with steel wool or with metal polish (Sidol or Brasso).

11
Clean the plate with parafin and remove all traces of grease with a little meths.

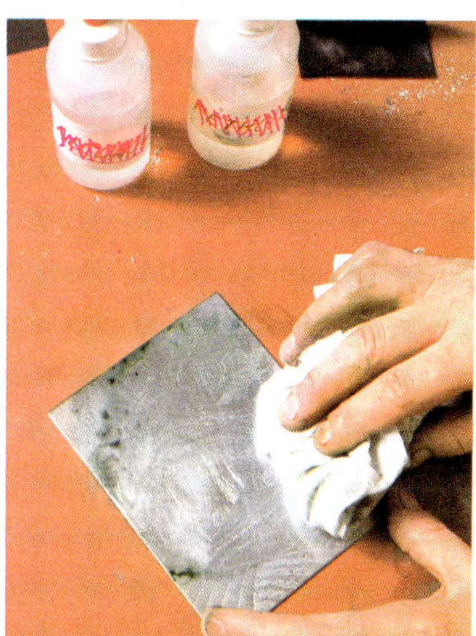

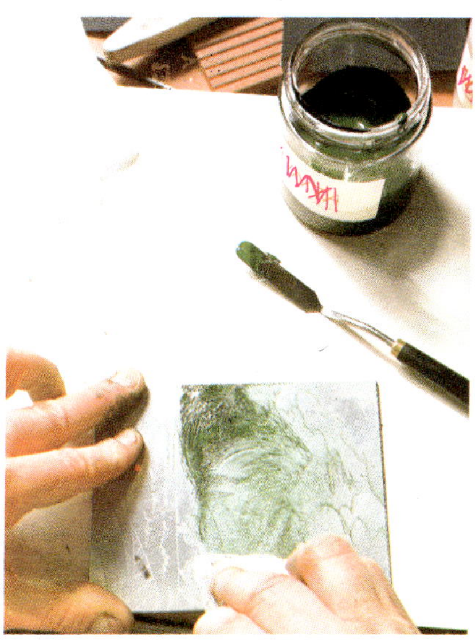

12
Spread the ink onto the plate with a piece of cheesecloth and remove the excess ink with another piece of cloth.

13
Finally, clean the plate with tissue paper (or strike it with the palm of the hand) before laying a sheet of printing paper on it.

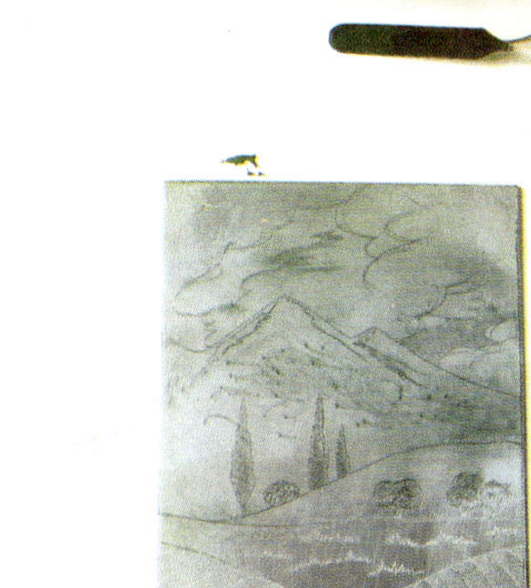

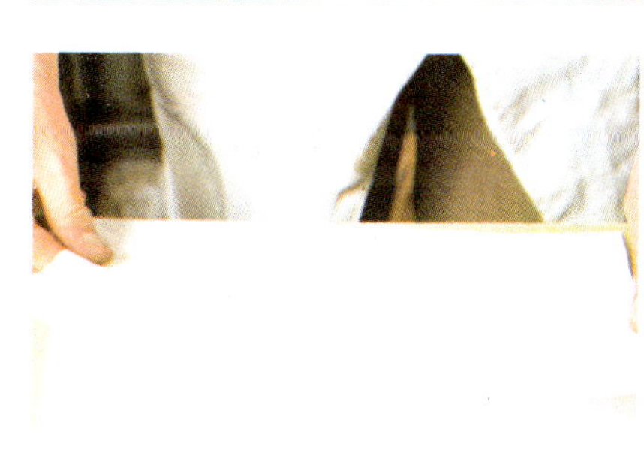

14
Take the paper out of the water and remove excess water with a few sheets of blotting paper.

15
Pass the corrected plate through the press to make a test print.

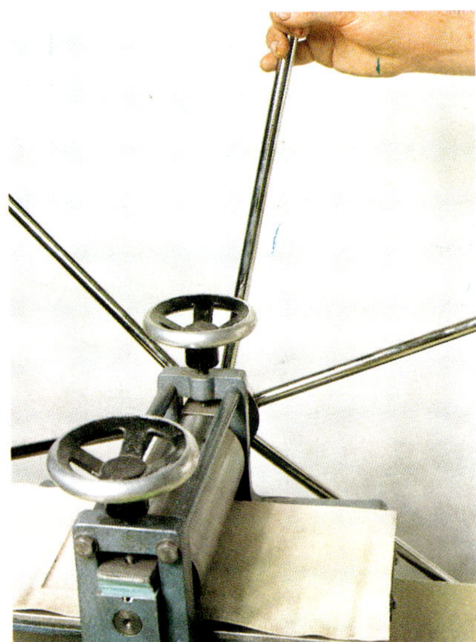

16
The test print will clearly show the differences with the first print. Many of the lines have disappeared.

17
Compare the first and last prints.

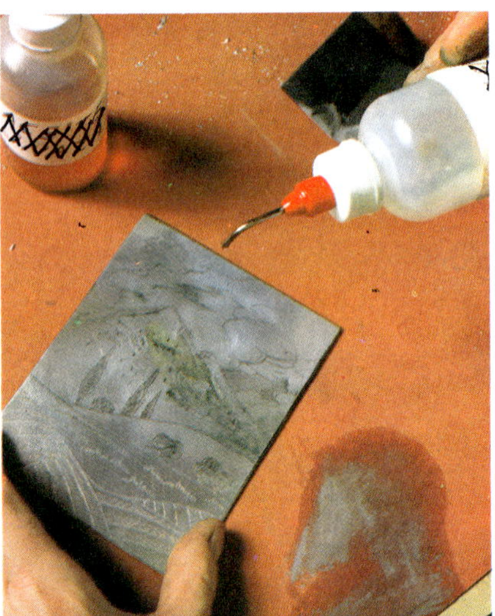

18
If any more changes have to be made to the etching, clean the zinc plate again with parafin and alcohol.

19
Scrape out the lines or areas that need to be removed with a steel scraper immediately.

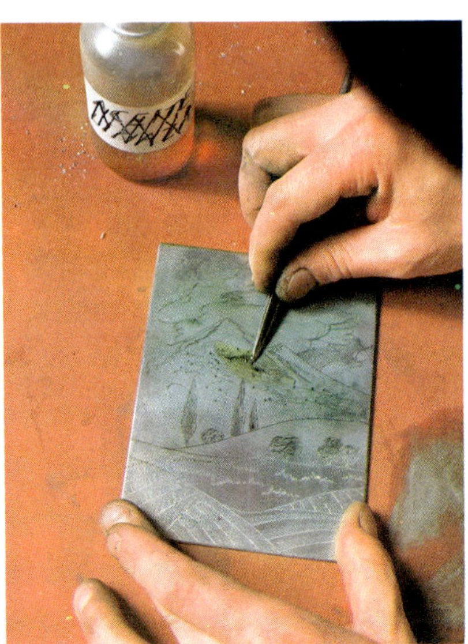

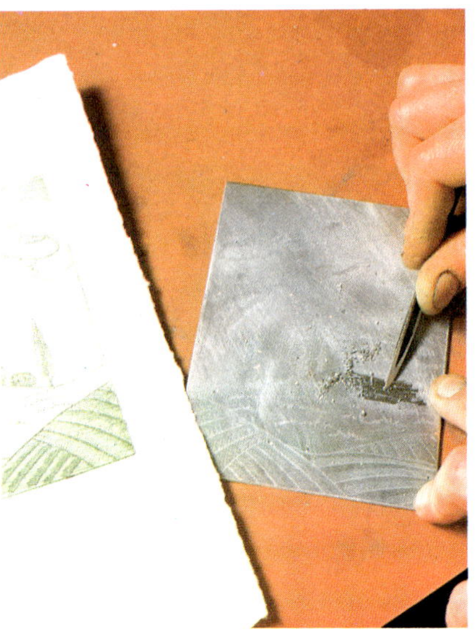

20
Always use a print for reference when making corrections.

21
Make the plate smooth again using sandpaper.

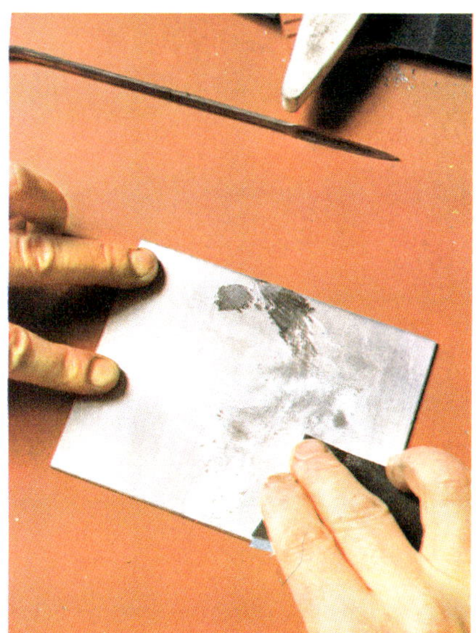

22
Now remove any remaining unevennesses with very fine sandpaper, linseed oil and parafin.

23
Go over all the sanded areas with a steel polisher.

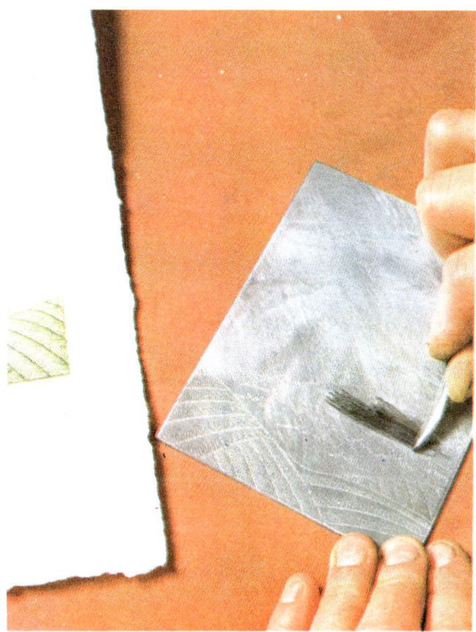

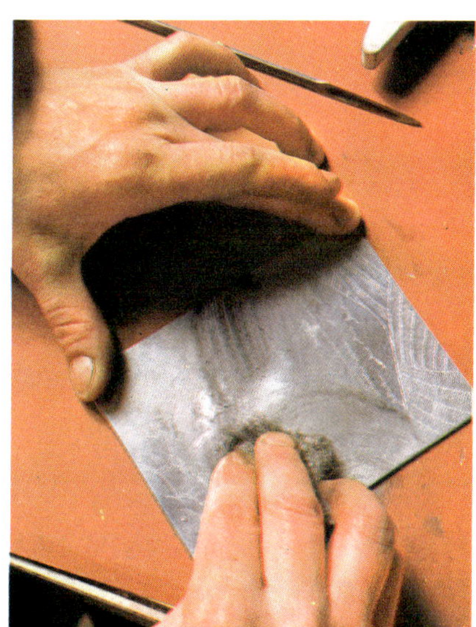

24
Smooth away all the irregularities by rubbing the corrected areas with steel wool and a little parafin.

25
Polish the plate with metal polish.

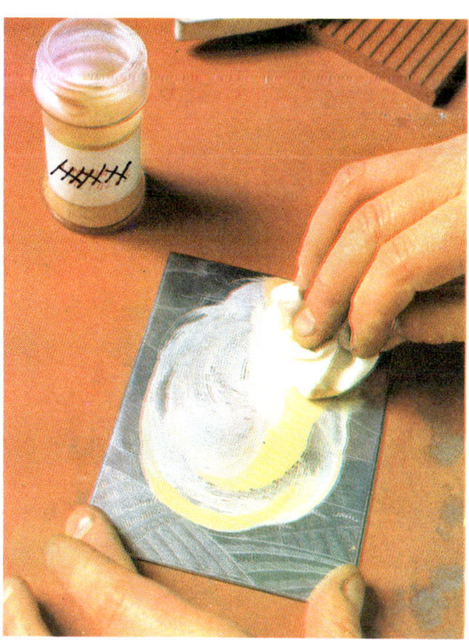

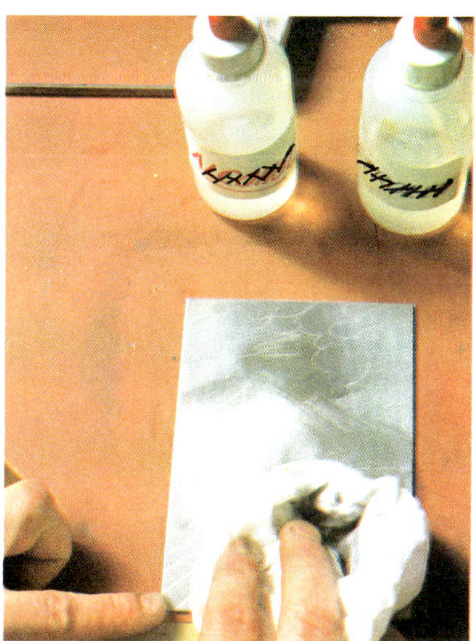

26
Finally, clean the zinc plate with parafin to remove all traces of grease with meths, and make another print.

Colour line etching

One line etching on a zinc plate can be used to make two different prints: one with lines without any colour onto a coloured base, and another in which the lines and the base are in contrasting colours. In the first example it is absolutely essential that the drawing (in this case, a playing card) is very clear. The lines should be drawn deeply and be completely free of ink. If both the surface and the lines are covered with ink, the colour combinations can produce very attractive prints. In both cases the lines therefore have to be etched quite deeply. This can be done by using a strong acid solution (one part of acid to four of water) and by leaving the plate in the acid bath for a relatively long time (two or three hours). During this period you must check that the etching ground has not come away and that the solution is strong enough. If it is not, add a little nitric acid. The etched lines should be eaten down to about 0.5 mm. Then use a roller to apply the ink onto the plate. The roller should be wider that the plate so that there are no lines or varying thicknesses in the layer of ink.

You will need the following: a press, a plate with the drawing, a tray, blotting paper, printing paper, nitric acid, water, meths, parafin, different coloured inks, a rubber spatula, a roller, a kitchen timer, cheesecloth, an engraving needle, a brush, tissue paper, a glass plate for the ink, and an acid bath for the acid solution.

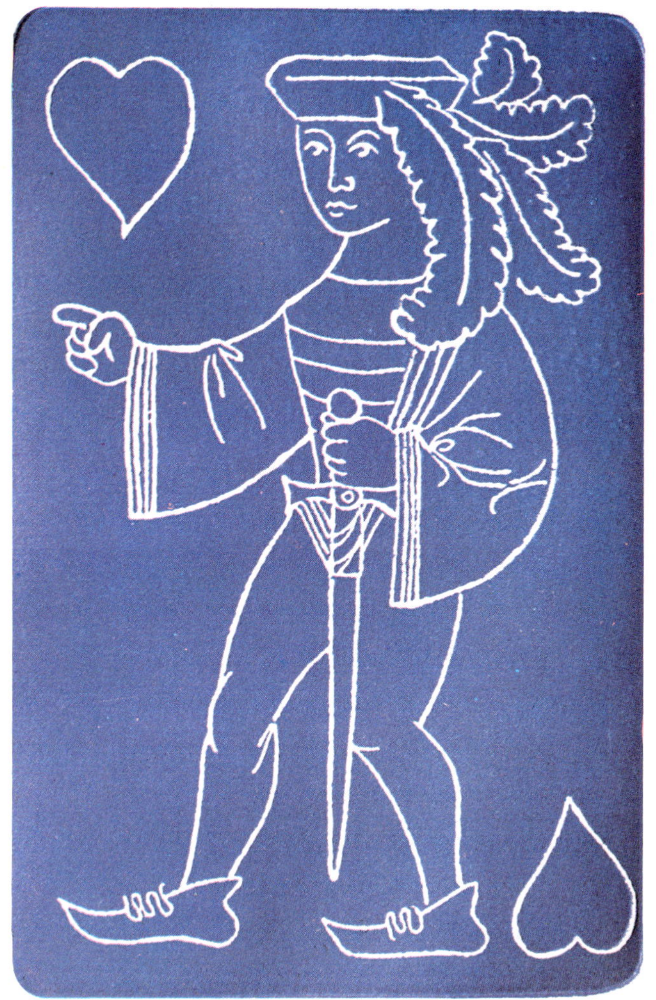

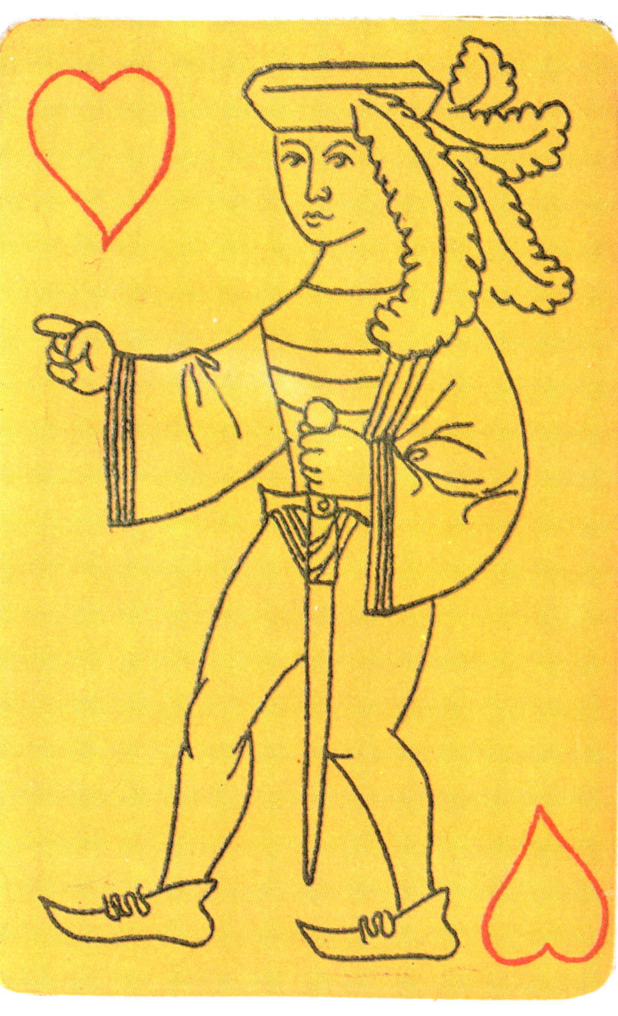

Two different prints of the same line etching on zinc: on the left ink has not been used, on the right it has.

1

Lay out all the tools and materials needed on the table.

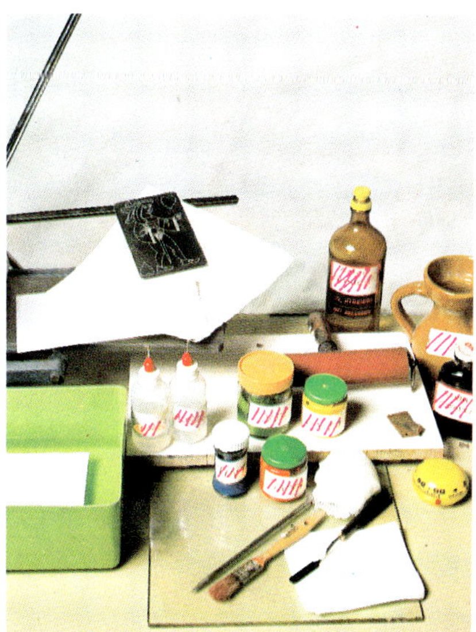

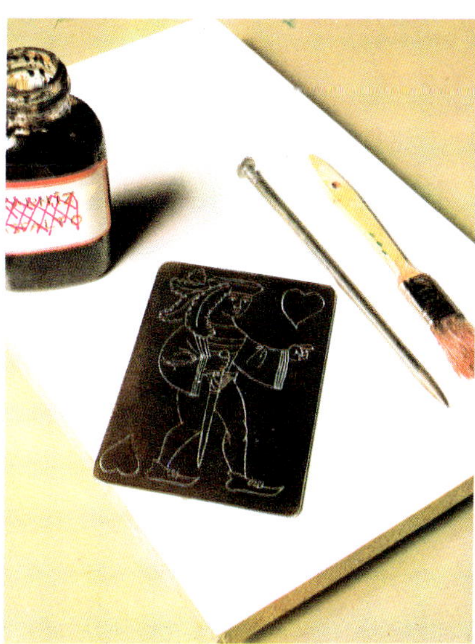

2

Cover the plate with etching ground and draw in the drawing of the playing card with an etching needle.

3
Mix the nitric acid with water (one part acid to four parts water). Leave the plate in the solution for two or three hours.

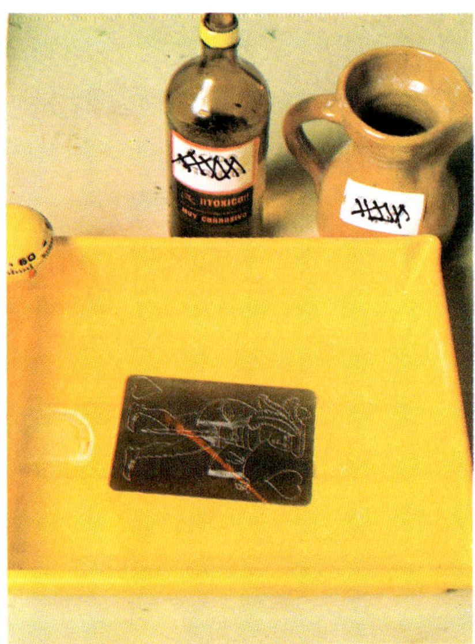

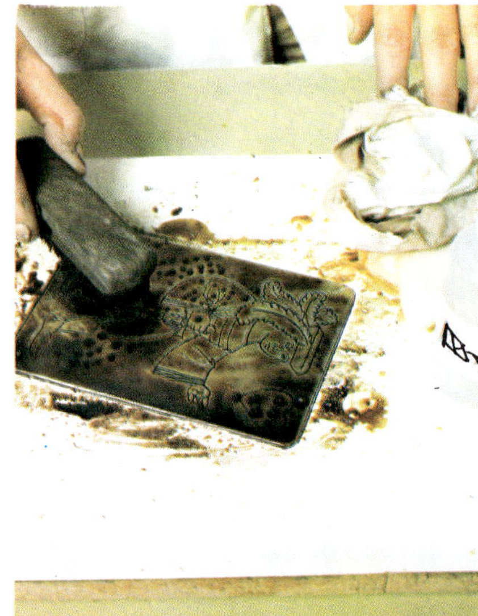

4
Remove the etched plate from the bath, clean the plate with parafin/turps and remove all traces of grease with meths.

5
The next step is carried out on the clean plate.

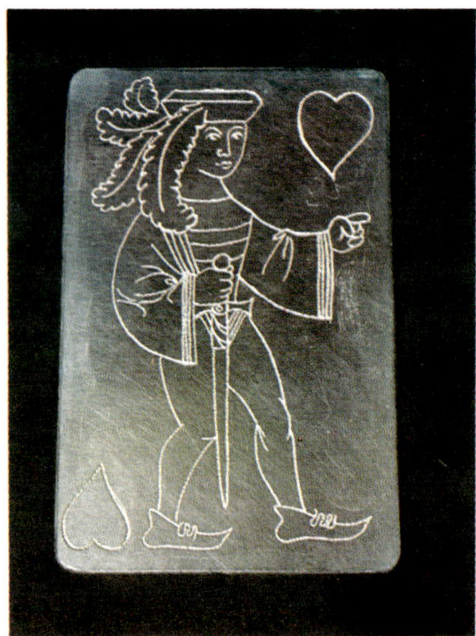

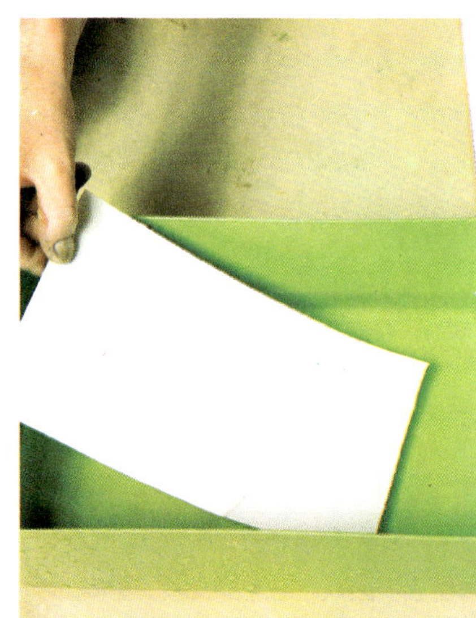

6
As usual, put the printing paper into water to soak.

7
Spread the ink over the glass plate with a spatula.

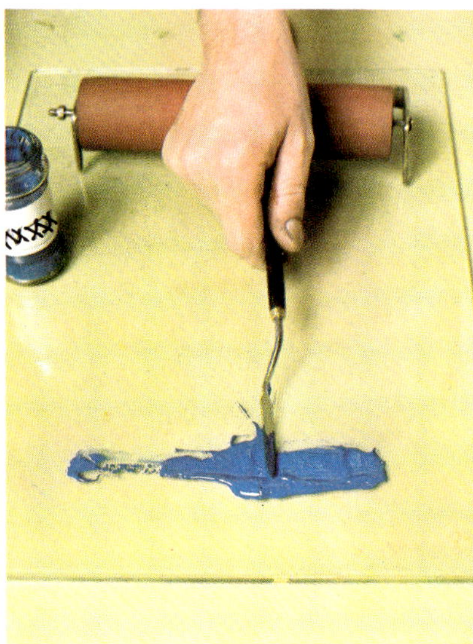

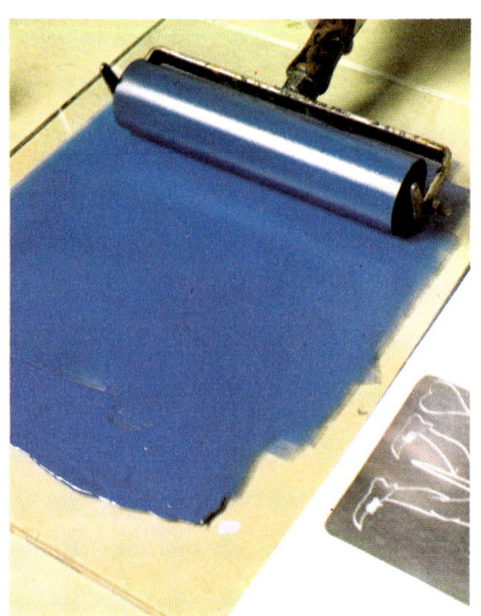

8
Go over the glass plate with a roller so that the ink has an even thickness everywhere. The glass plate should be covered with a thin, even layer of ink.

9

With the roller, cover the zinc plate with a thin layer of ink.

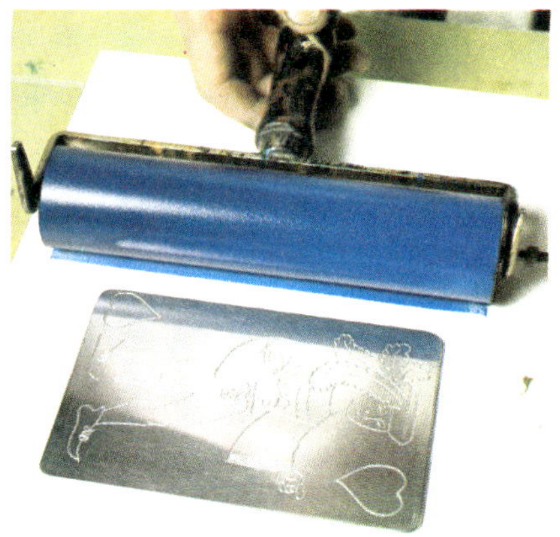

10

Go over the glass plate again with the roller.

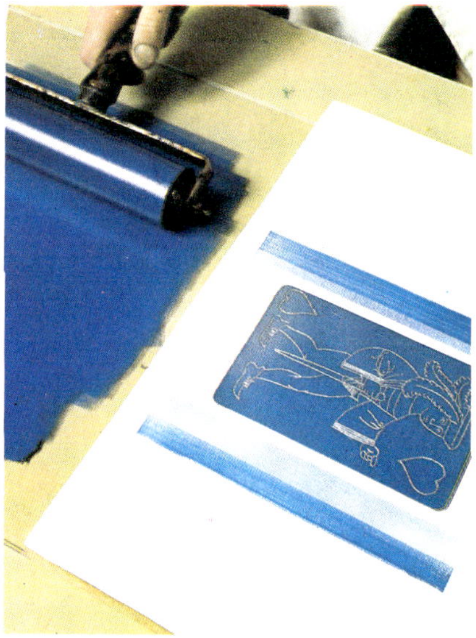

11

Now go over the zinc plate again with the roller so that the ink is evenly distributed.

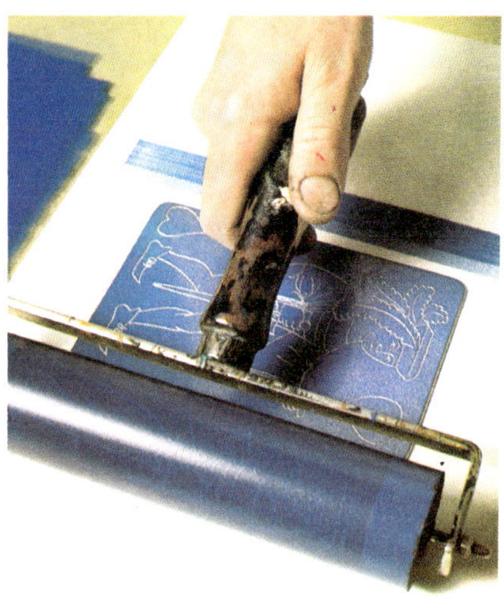

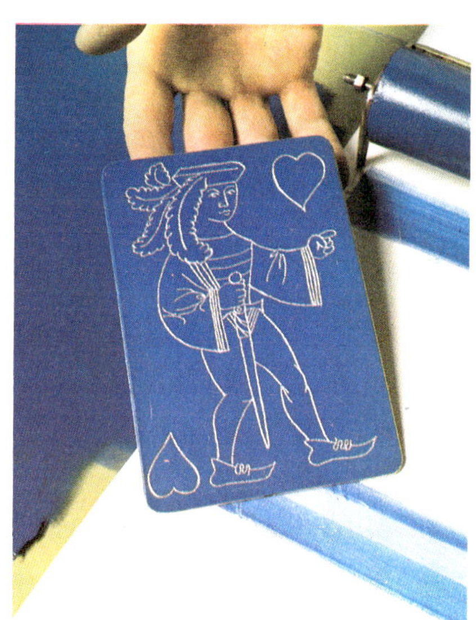

12

The plate is now ready for printing.

13

Take the printing paper out of the water and place it between two sheets of blotting paper to remove any excess water.

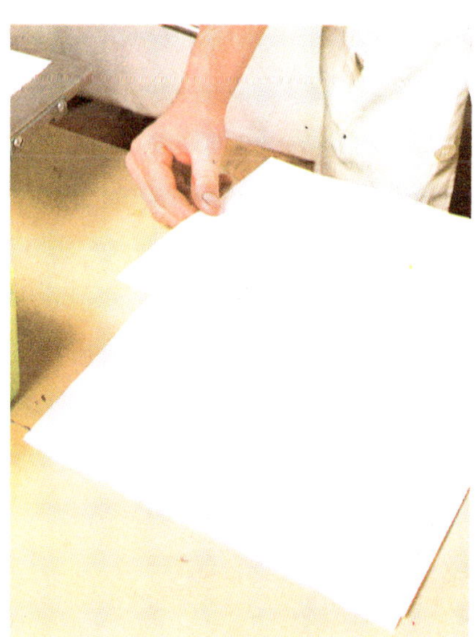

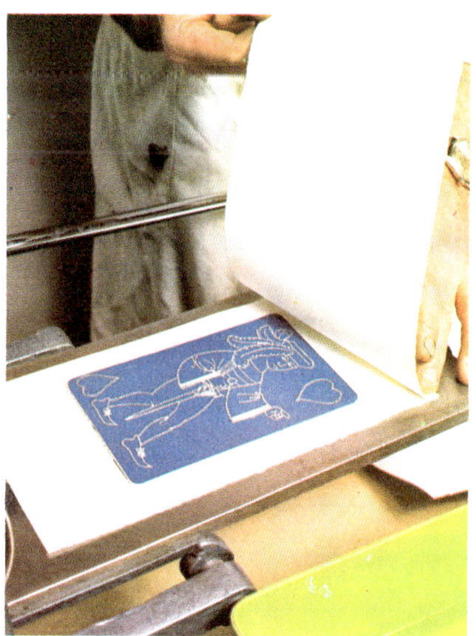

14

Place the plate in the press and lay the printing paper on top of it.

15

Place the plate in the middle of the press, cover it with the felt and pass the plate through the press.

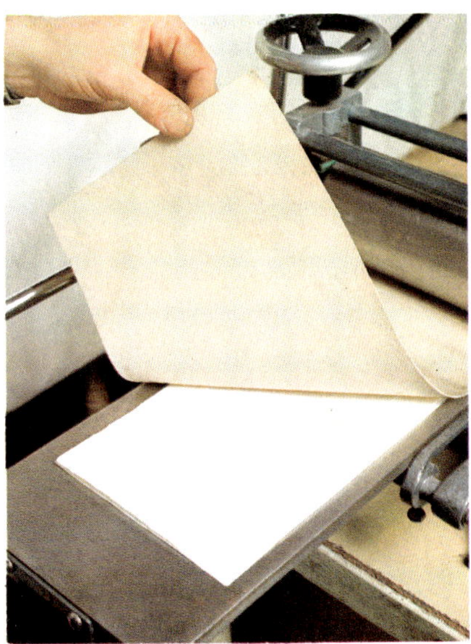

16

In this way a print is obtained in which there is no ink on the lines.

17

Clean the glass plate and the roller with a spatula and parafin, and then remove all traces of grease.

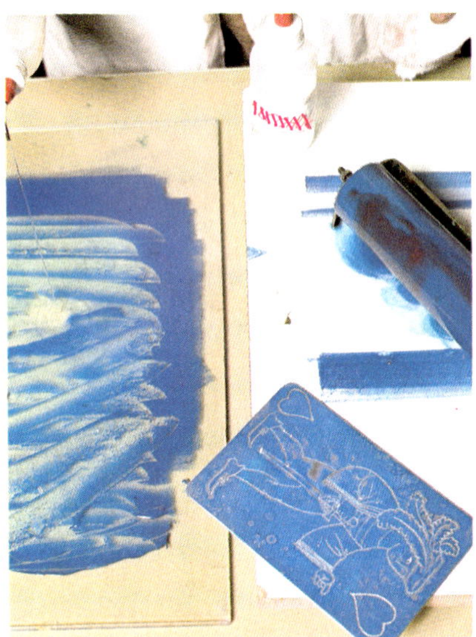

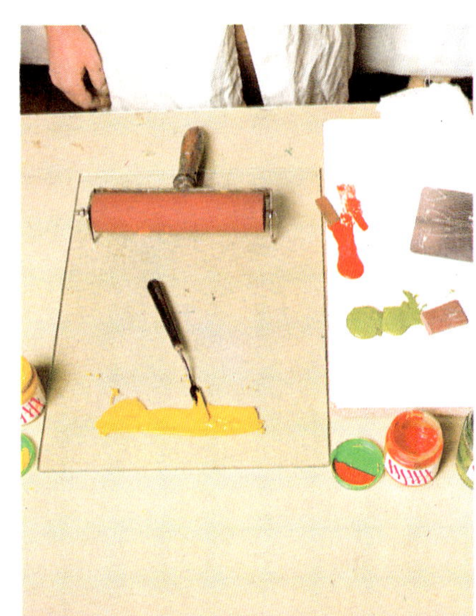

18

For the second part of the process you need different coloured inks, a spatula, the same zinc plate, a roller, a glass plate, and a small rubber spatula.

19

Using the rubber spatula, cover the whole plate, except for the hearts, with green or yellow ink.

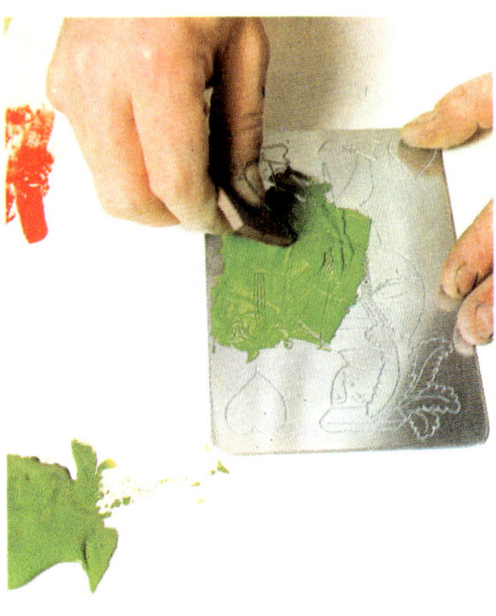

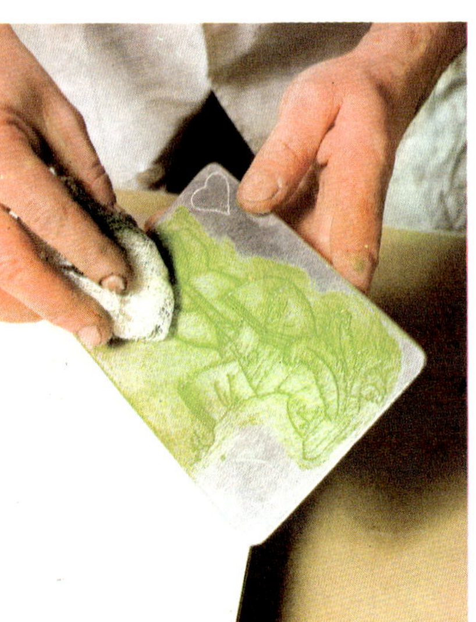

20

Go over the plate with a piece of cheesecloth so that the ink goes into the lines.

21
Go over the plate with tissue paper to remove excess ink.

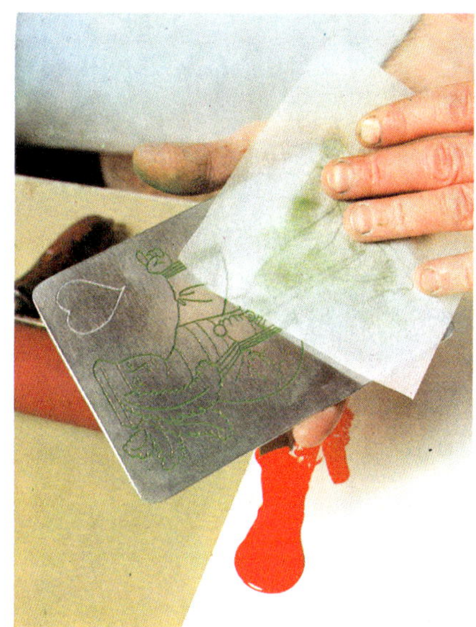

22
Just cover the corners of the plate – where the hearts have been etched – with red ink.

23
Go over these areas with a cheesecloth and then with tissue paper.

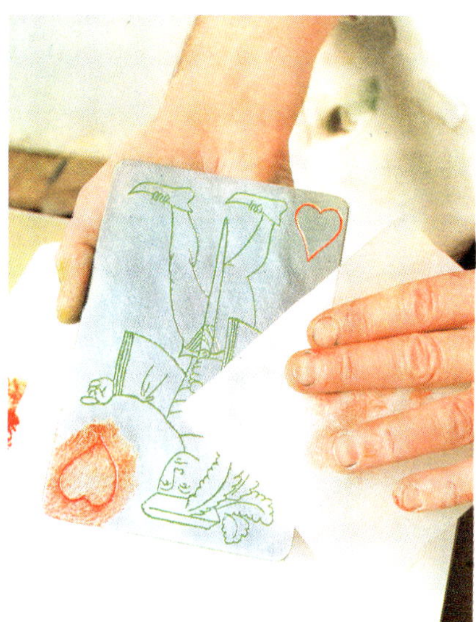

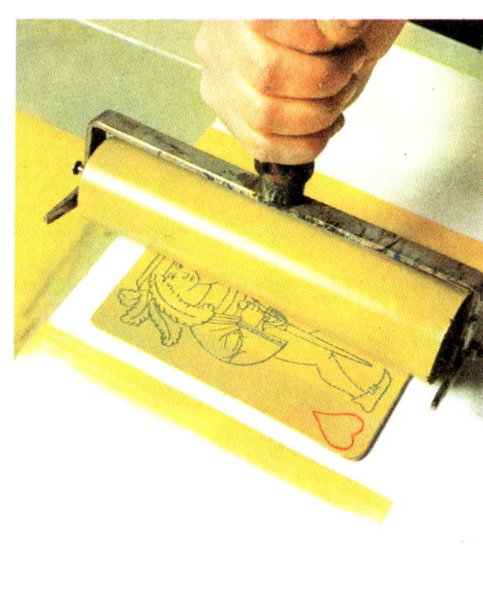

24
Put the ink on the roller and go over the plate so that it is evenly covered.

25
Put the plate in the middle of the press to make a print.

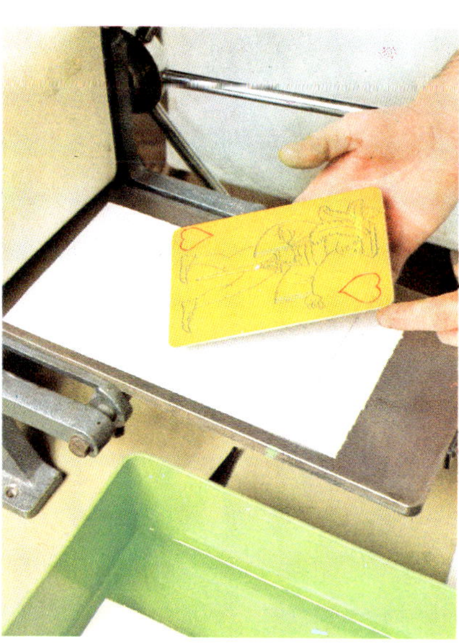

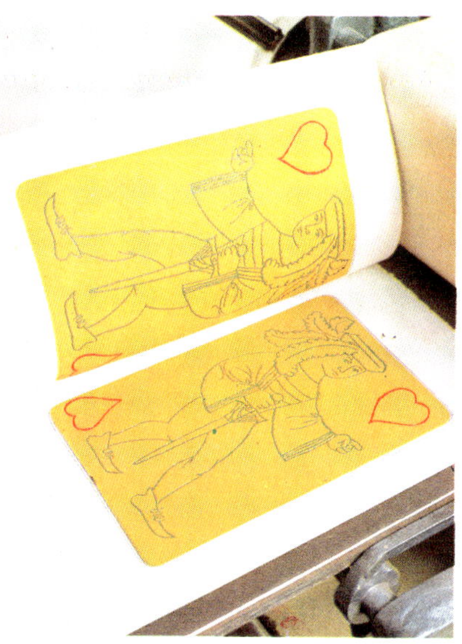

26
This time both the surface and the lines are covered.

Aquatint with resin

If different shades are required in etching, for example, contrasting shades of grey or a deep black colour, the best way of achieving this is to use powdered resin.
The powdered resin, which is melted onto the metal plate, determines the corrosive effect of the acid, which only works in the spaces between the particles of resin.
The most common method used by etchers when applying the powdered resin is to sieve it through a fine sieve onto a plate. It is also possible to use a small glass pot filled with powdered resin with a nylon stocking stretched tautly over it. This produces the same effect as a sieve. It is important to try and distribute the powder as evenly as possible.
The drawing used in our example is a seascape at night, because this clearly shows the effects that can be achieved with this technique.
The acid solution used consists of one part of nitric acid to ten parts of water. It's advisable to put the printing paper into a bowl of water before starting. The excess water can be absorbed between sheets of blotting paper.
Requirements: a zinc plate, printing paper, printing ink, water, nitric acid, linseed oil, powdered resin, meths, varnish, parafin, a brush, a spatula, a file, a fine brush, blotting paper, some cotton, something to hold the plate in place, and a press.

The effect of the resin on the plate

The resin should be sprinkled over the surface of the metal very evenly through an extremely fine sieve, or using a small dish covered with a piece of cloth. Spaces remain between the grains of resin where the acid can penetrate.

The resin coated plate is heated so that the resin melts and adheres to the plate. This should be done very carefully because if there is too much heat, the resin will melt completely and no spaces will remain where the acid can penetrate. On the other hand, if there is not enough heat the resin will melt unevenly, leaving too large spaces in between. The right time is just when the resin begins to melt.

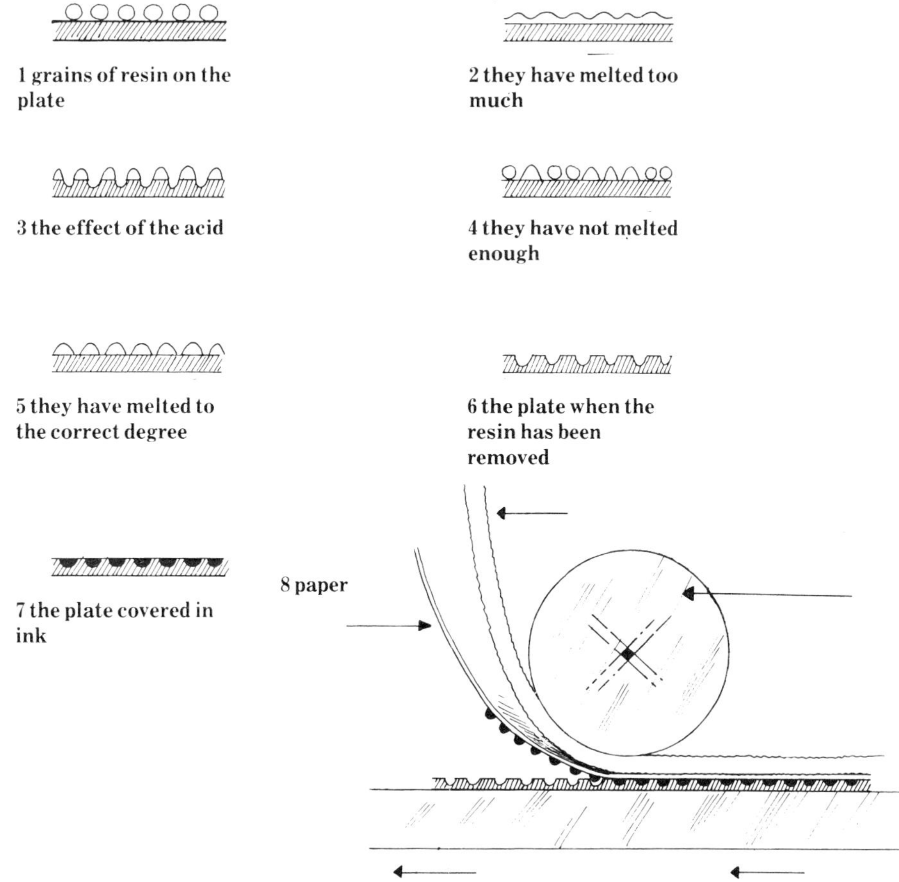

1 grains of resin on the plate

2 they have melted too much

3 the effect of the acid

4 they have not melted enough

5 they have melted to the correct degree

6 the plate when the resin has been removed

7 the plate covered in ink

1
The materials required.

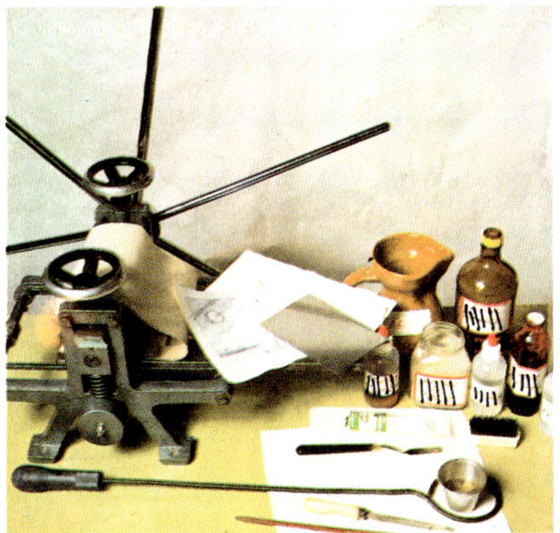

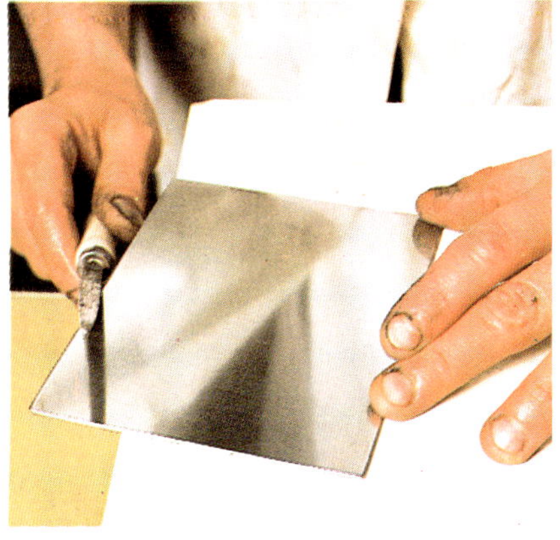

2
The edges of the zinc plate.

3
Remove all traces of grease from the plate with a cloth soaked in meths.

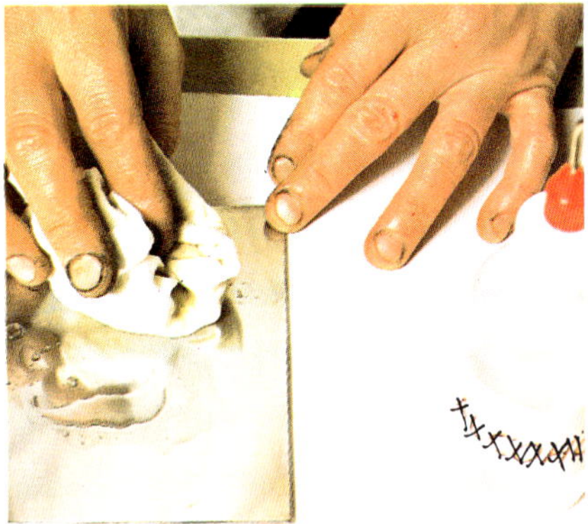

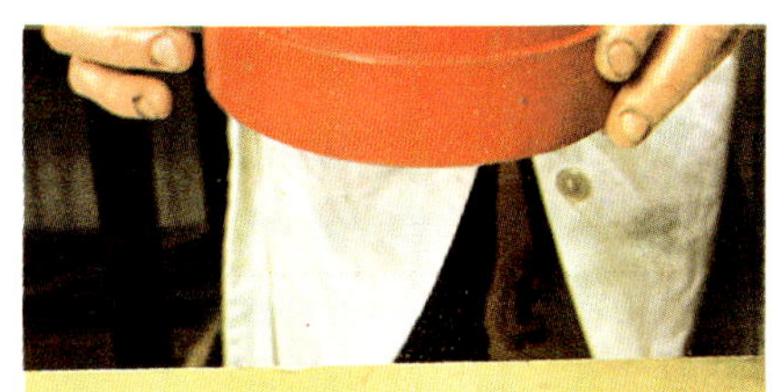

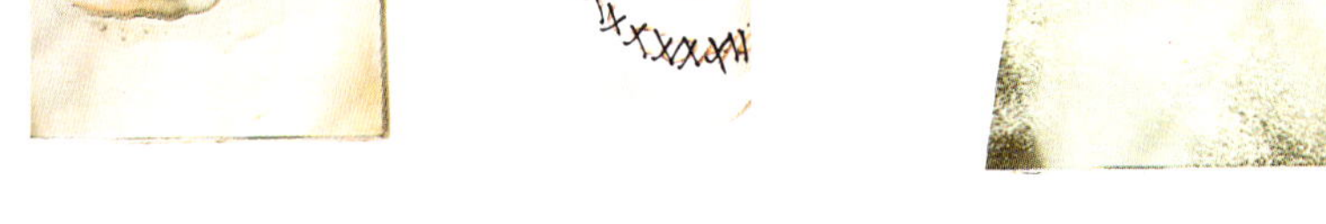

4
Sprinkle the powdered resin evenly over the plate.

5
In a metal bowl sprinkle a little fibreglass wool with meths, light it and heat the plate above it until the resin melts and adheres to the plate.
Never add meths to the bowl while there is a flame or while it is still hot. Put out the flame by placing a metal plate over it.

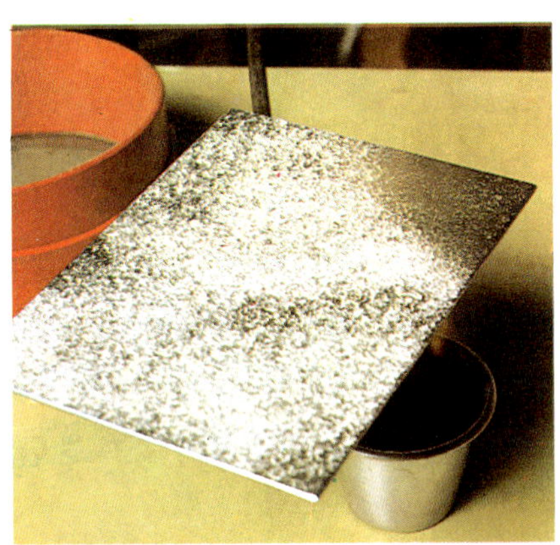

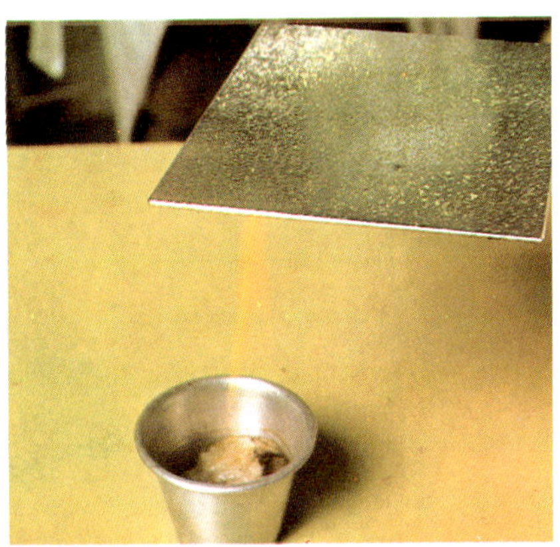

6
Make sure that the resin does not burn, as this produces a sticky layer that the acid cannot penetrate.

7
When the plate has cooled down cover those parts which should not be affected by the acid with varnish.

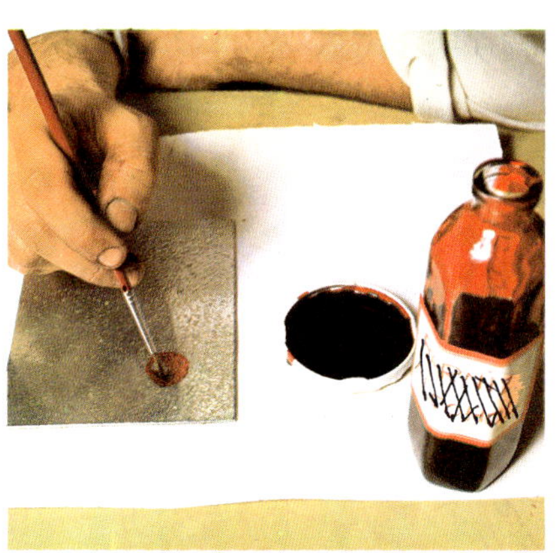

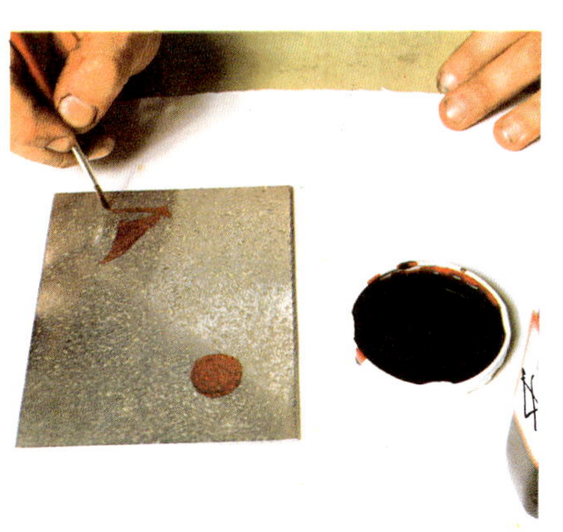

8
The areas covered with varnish will come out white when the print is made.

9

When the varnish has been applied, leave the zinc plate to dry before putting it in the nitric acid.

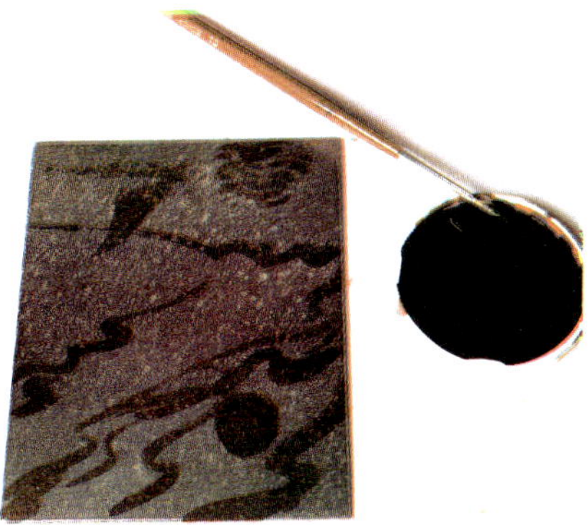

10

Pour some water into a plastic bowl.

11

Add the nitric acid (N.b. One part of acid to ten parts of water).

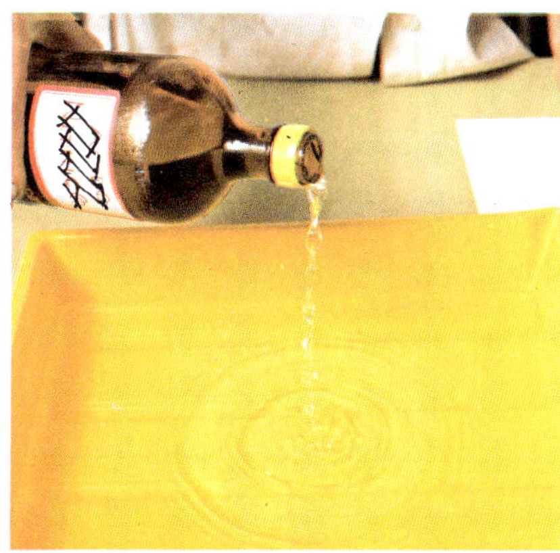

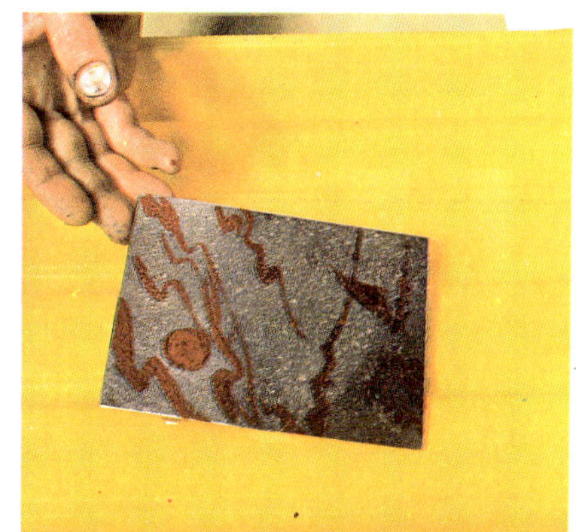

12

Place the zinc plate in the bath with acid solution.

13

Leave the plate in the acid solution for about ten minutes.

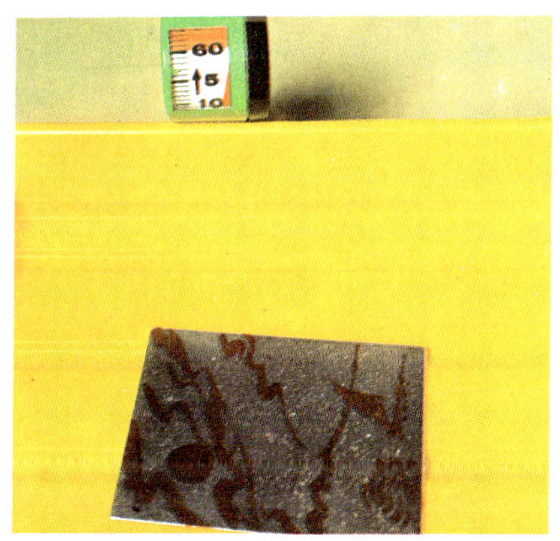

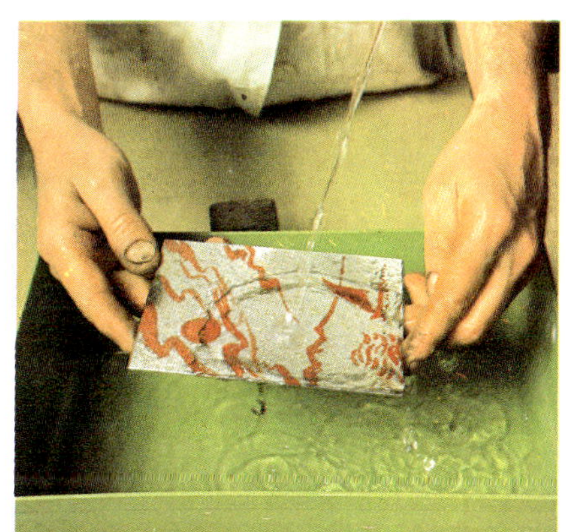

14

Take the plate out of the bowl and rinse thoroughly with water.

15

Dry the plate very carefully with a cloth without removing the resin.

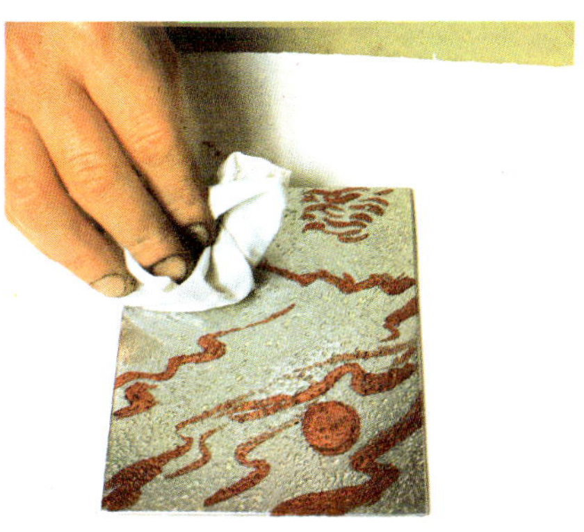

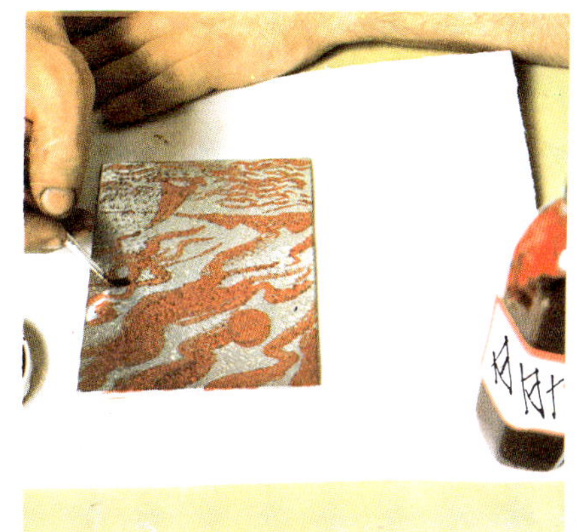

16

Now cover other areas with varnish. (The areas which have already been affected by the acid remain grey.)

17
Place the zinc plate in the acid solution again, this time for twenty minutes.

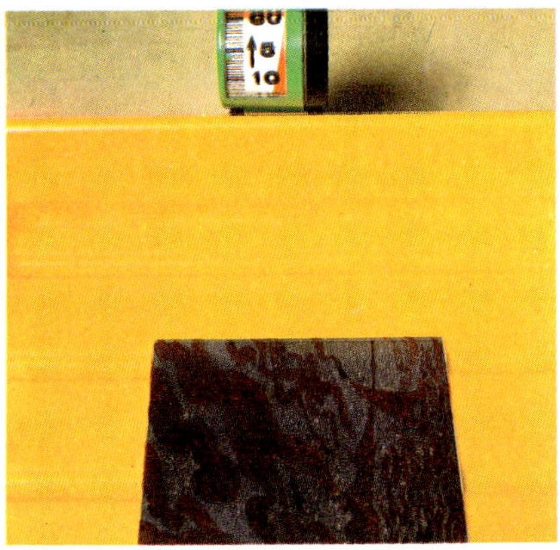

18
After twenty minutes take out the plate and rinse thoroughly with water.

19
Apply varnish to the other parts which must not be any darker, and this time leave the plate in the solution for an hour.

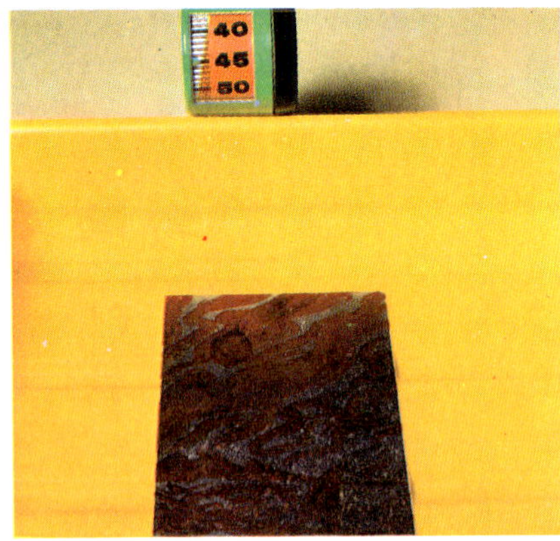

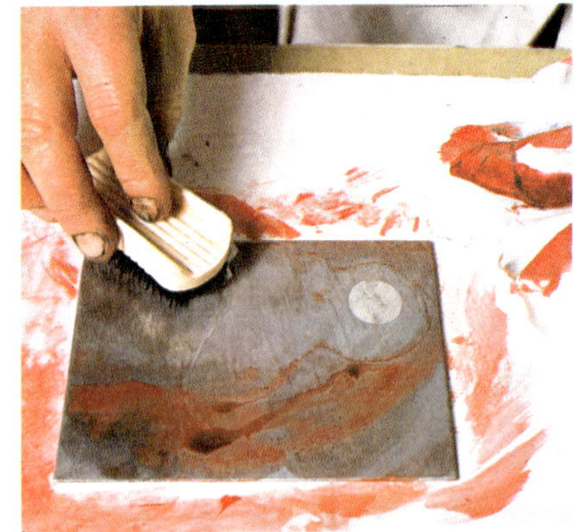

20
Take the plate out of the solution and rinse with water, remove all the varnish with a brush and meths.

21
Clean the plate with a cloth and then apply the ink with a piece of cheesecloth.

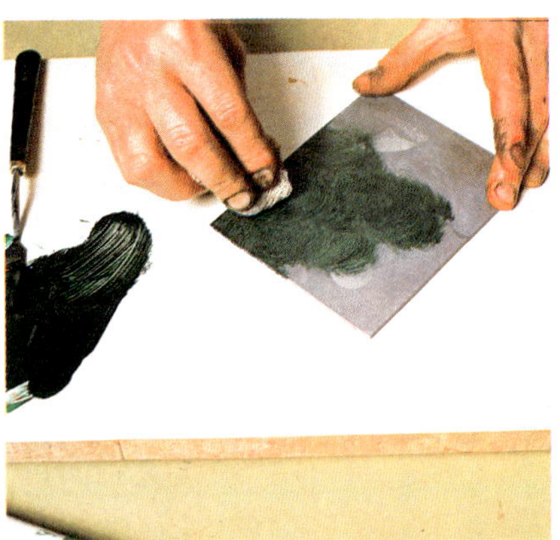

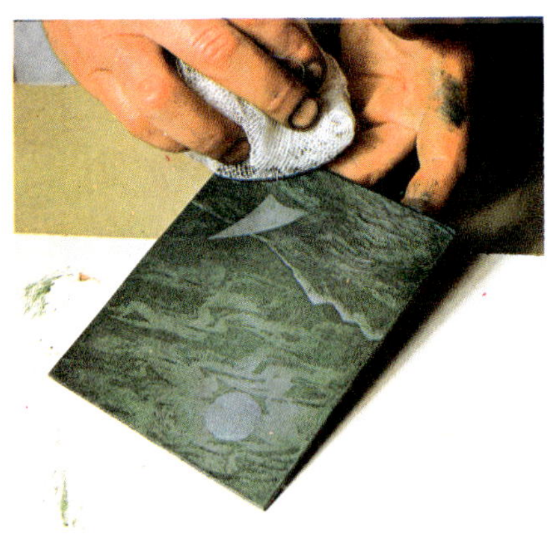

22
Carefully remove the excess ink with a piece of cheesecloth.

23
Take the printing paper out of the water (where it has been soaking).

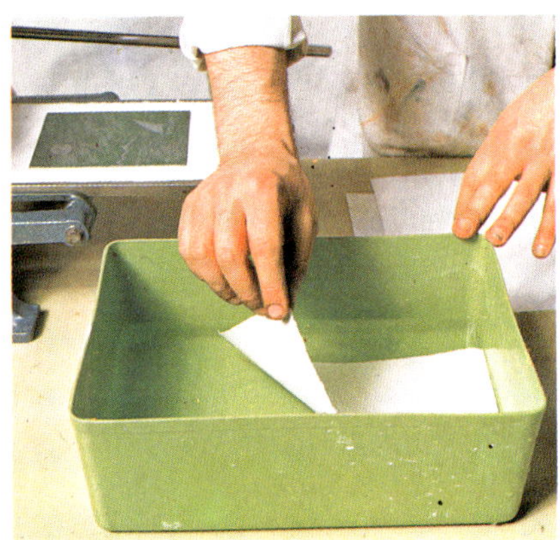

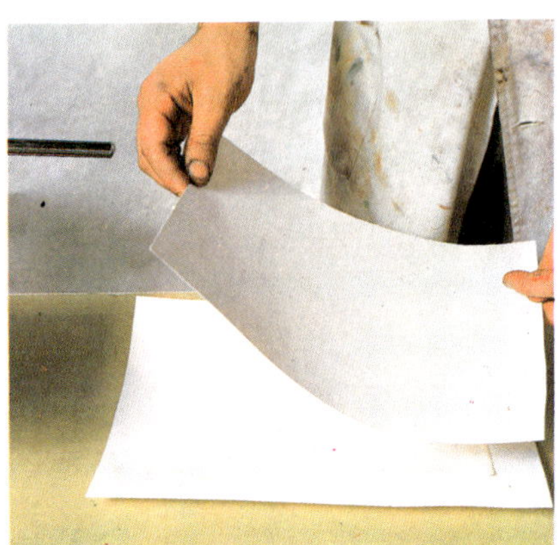

24
Place the paper between two sheets of blotting paper to absorb the excess water.

25

Place a sheet of paper in the press and put the zinc plate on top of this. Then place the printing paper in the correct position.

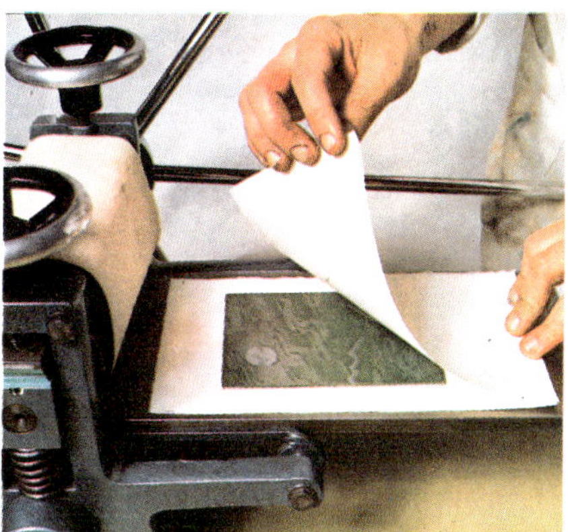

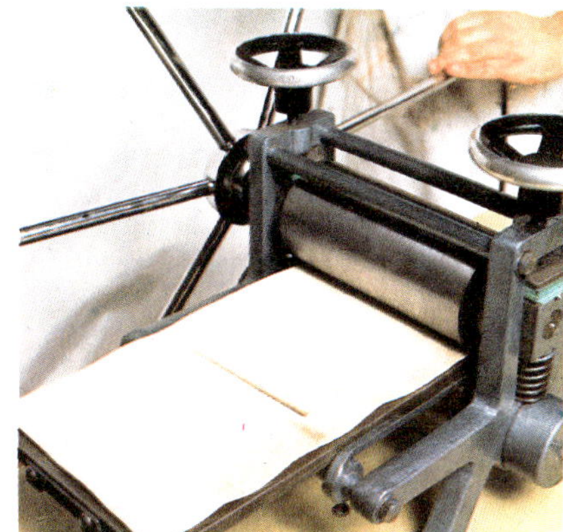

26

Pass the plate through the press so that the paper is printed.

27

When the plate has passed through the press, carfully lift off the print.

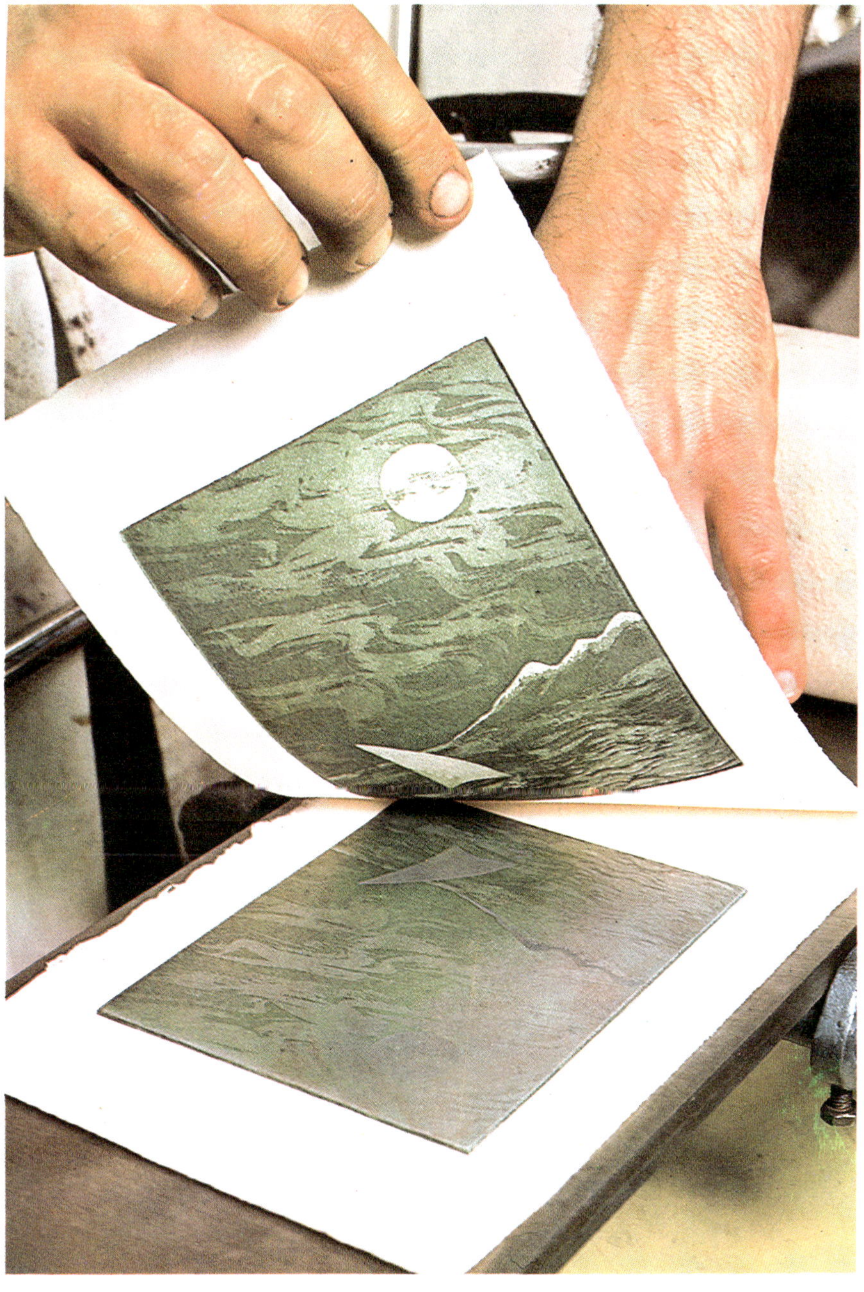

Correcting aquatint plates

In a preceding section the procedure for correcting a line etching was described, using mainly steel scrapers and sandpaper. The same technique can also be used to correct an aquatint. In both cases virtually the same tools are used. Nevertheless, correcting an aquatint takes more time because the areas that have to be removed are larger – entire parts of the drawing rather than lines.
When correcting an aquatint keep making prints regularly so that you are aware of the changes being made. Successive prints will clearly show what has been corrected. Remember that this is a practice exercise and do not be surprised if the corrections actually detract from the original.
To correct an aquatint the following tools and materials are required: the aquatint, a print of the aquatint, a tray, printing paper, blotting paper, ink, tissue paper, a rubber block, cheesecloth, metal polish, parafin, meths, steel wool, files of varying degrees of fineness, a whetstone, waterproof sandpaper and polishing paper, a fine brush, a spatula, a number of steel scrapers, linseed oil and a printing press.

1
All the tools and materials required for this exercise.

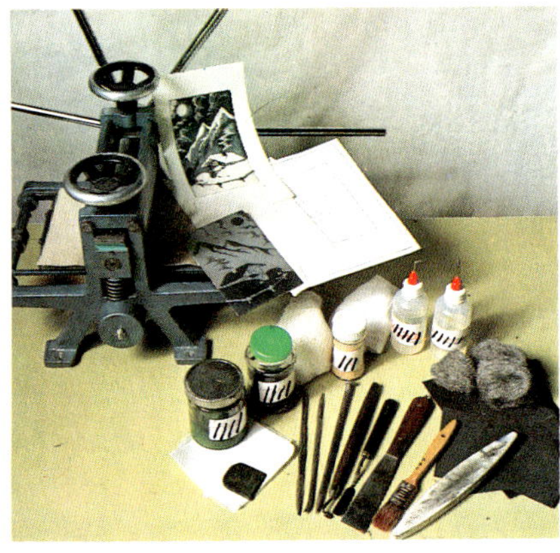

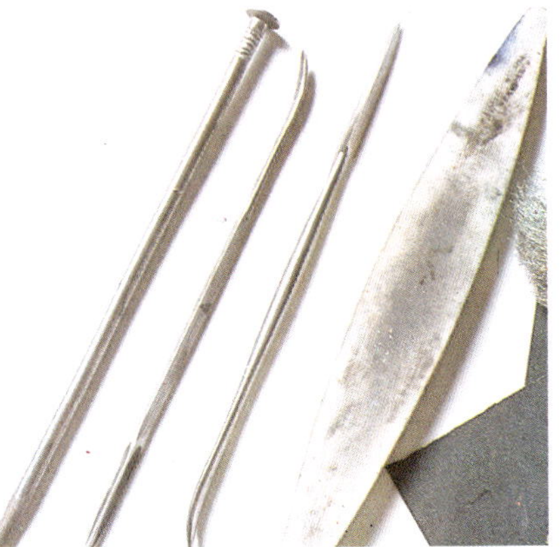

2
The most important tools are: the steel scrapers, a whetstone, an engraving needle, waterproof sandpaper and steel wool.

This etching is corrected by removing a number of lines and shapes, such as the sky and some other details.
The result makes a less cluttered impression.

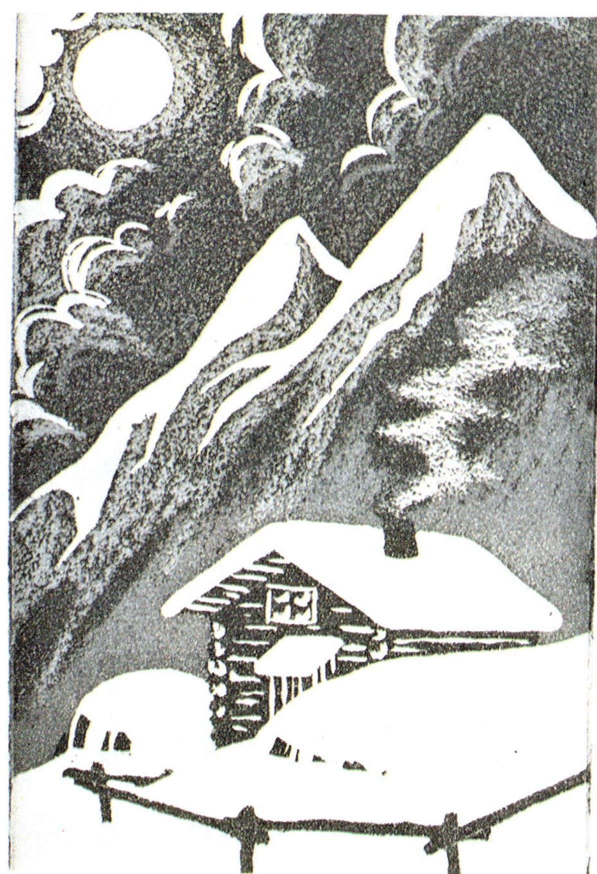

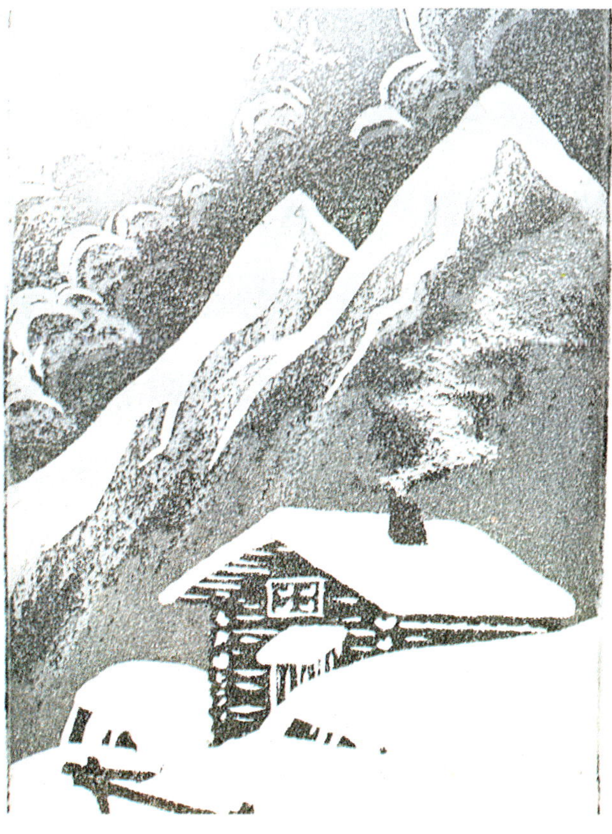

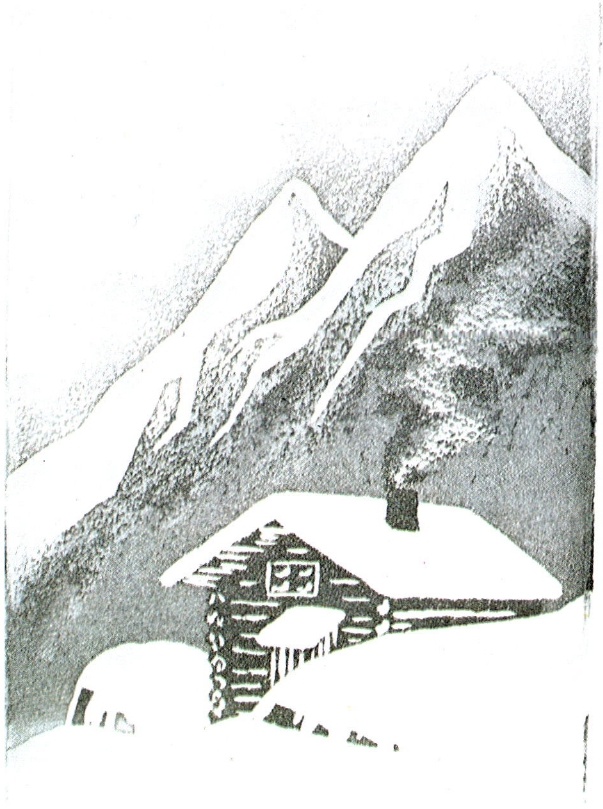

3
Before sharpening the tools, put a few drops of linseed oil on the whetstone.

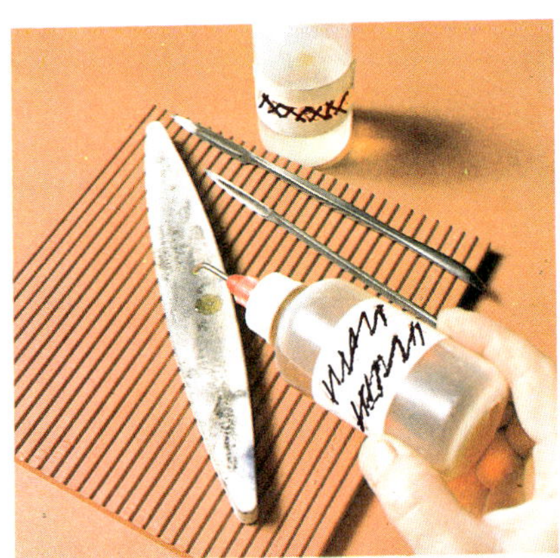

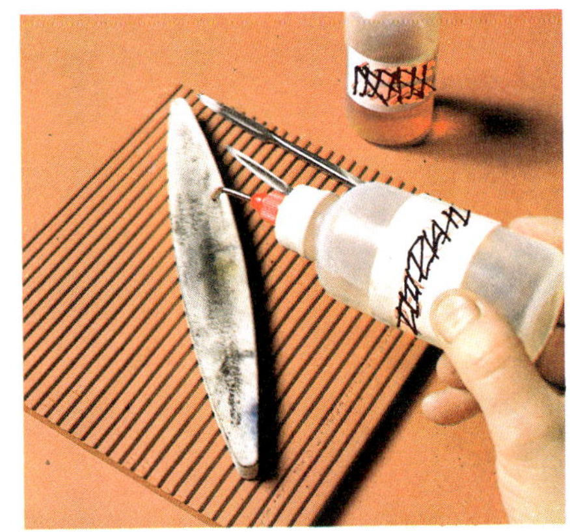

4
Add a little parafin to the linseed oil so that the whetstone is quite wet.

5
Always sharpen the steel scrapers on the flat side and in the same direction.

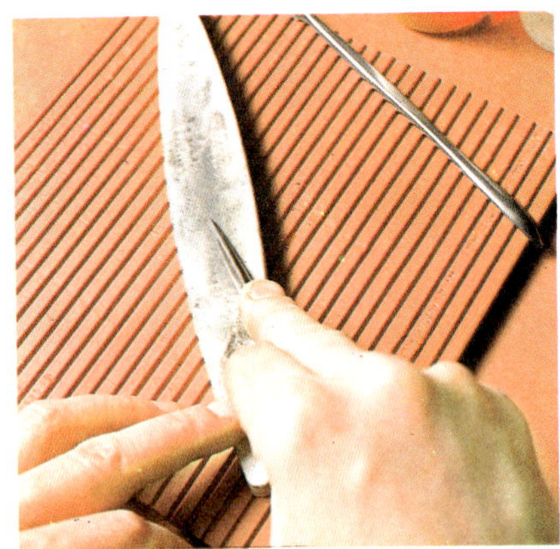

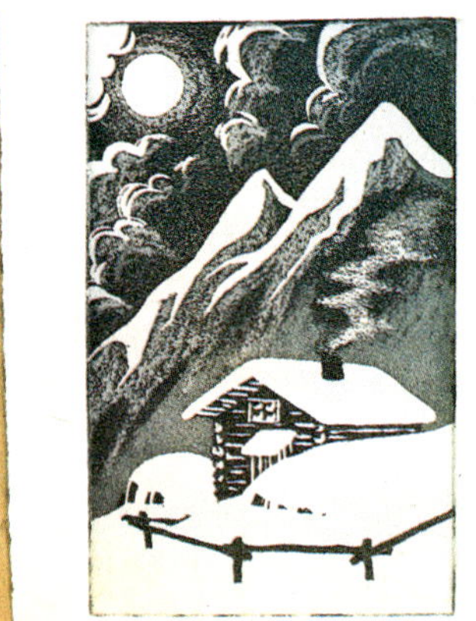

6
Closely examine a print of the etching which you want to correct.

7
Then examine the plate to which the corrections are to be made with the steel scraper.

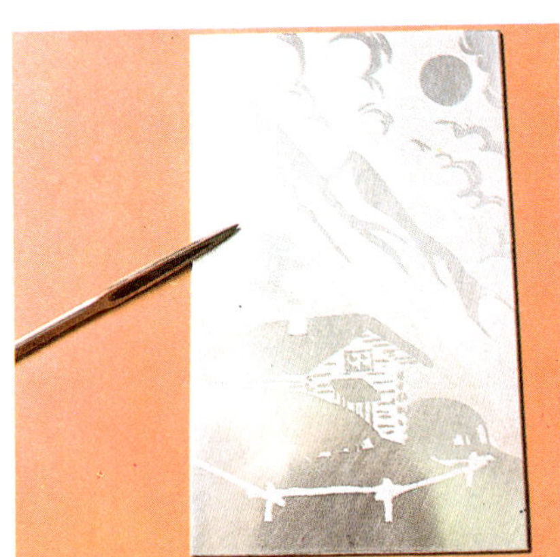

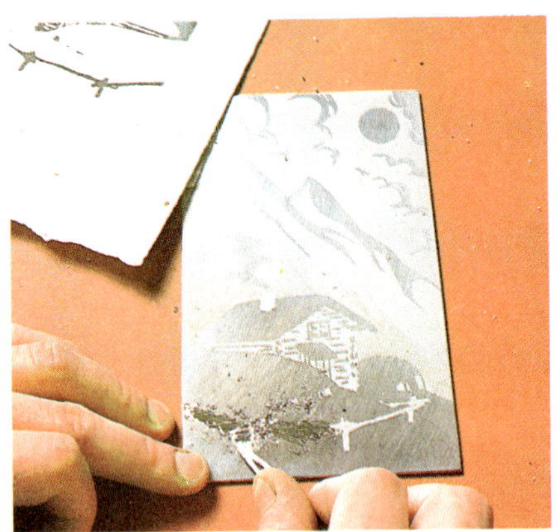

8
Remove lines from the metal plate by carefully going over them with the steel scraper.

9
Brush away the metal powder left by the scraping process with a fine brush.

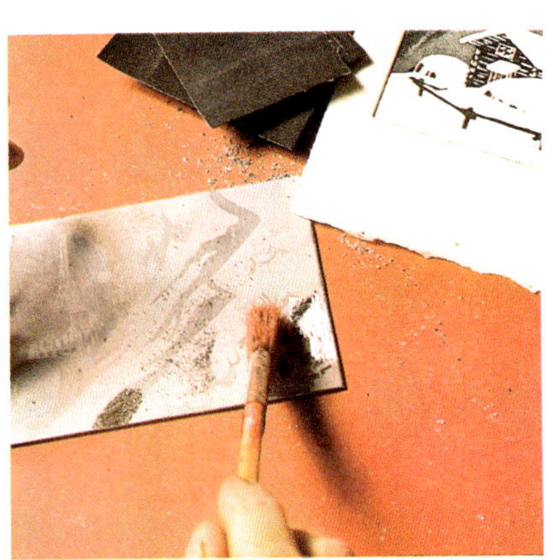

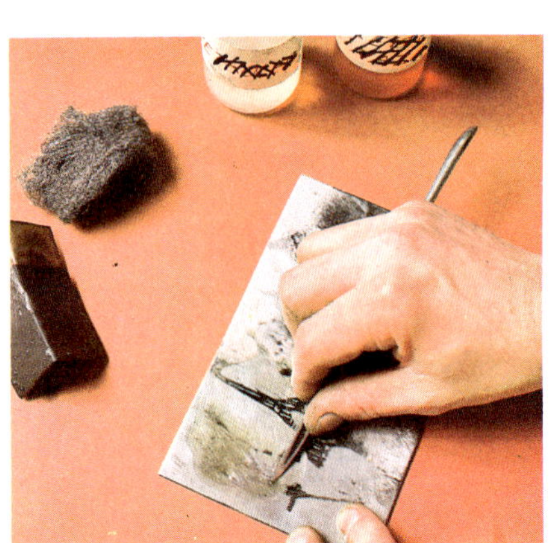

10
Make sure that you scrape the required area thoroughly, and then clean it.

11
When the parts of the plate that have to be changed have not been etched very deeply, it is best to use linseed oil when you are scraping.

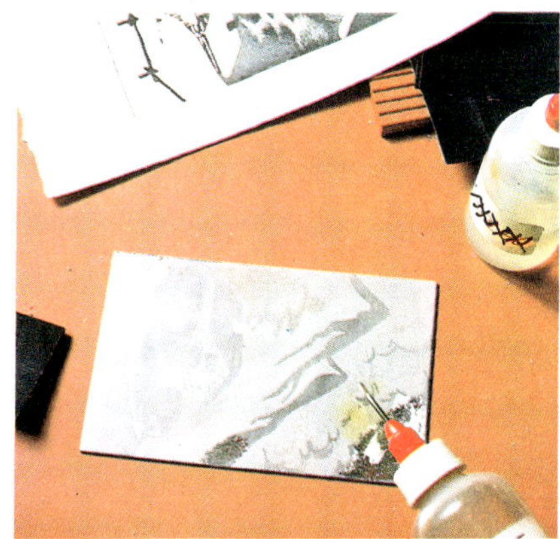

12
Then polish the plate thoroughly with linseed oil, parafin and sandpaper of various grades.

13
The part that has not been very deeply etched is finally polished with fine steel wool, linseed oil and parafin.

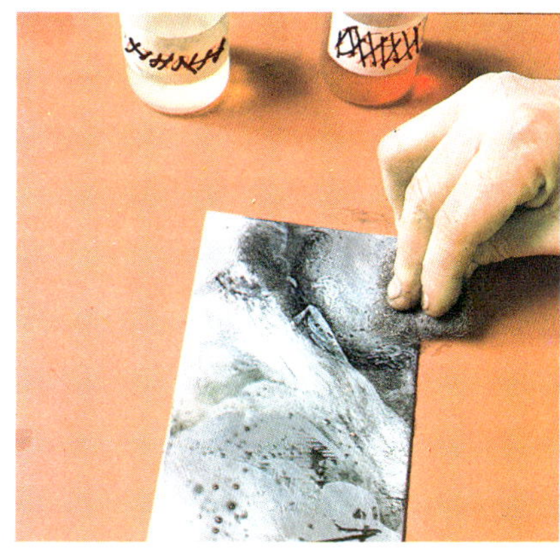

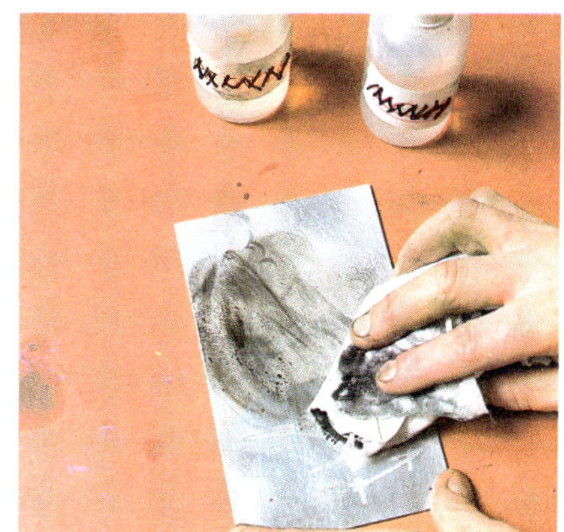

14
Then clean this area with a cloth soaked in parafin and remove all traces of grease with another cloth and some meths.

15
Firmly rub over the plate with a piece of cheesecloth and some ink so that a test print can be made.

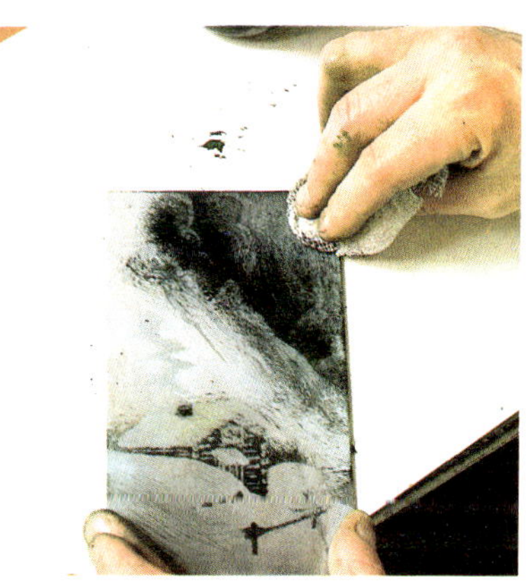

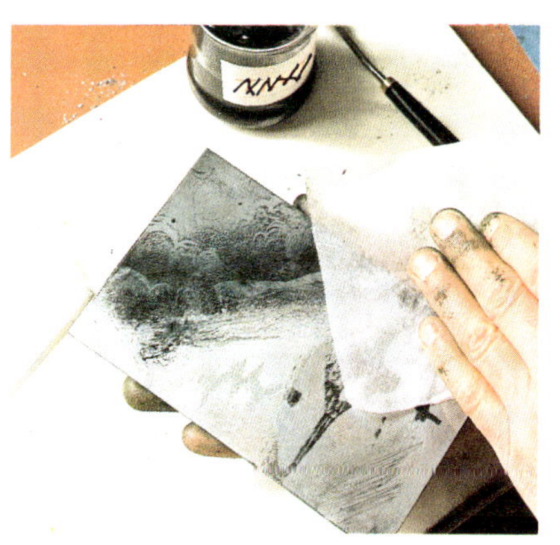

16
Remove the excess ink with tissue paper, cheesecloth, or the palm of your hand. If paper is used, it should not be folded.

17
Lay the plate and the printing paper in the middle of the bed of the press.

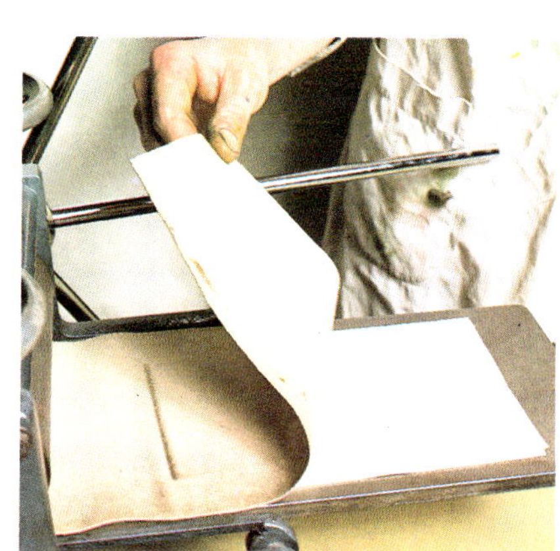

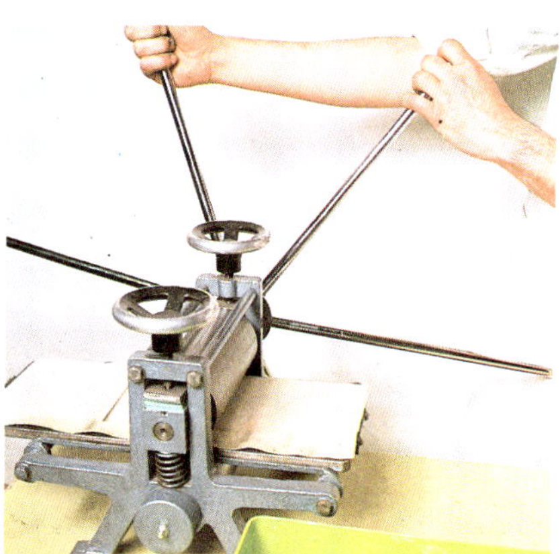

18
To make a good print it is important to pass the plate evenly through the press.

19
This clearly shows that the sun, which was in the top right hand corner of the plate, has disappeared.

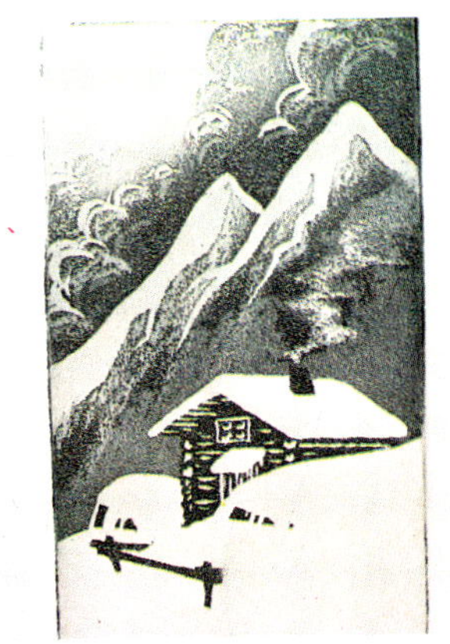

20
The two test prints are now compared: the first, which was used as a basis, and the second, made after the changes were made to the plate.

21
Other lines and shapes are removed and the steel scraper is again used on the top half of the plate.

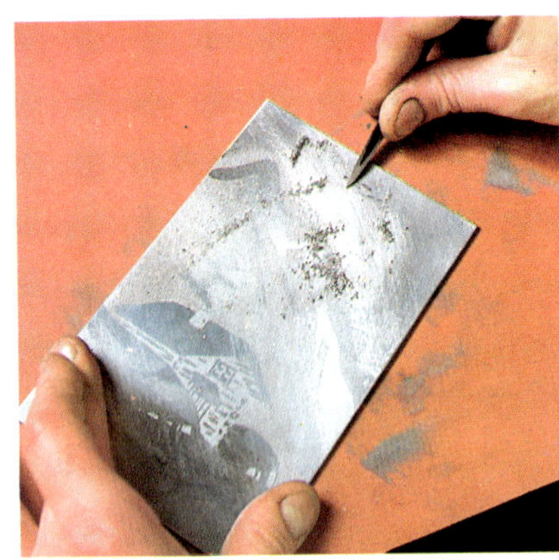

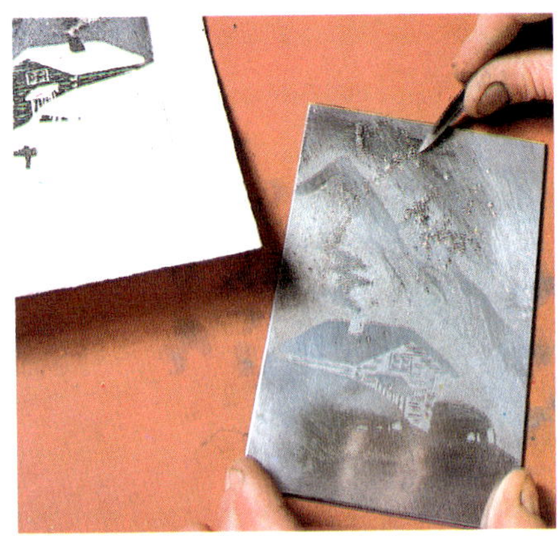

22
Using the print as a starting point, the alterations required are carried out.

23
The clouds over the mountains are removed.

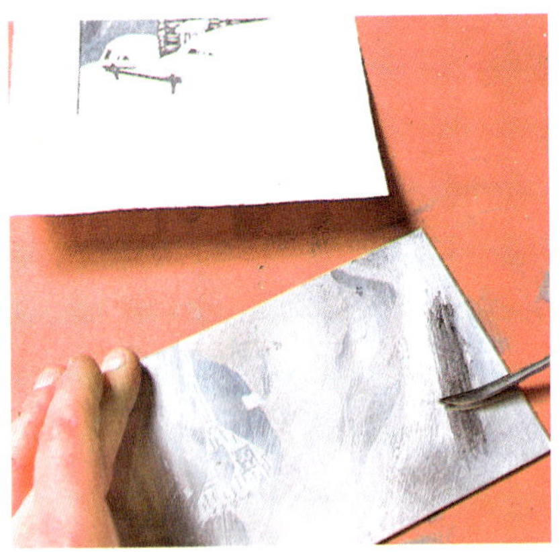

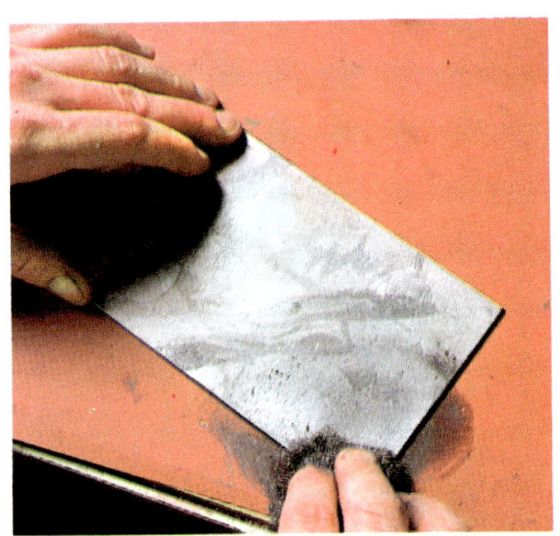

24
Again polish the area with steel wool and then polish with linseed oil and a few drops of parafin.

25
Polish the metal plate with a cloth and some metal polish.

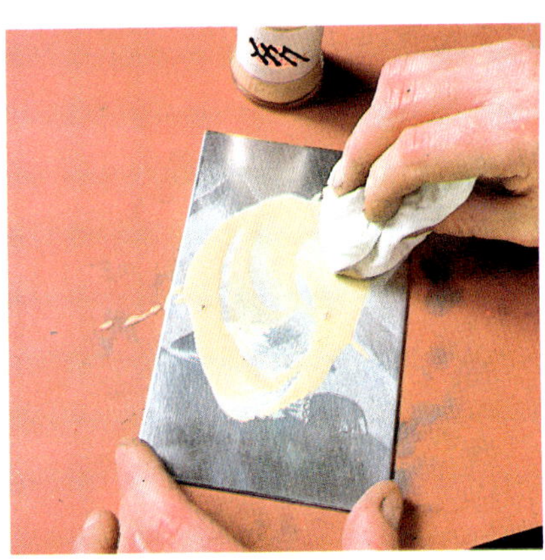

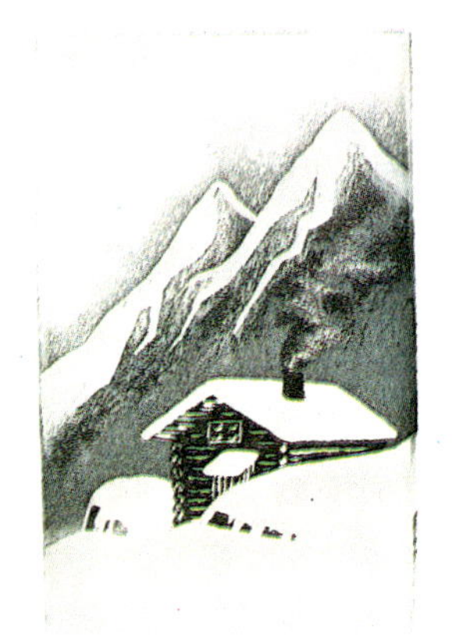

26
By removing different lines and areas, this version is finally obtained.

Making an etching using lithographic chalk

If you wish to make an etching in different shades of grey, or even with white and a deep black, you can use a lithographic crayon (lithographic chalk) as well as the aquatint technique. It is easy to achieve the desired results with this sort of crayon although the procedure may be rather lengthy.

The crayon protects the metal by inhibiting the action of the acid on the plate. The degree of protection depends on the intensity and thickness of the lines and on the length of time that the plate is left in the acid solution. Cover the parts which are to be completely white with methylated spirit based varnish as this forms an even better protection. The lithographic crayon is an ideal way of creating subtleties of tone. With the following simple exercise you can learn to use this pencil and discover some of the possibilities of the technique. For this exercise you will need: a printing press, carbon paper, a zinc plate, a lithographic crayon or lithographic chalk, a ballpoint, fine brushes, nitric acid, water, powdered resin, methylated spirit based varnish, linseed oil, alcohol, parafin, a bath for the acid, a cheesecloth, another piece of cloth, a scrubbing brush, a bowl containing fibreglass wool and alcohol, ink, a spatula, a kitchen timer, a small block of rubber and a nylon stocking.

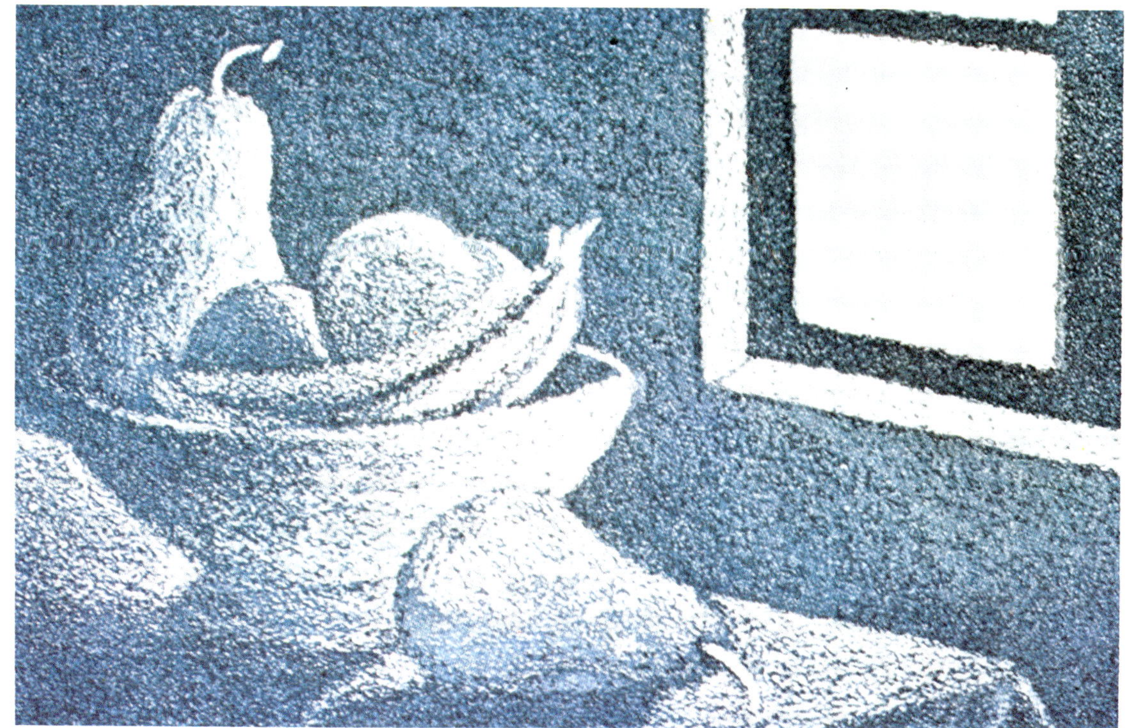

When you compare the final print of the etching with a test print made during the procedure, you can clearly see the differences in shade and colour obtained with the lithographic pencil.

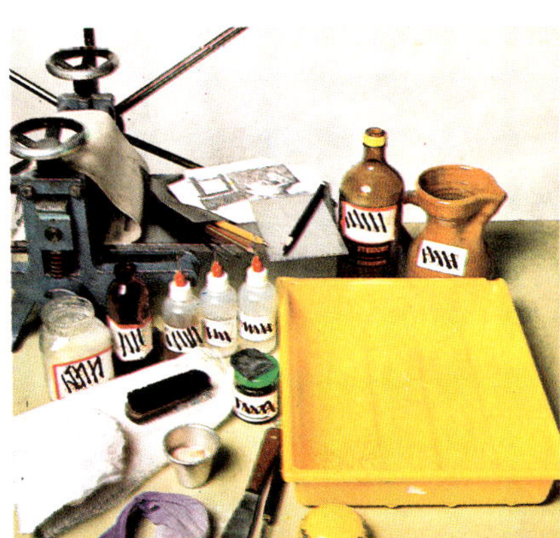

1
All the tools and materials required.

2
Clean the zinc plate and remove all traces of grease.

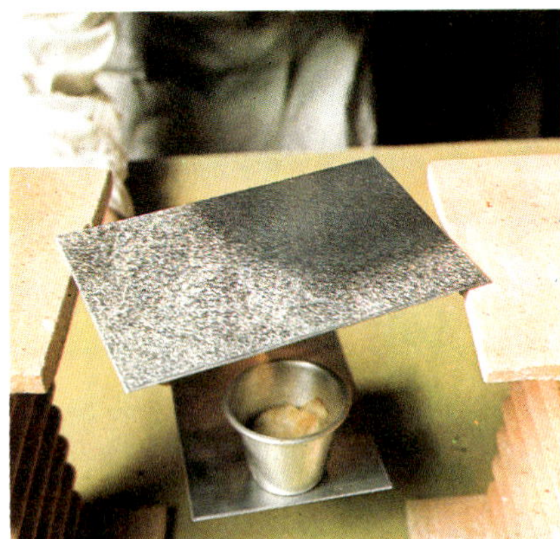

3
Heat the zinc plate covered in resin without burning the resin, and then leave it to cool.

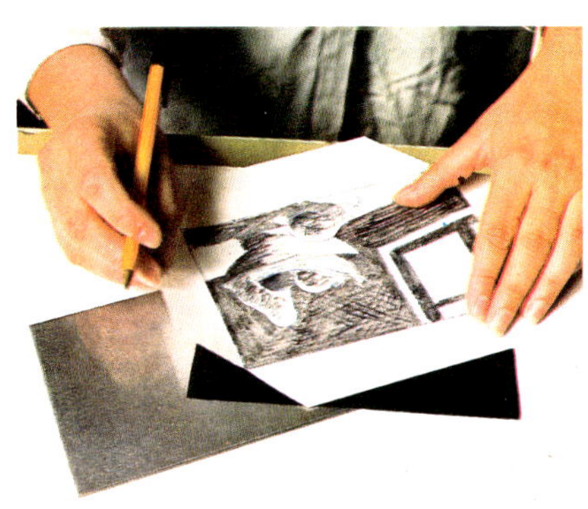

4
Transfer the design to the plate with carbon paper and a ballpoint.

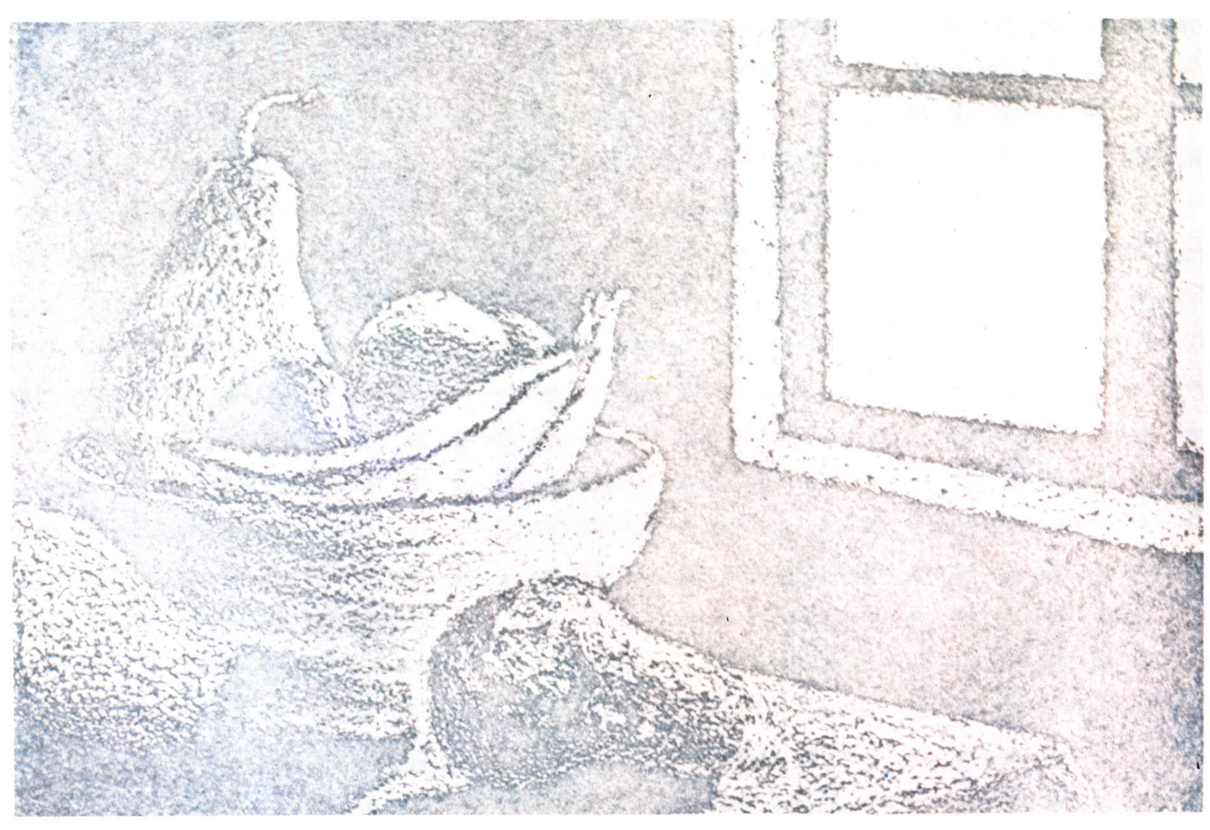

5

Go over the drawing on the plate with the crayon.

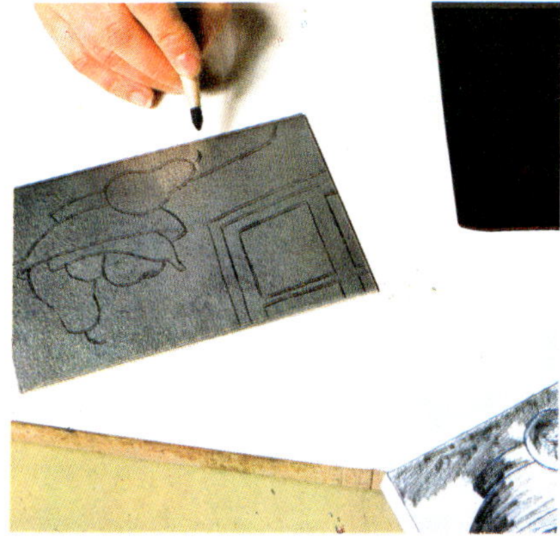

6

Those parts which have been drawn in with the crayon are not affected by the acid and will be light coloured when the print is made.

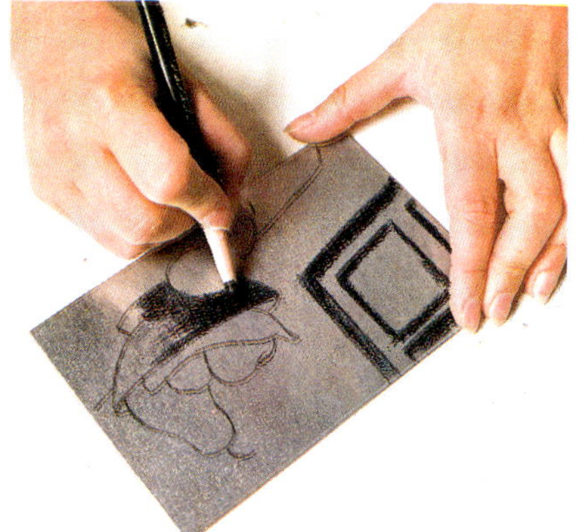

7

Cover the areas which are to remain completely white with varnish, using a brush.

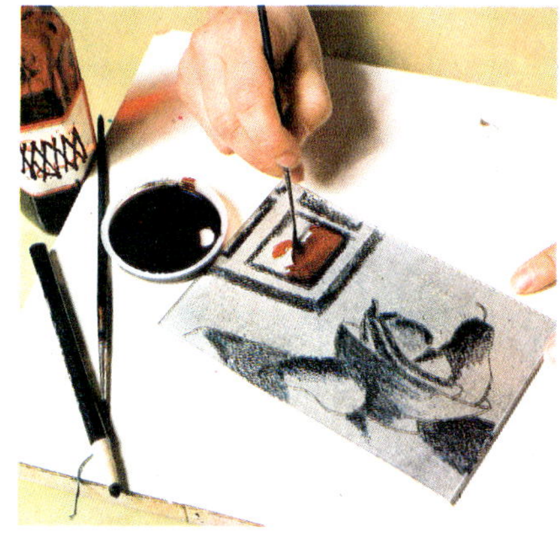

8

Prepare the acid solution. Pour the water into the bath.

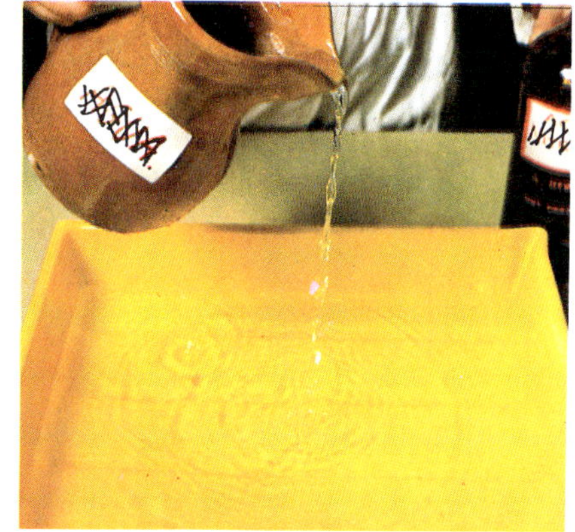

9

The solution does not have to be particularly strong, so add one part of nitric acid to eight parts of water.

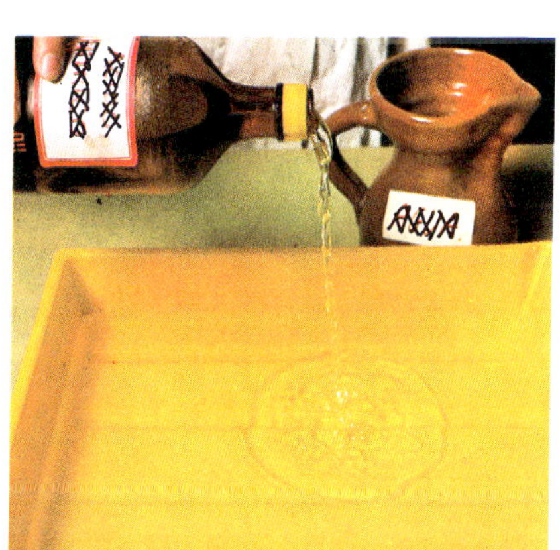

10

Leave the zinc plate in the acid solution for about ten minutes.

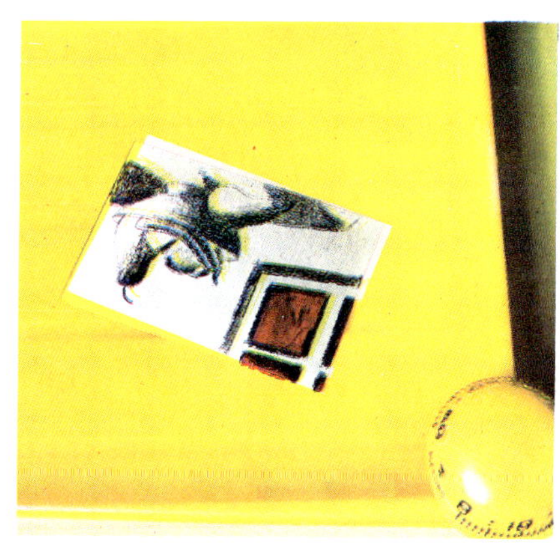

11

Take the plate out of the bath and rinse thoroughly with water.

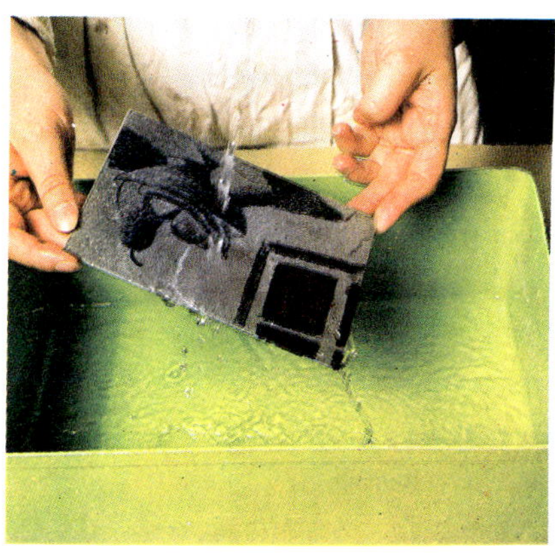

12

Pat the plate dry with an absorbent cloth.

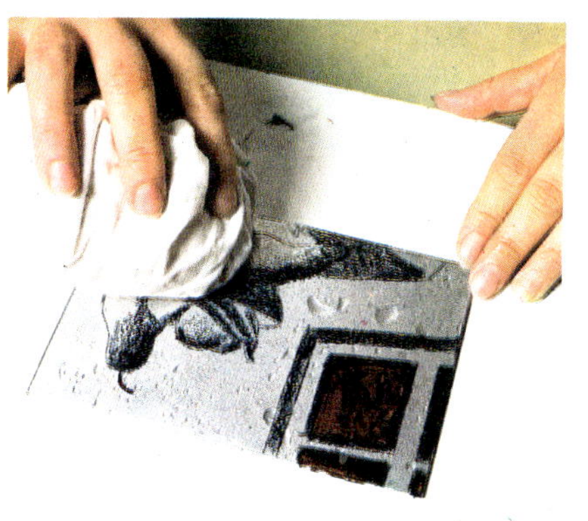

13
Go over the pattern created by the acid solution with the lithographic crayon. This time also cover other parts of the drawing.

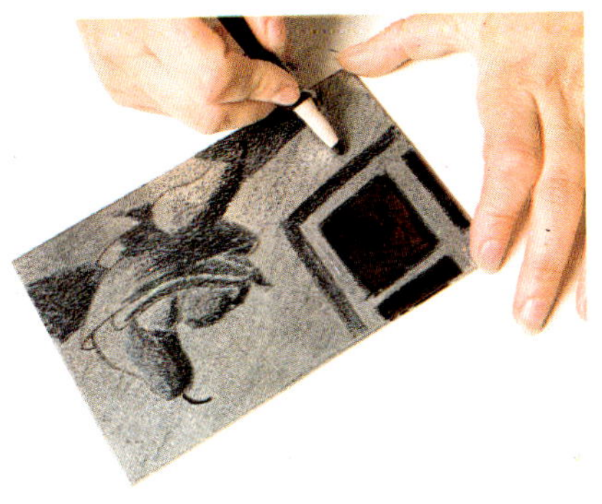

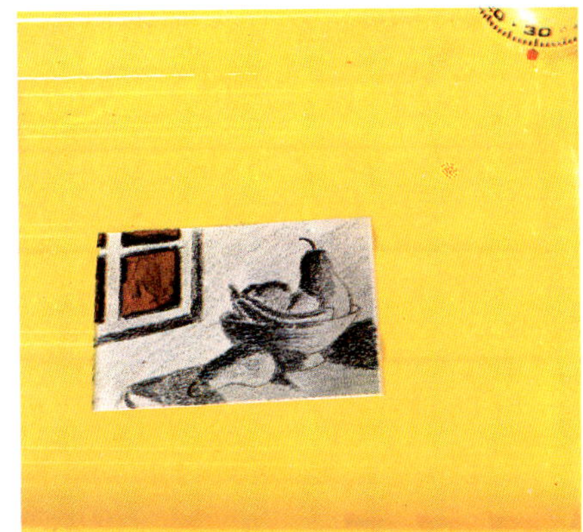

14
Leave the plate in the acid solution for about thirty minutes.

15
Take the plate out of the bath and rinse thoroughly with water.

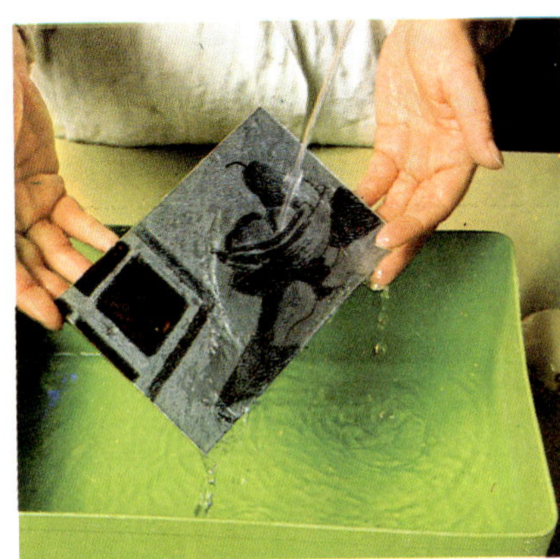

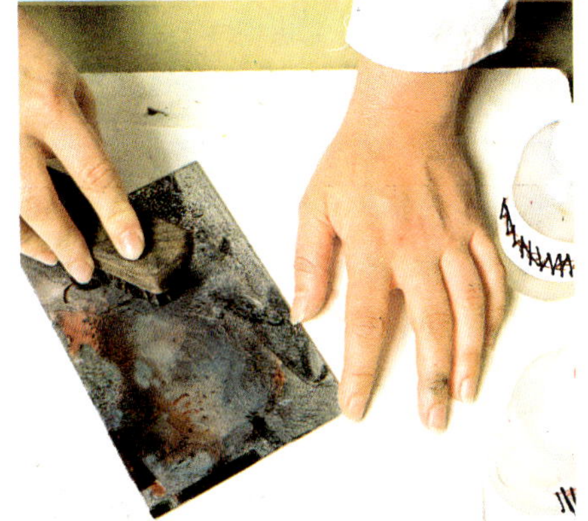

16
Using a brush, clean the plate with parafin/turps and then remove all traces of grease with meths.

17
Now clean the plate thoroughly with a cloth and a little bit of meths, and dry it.

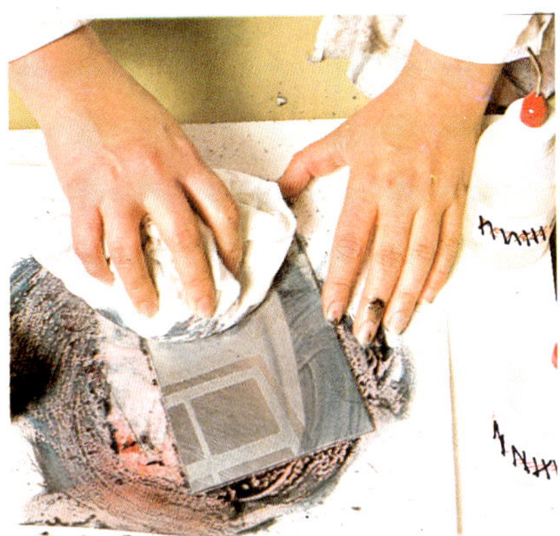

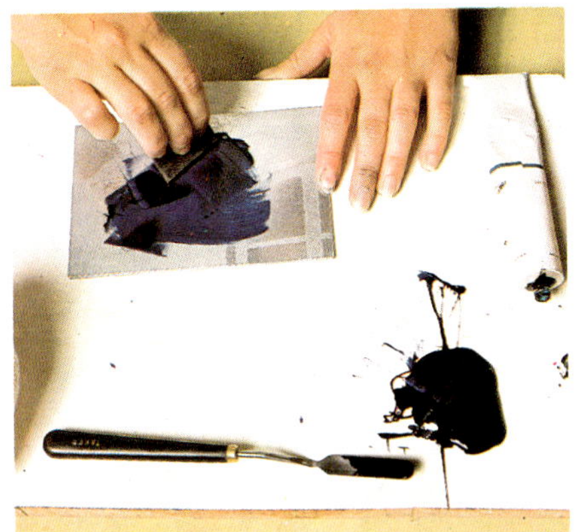

18
Using the block of rubber, cover the plate with a layer of ink.

19
Remove the excess ink from the plate with a piece of cheesecloth.

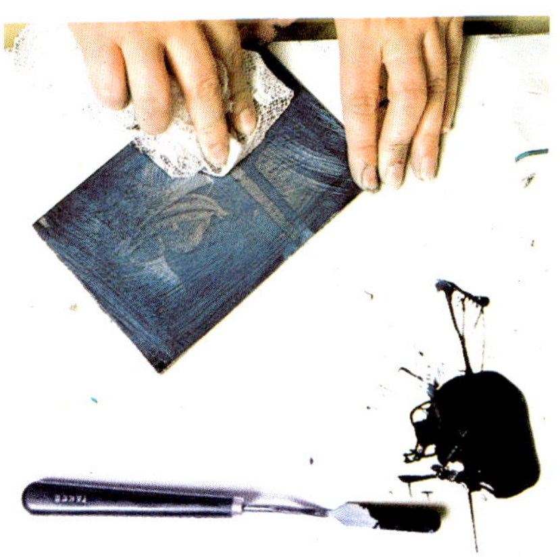

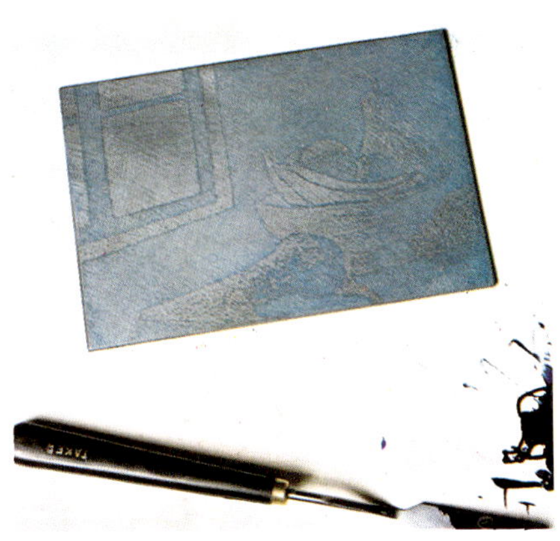

20
At this stage in the procedure the plate looks like this. It has not yet been sufficiently affected by the acid.

21
Lay the plate in the middle of the printing press to make a test print.

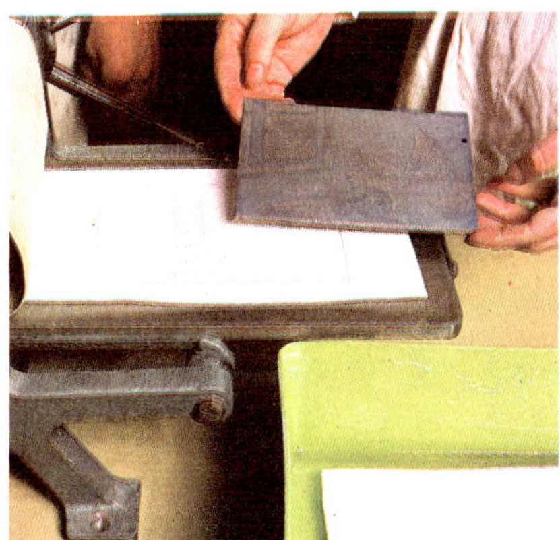

22
Remove the printing paper from the water and place between two sheets of blotting paper.

23
Press the sheets of blotting paper with a cloth to accelerate the drying out.

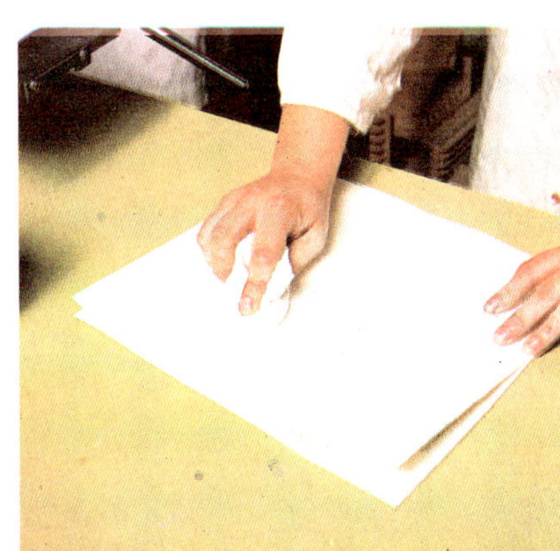

24
Place the zinc plate on the tray of the press and cover with the printing paper.

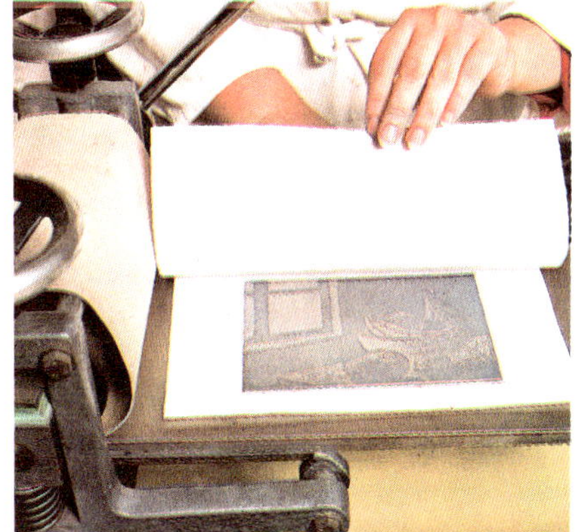

25
Remove the test print of the etching in its first version of this procedure.

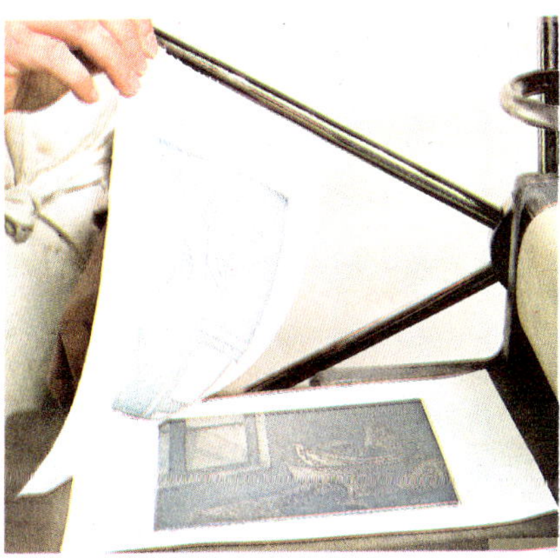

26
Again sprinkle resin over the plate and heat until it starts to melt. Cover the parts of the etching which are to remain white with varnish.

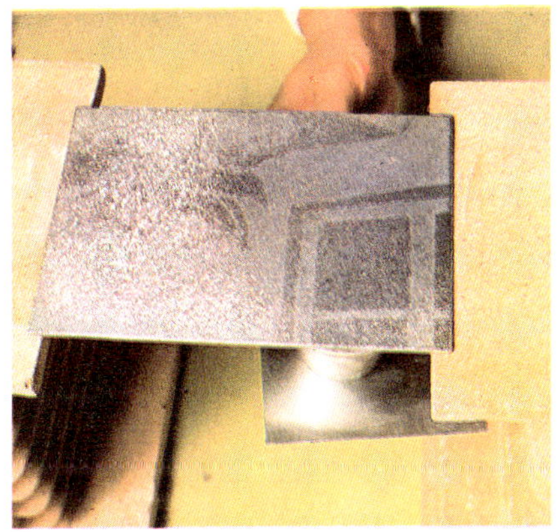

27
Leave the plate in the acid solution for about twenty minutes.

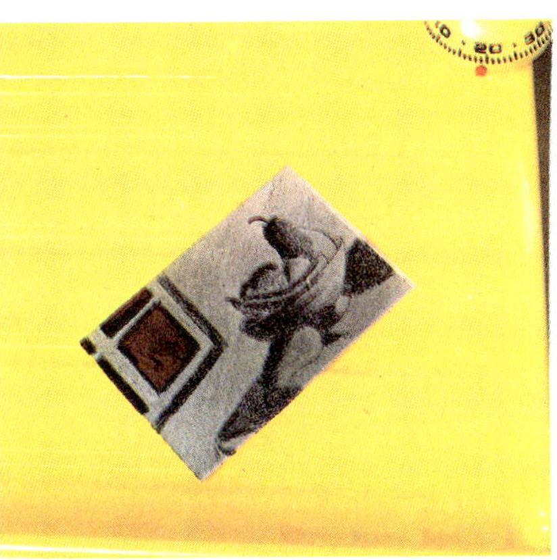

28
Rinse the plate thoroughly in water. Dry with a cloth. Do not rub, as the resin might come off.

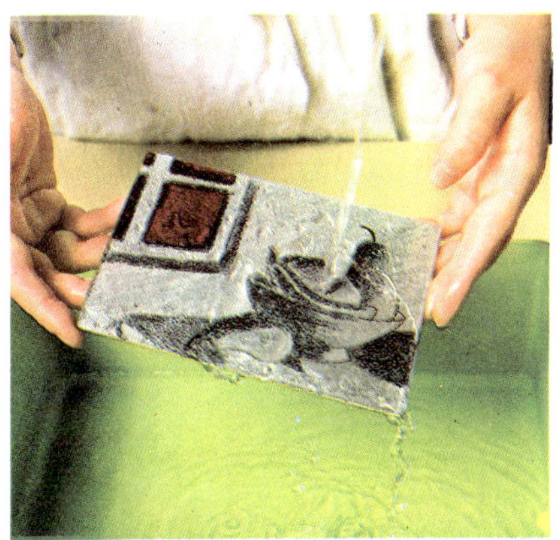

29
There are now three shades, one of which is white. These are now covered with the lithographic crayon, except for the areas which are to be completely dark.

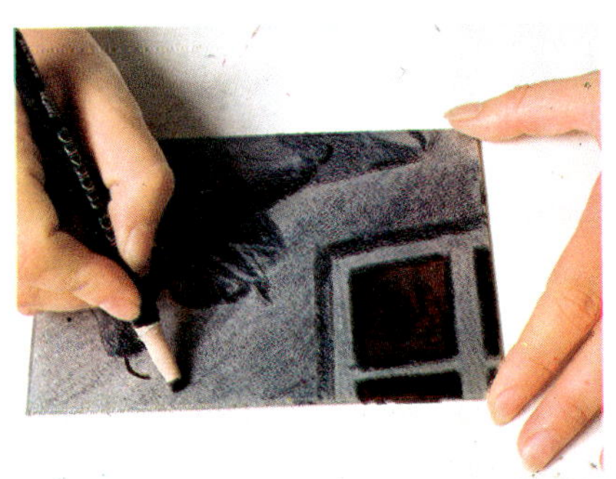

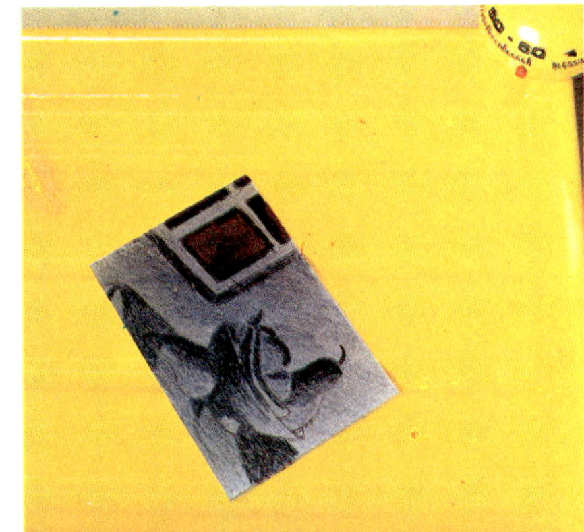

30
Leave the plate in the acid solution for approximately one hour.

31
Clean the plate with a brush when it has been taken out of the acid, and remove all traces of grease with parafin and meths.

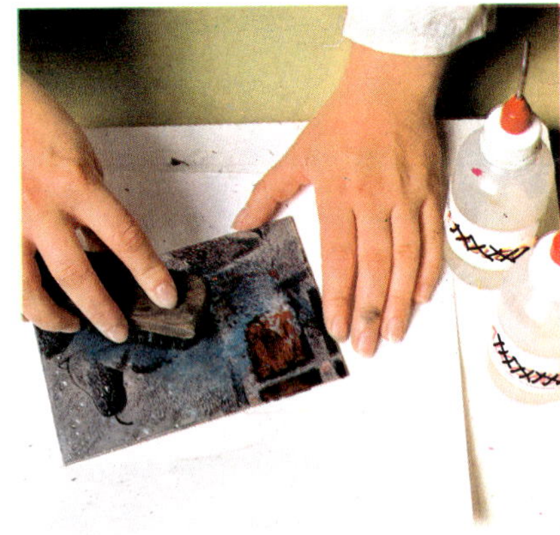

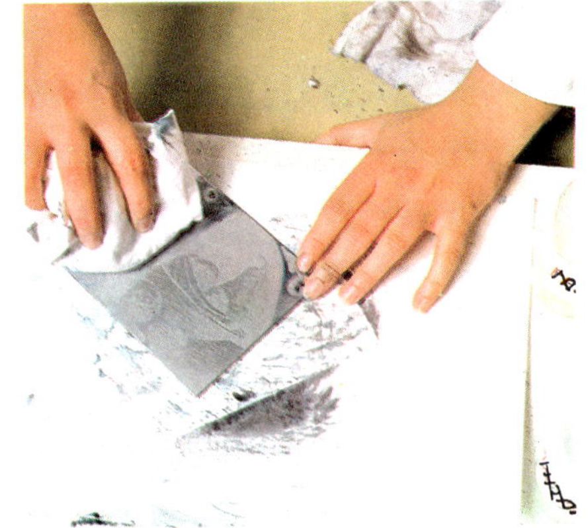

32
Clean and dry the zinc plate with a clean cloth without rubbing it.

33
Using a rubber block, cover the plate with a layer of ink.

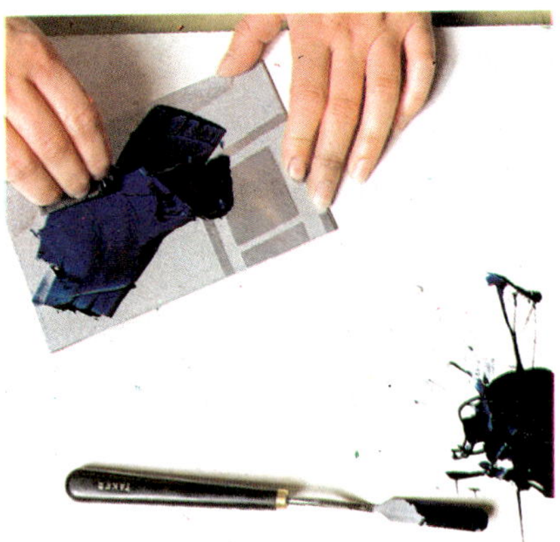

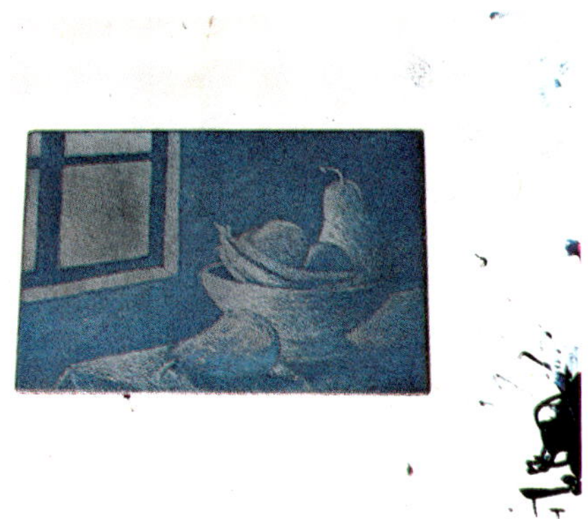

34
The plate is covered in ink and the excess ink is removed with a cheesecloth. Now make a print.

35
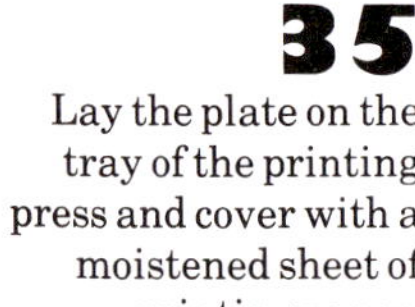
Lay the plate on the tray of the printing press and cover with a moistened sheet of printing paper.

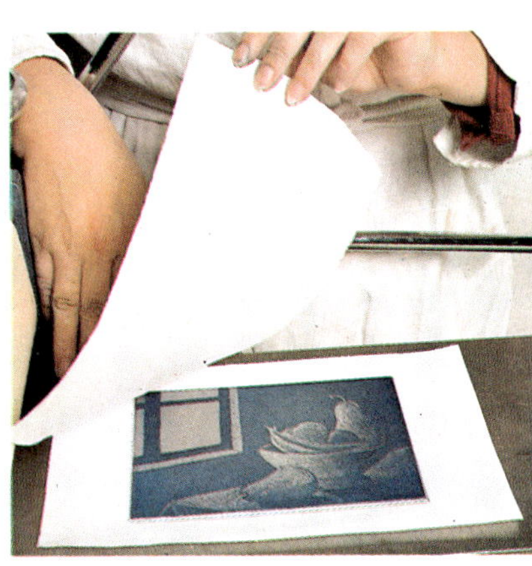

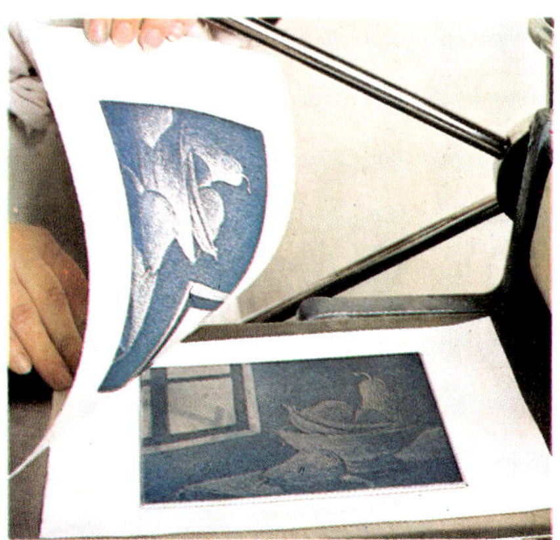

36
Pass the plate through the press to obtain the final print of the etching.

Line etching with resin (aquatint)

The aquatint technique makes it possible to put finishing touches or to enrich line etchings by adding shades of grey.
If you have a linear etched plate this can be used to try out this unique possibility.
In principle there is no difference from the aquatint technique described in the previous section, but all the steps will be illustrated and described in more detail in this section.
The print of the original line etching to which the shades of grey are to be added with pencil or watercolours, forms the basis for this exercise.
This print serves as a standard of comparison and should be consulted at every step throughout the experiment.
The zinc plate should have powdered resin sprinkled onto it; this is then melted on. The areas which should not be etched and which are therefore white in the print, should be covered with methylated spirit based varnish or lithographic pencil.
For this exercise you will need the following materials: a printing press, a tray, printing paper, blotting paper, cheesecloth, meths, parafin, a scrubbing brush, fine brushes, a spatula, lithographic pencil or lithograpic chalk, a block of rubber, resin, a bowl of fibreglass wool and some meths or the gas ring of a cooker, methylated spirit based varnish, various sorts of ink, water, nitric acid, an acid bath, a kitchen timer and a plate with a line etching.

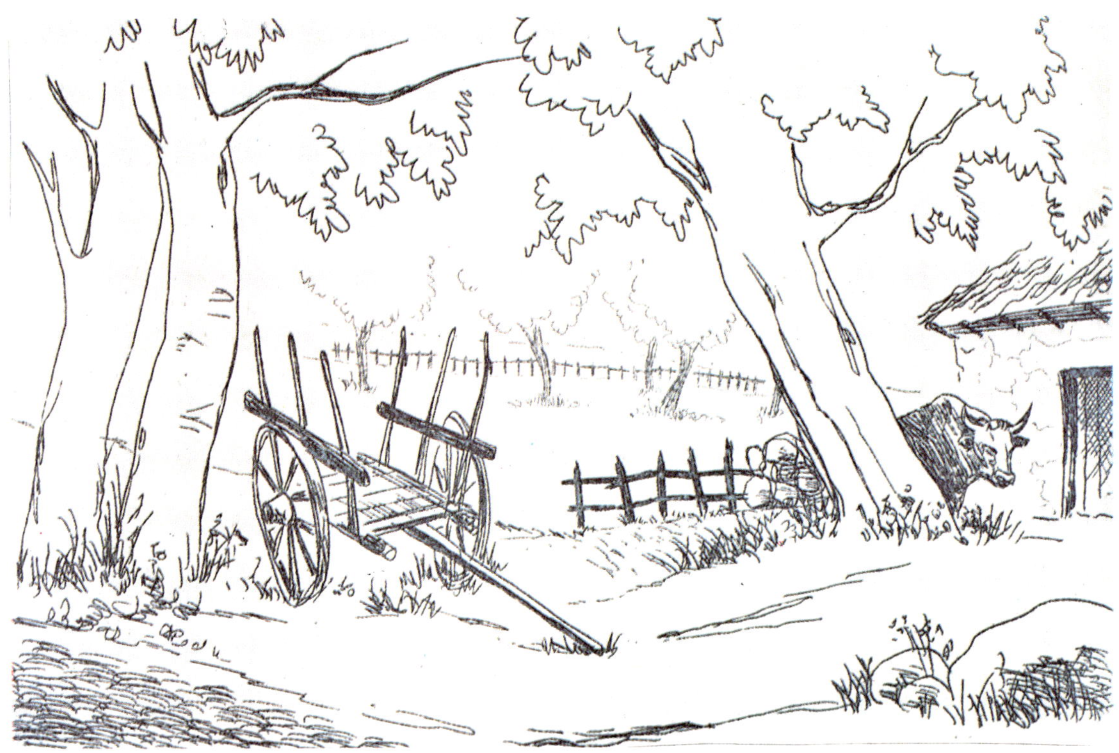

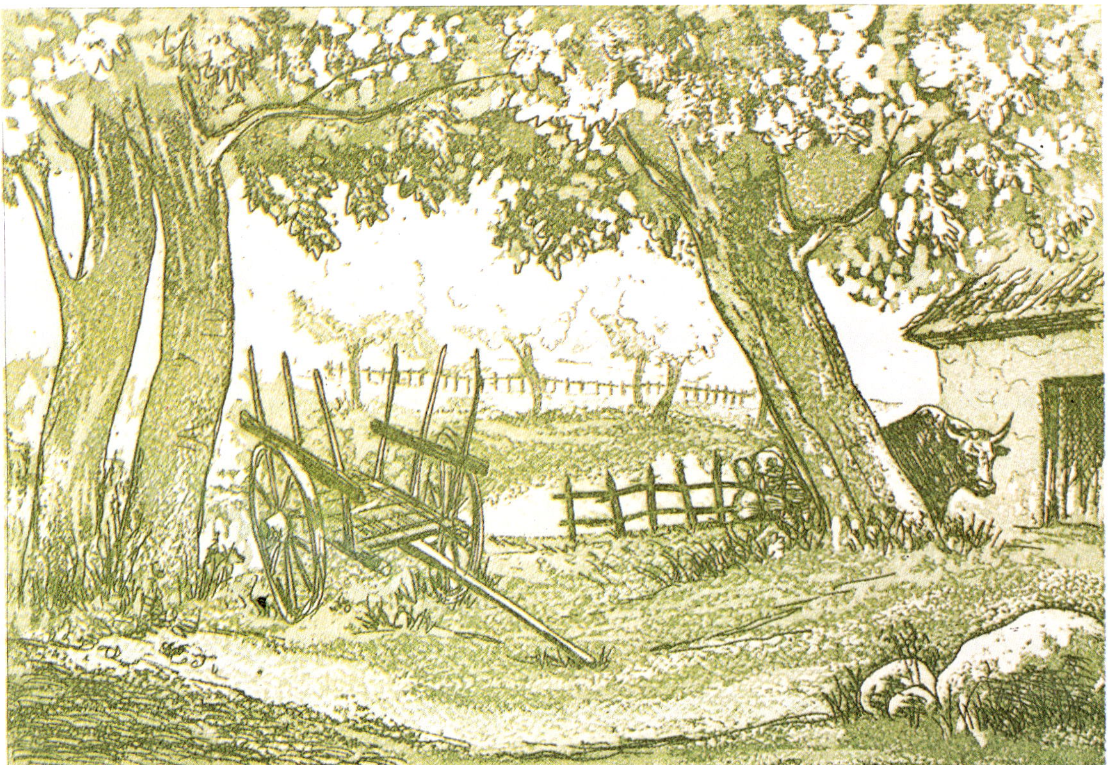

First and second version.
The extra shades of colour in the second version are clearly visible.

1
The tools and materials required.

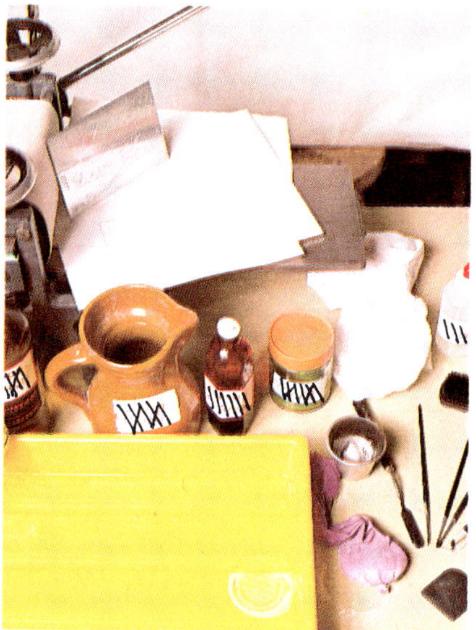

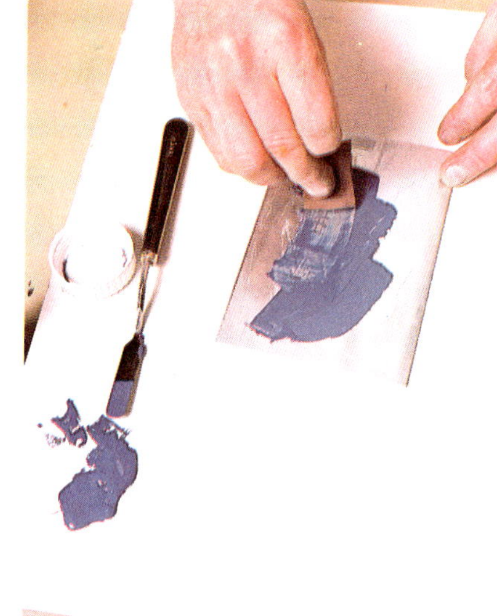

2
The zinc plate which has only the line etching is covered with ink. Press the ink firmly into the grooves with a rubber block.

3
Now remove the excess ink from the plate with a piece of cheesecloth so that the ink only remains in the lines.

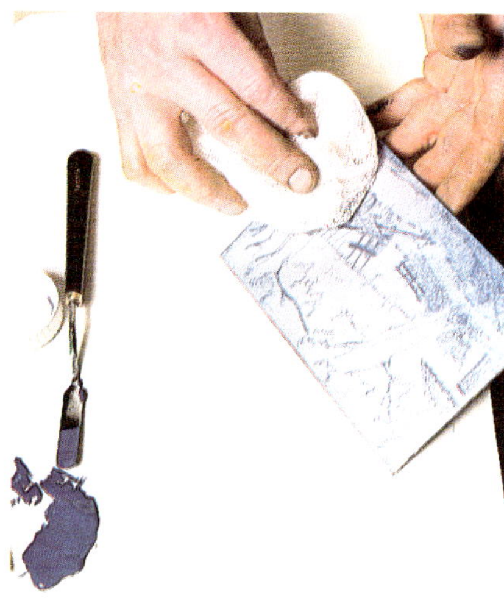

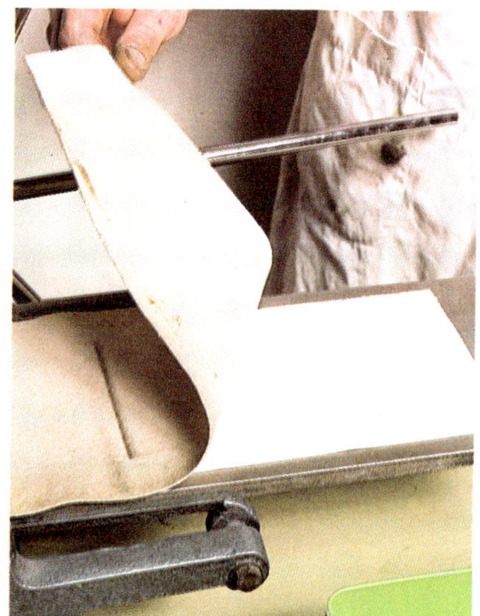

4
Prepare the printing press. Lay the plate and a sheet of printing paper in the press to make a print.

5
Make the print.

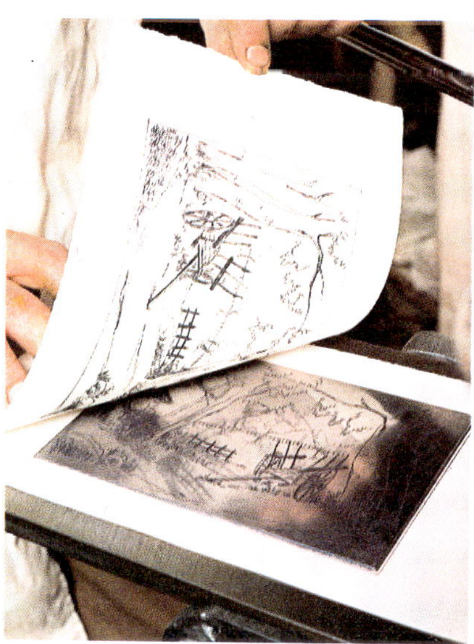

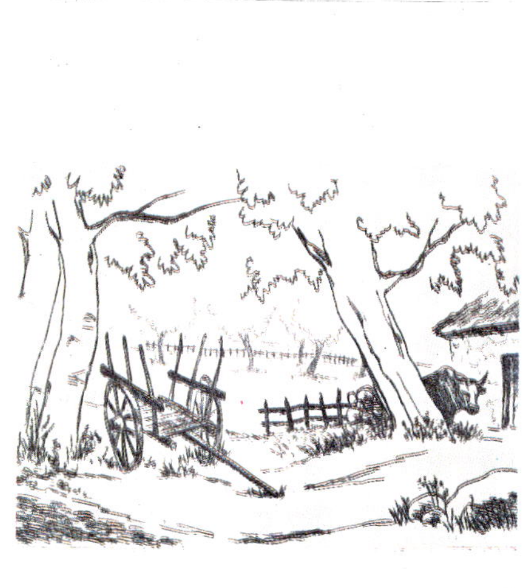

6
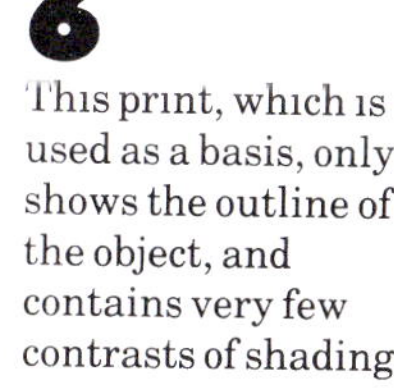
This print, which is used as a basis, only shows the outline of the object, and contains very few contrasts of shading.

7

Clean the etched plate with a cloth and some parafin. Remove all traces of grease with meths.

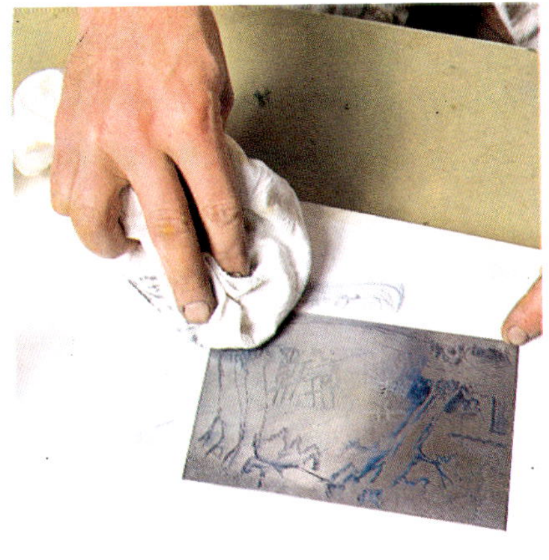

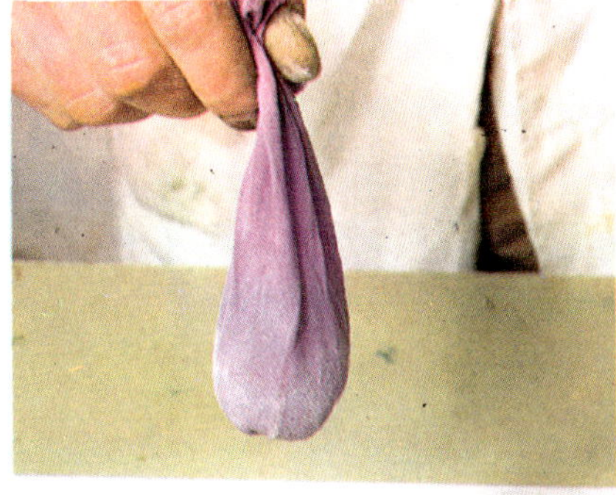

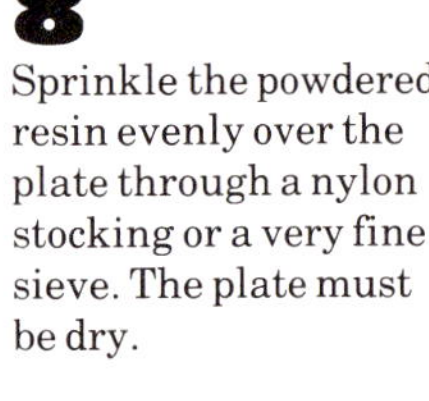

8

Sprinkle the powdered resin evenly over the plate through a nylon stocking or a very fine sieve. The plate must be dry.

9

Heat the plate above the gas flame or burning meths until the resin starts to melt and adhere to the plate.

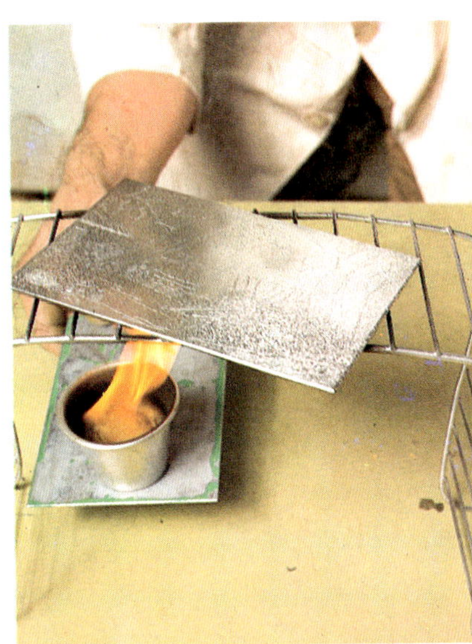

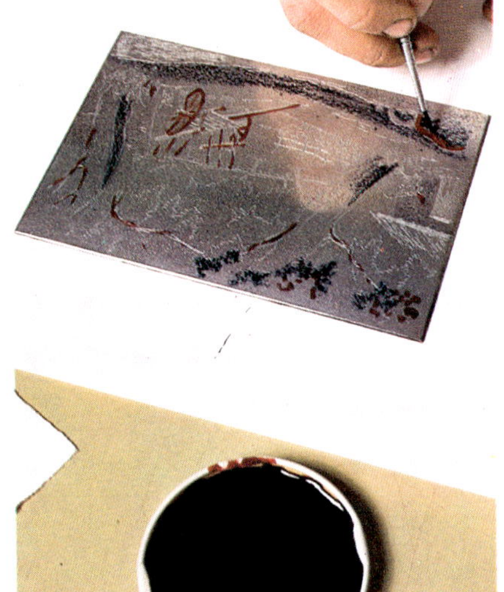

10

Cover the areas which are to remain white with varnish or lithographic pencil.

11

Prepare the acid solution. It does not have to be very concentrated. A solution of one part acid to eight parts water is sufficiently strong.

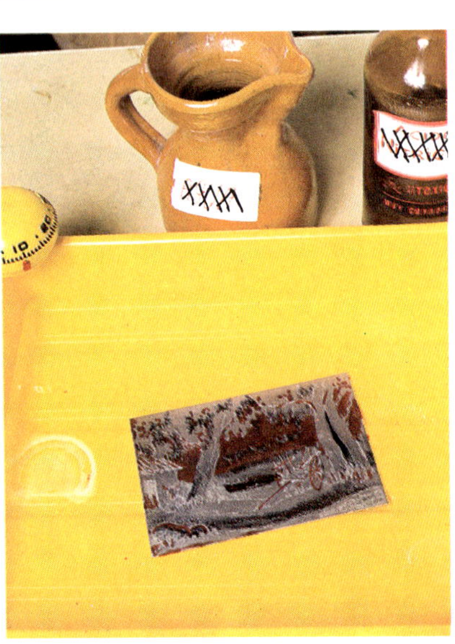

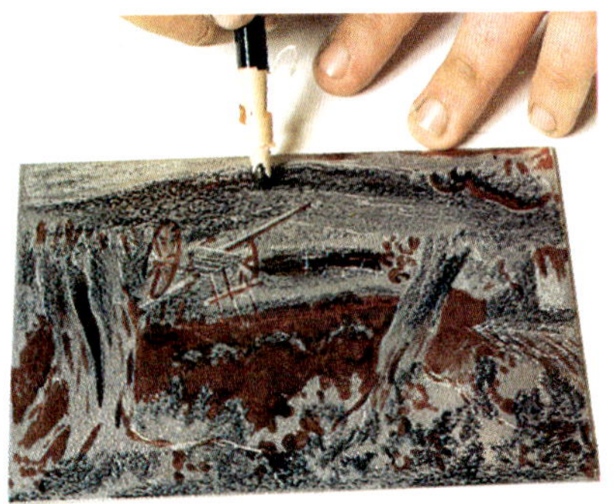

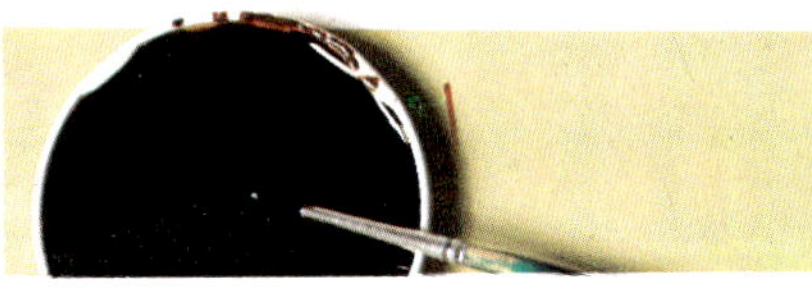

12

Take the plate out of the bath after about ten minutes and dry carefully. This first step has produced the lightest shade and this therefore has to be protected against any further effect of the acid by covering with lithographic pencil or varnish.

13
The second etching; lay the plate in the acid solution and this time leave it in for about thirty minutes to produce a darker shade.

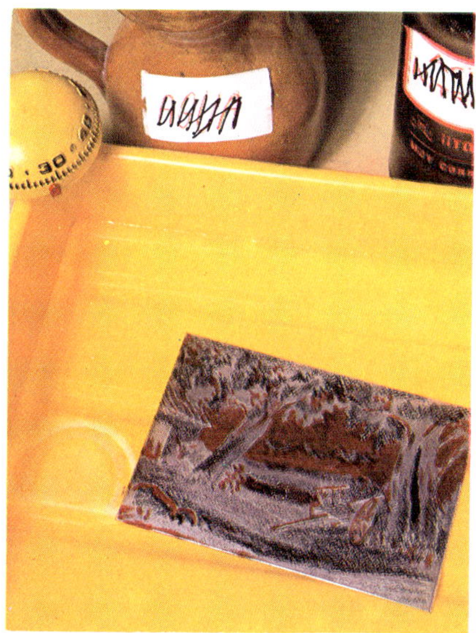

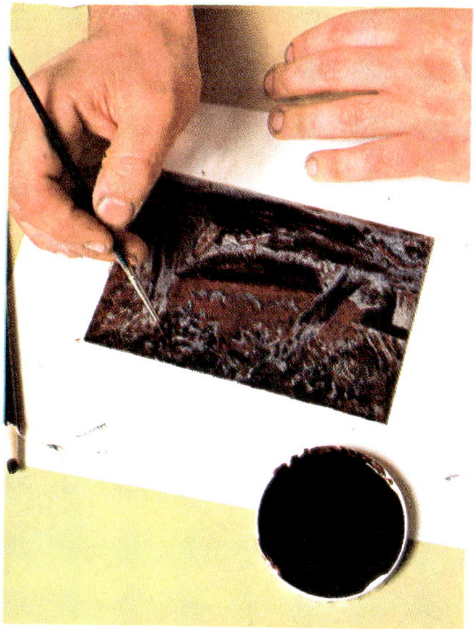

14
Again cover the areas which must not become any darker with methylated spirit based varnish, after the plate has been rinsed and cleaned.

15
Third etching. Place the plate in the acid solution and this final time leave it in the solution for about an hour.

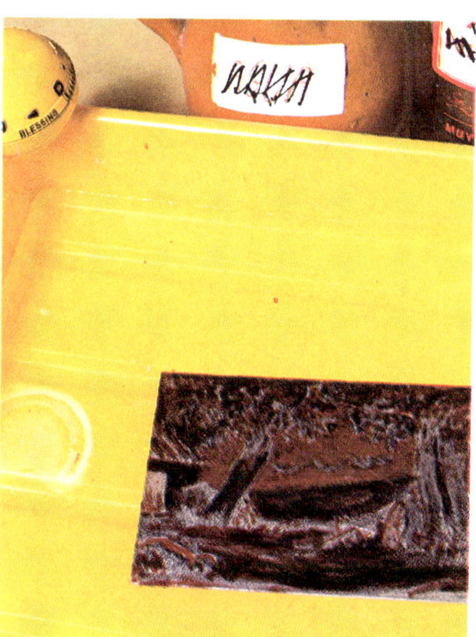

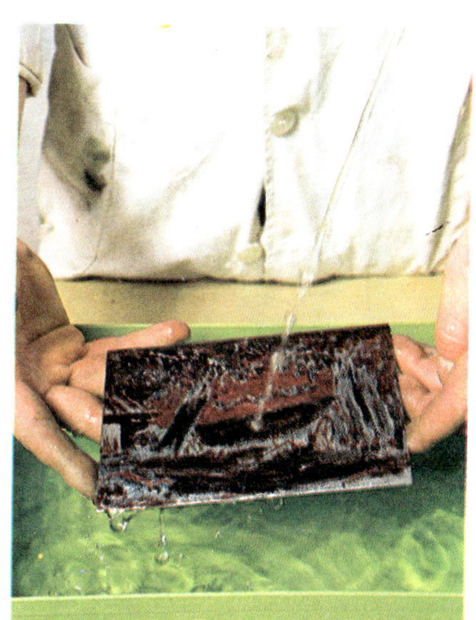

16
Take the plate out of the acid solution and rinse thoroughly with water.

17
Clean the plate with a brush and then remove all traces of grease with parafin and meths.

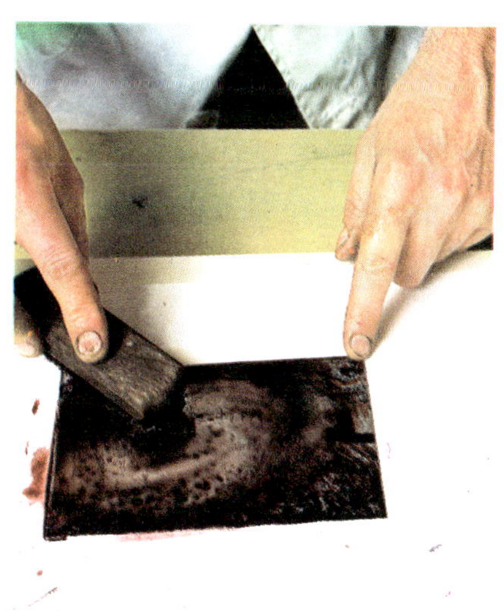

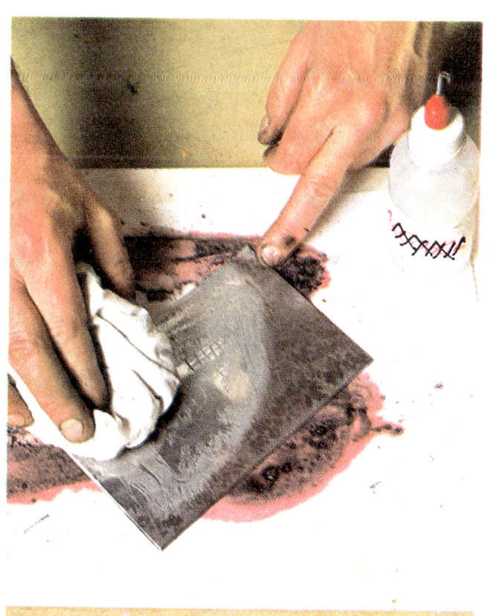

18
Now dry the plate thoroughly.

19

Using a rubber block, cover the plate with ink in the usual way.

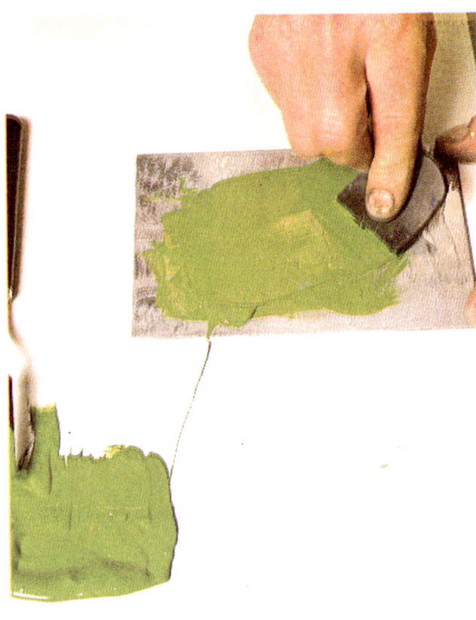

20

Rub the ink into the plate with a piece of cheesecloth so that it penetrates all the grooves; then remove the excess ink.

21

Take the printing paper out of the water where it has been soaking since the beginning of the exercise, and pat dry.

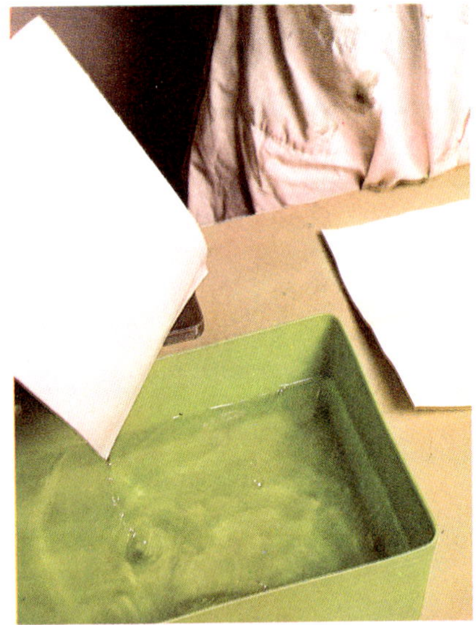

22

Place the plate in the press to make a print.

23

Pass the plate through the press to obtain the final version.

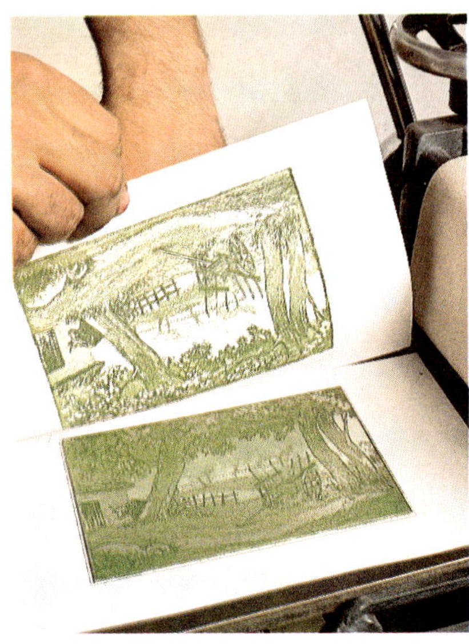

24

When you have finished this process the original line etching is enhanced with a lot of added detail.
You can now make a large number of prints from this plate.

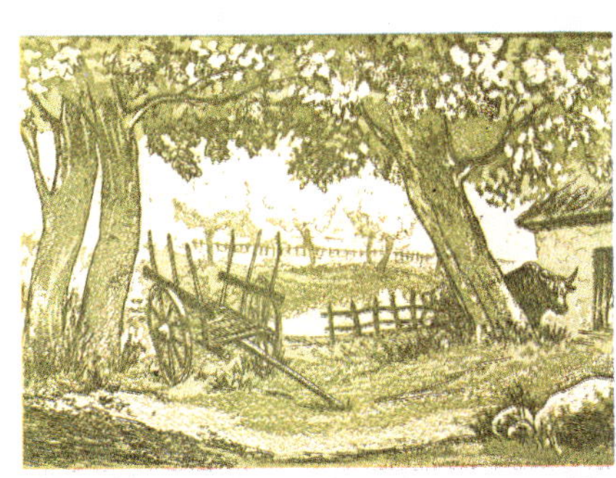

Etching with sugar (sugar aquatint)

A very attractive result can be obtained by using sugar in etching. The sugar is caramelised and a small amount of analyne is then added to the transparent substance to give it colour. The mixture is sometimes known as 'lift ground' and should be prepared in such a way that it does not go hard straightaway, as this prevents it from sliding smoothly over the metal.

The lift ground is later removed with warm water.

In this exercise a drawing is first transferred onto the plate. This might be a view of some buildings seen through a window glazed with rain. Instead of powdered resin, an aerosol can of varnish is used to do the buildings.

For this exercise you will need the following materials: analyne, sugar, water, a spatula, fine brushes, a rubber block to apply the ink, an aluminium bowl for the sugar, alcohol based varnish, nitric acid, solvent, parafin, meths, ink, a gas flame, a tray, blotting paper, printing paper, tarlatan, car varnish in an aerosol can, a bowl of water for rinsing the plate, and an acid bath.

1

All the materials and tools needed to make an etching using sugar.

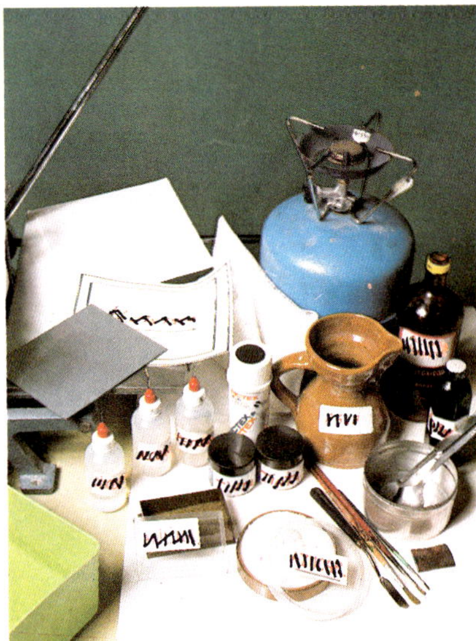

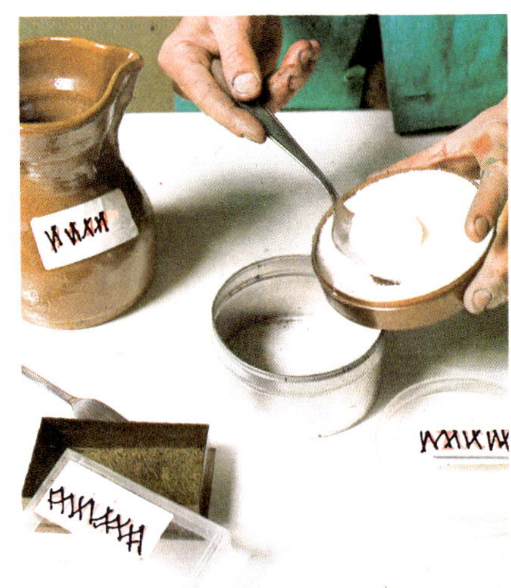

2

Place a small amount of sugar in an aluminium bowl.

The result: an etching showing the view from a window glazed with rain. This effect is achieved by using sugar and it is a way of evoking the feeling of a rainy day in the city.

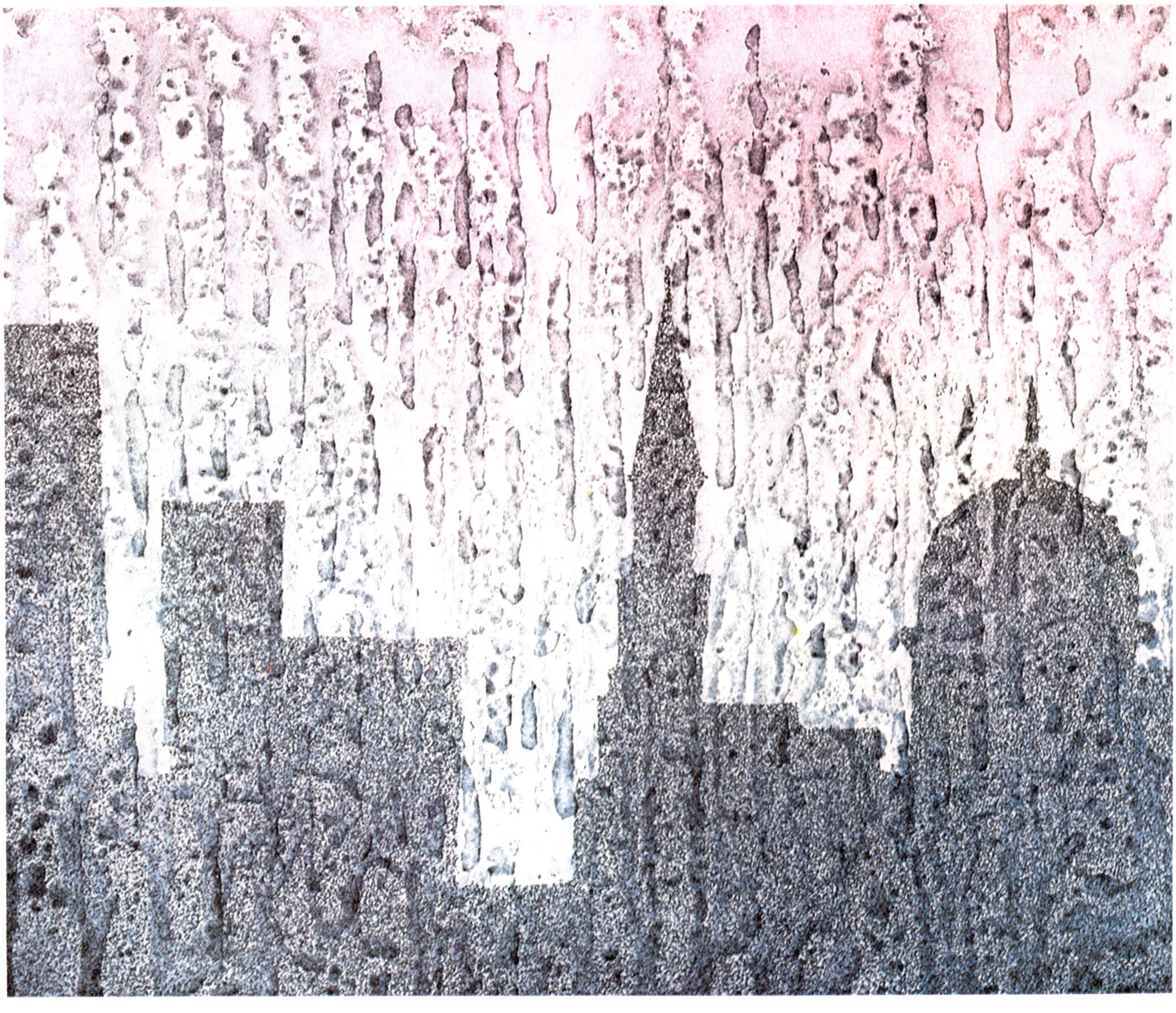

3
Add a little bit of analyne or another water soluble colorizer for the colour.

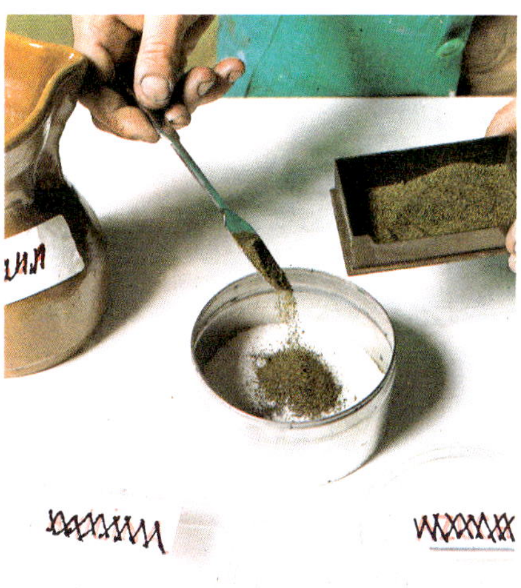

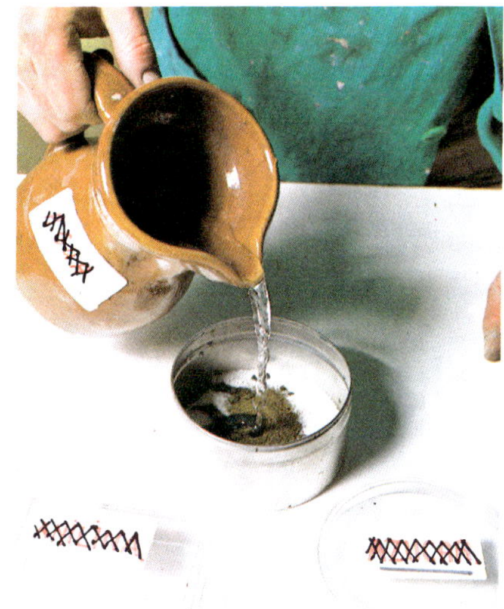

4
Add enough water to achieve the consistency of honey.

5
Heat the bowl over a gas burner until the sugar is dissolved and the required consistency is achieved.

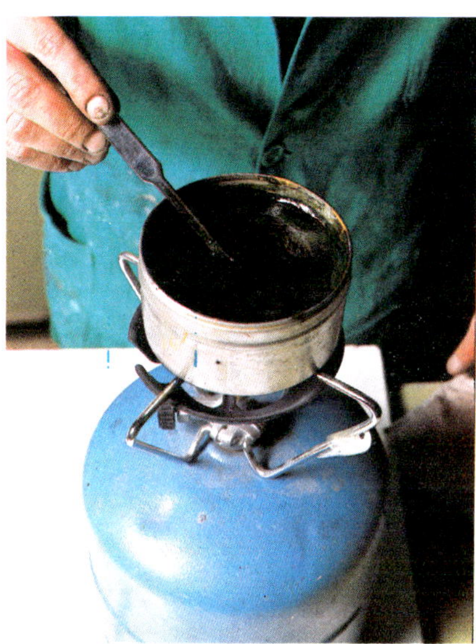

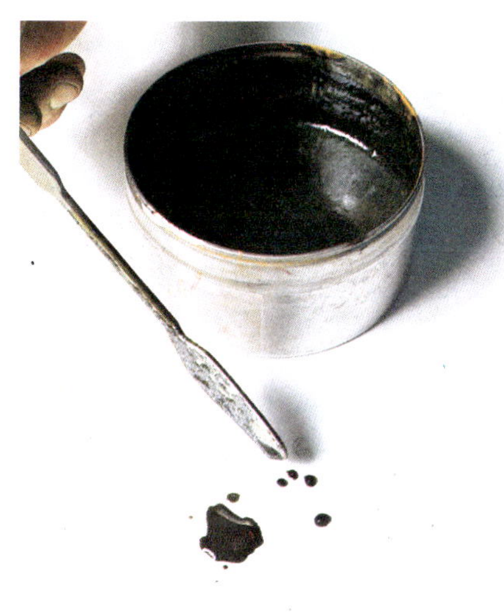

6
See how long it takes for a small quantity of lift ground to dry on the table.

7
Attach a zinc plate to a piece of wood and let the liquid slide down the plate.

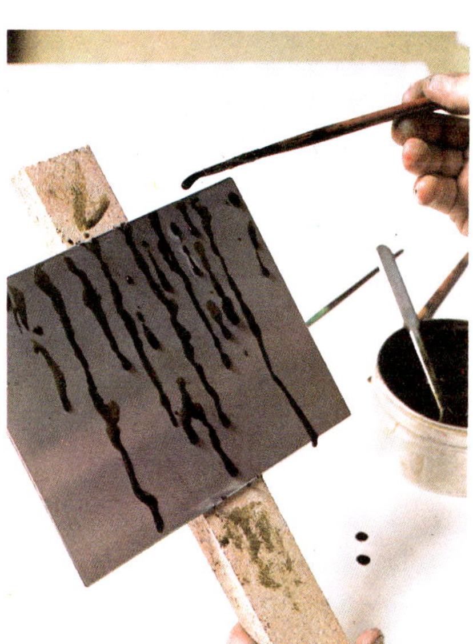

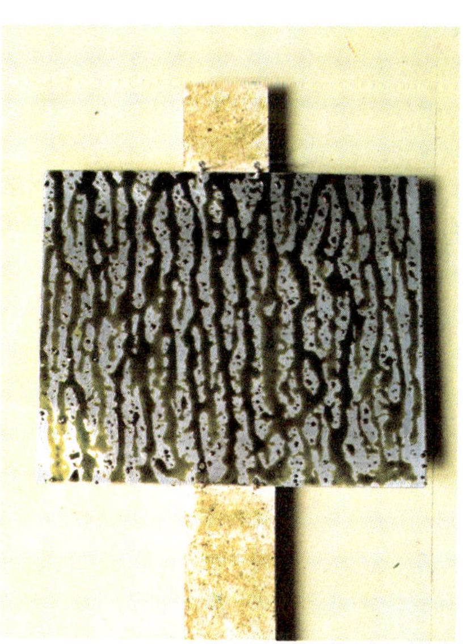

8
Sufficient liftground has been applied to the plate.

9

When the sugar has gone hard – this takes a few hours – cover the plate with varnish and leave to dry.

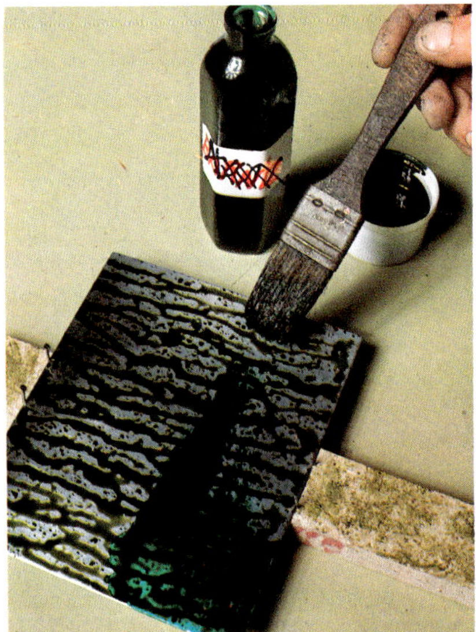

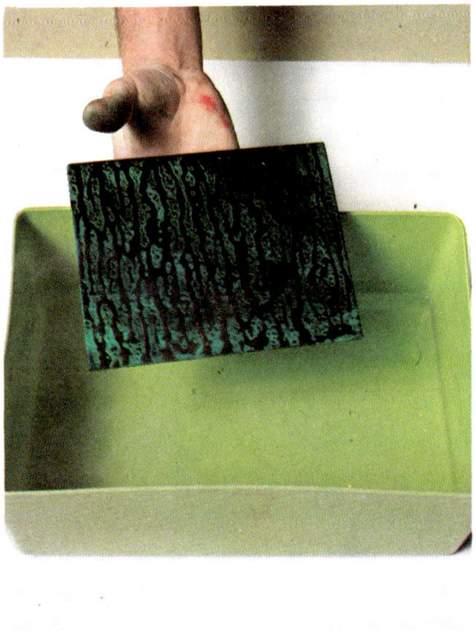

10

When the varnish has dried, place the plate in warm water to dissolve the sugar.

11

The warm water will dissolve the sugar but does not affect the varnish.

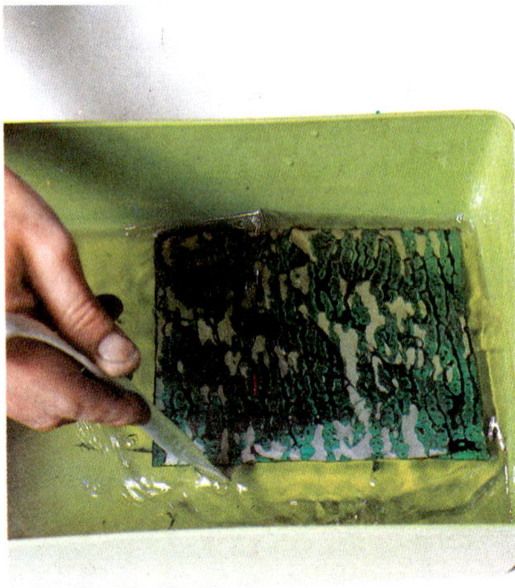

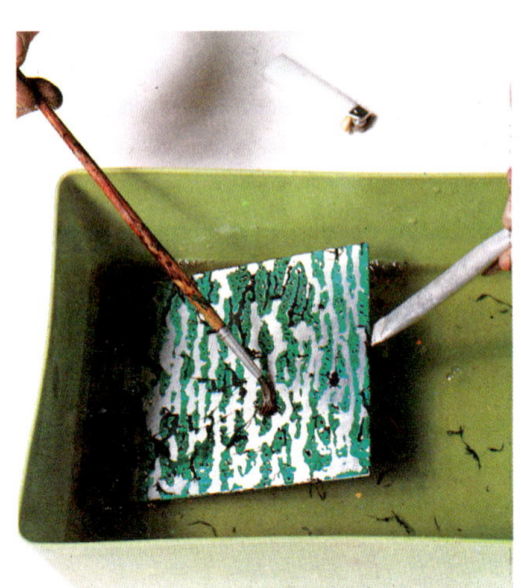

12

Move the plate about in the bowl and use a brush to help remove the sugar.

13

When the sugar has been removed, prepare the acid solution. Put five parts of water into the acid bath.

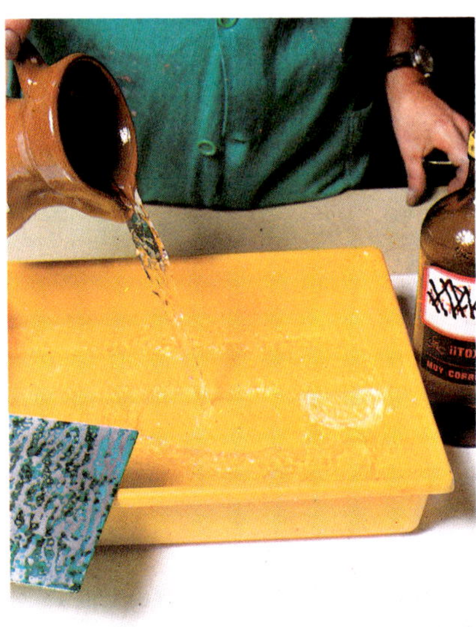

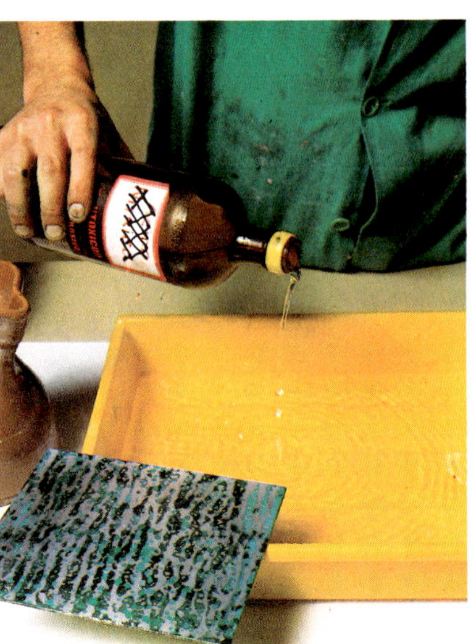

14

Add one part of nitric acid. This is a fairly concentrated solution. Place the zinc plate in the acid solution.

15
Leave the plate in the solution for about four hours so that it is thoroughly etched.

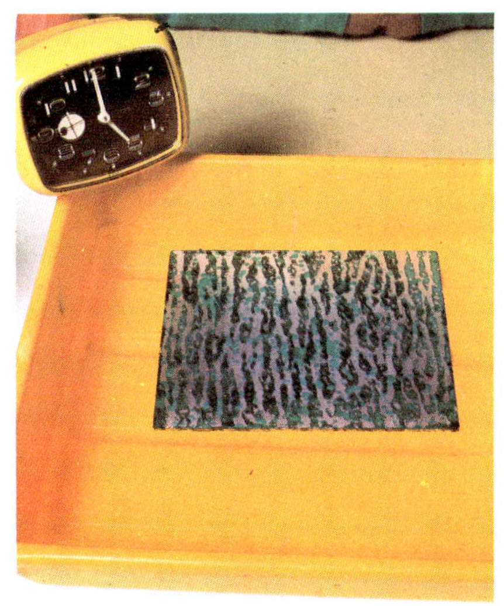

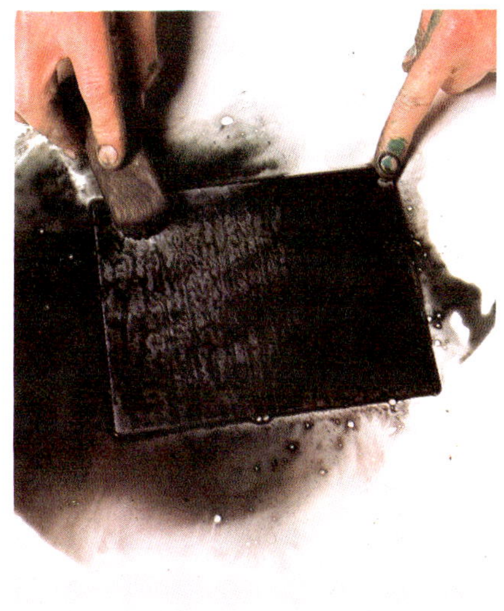

16
Take the plate out of the bath and clean with a scrubbing brush and some meths.

17
Make a test print. Compare the plate and the print.

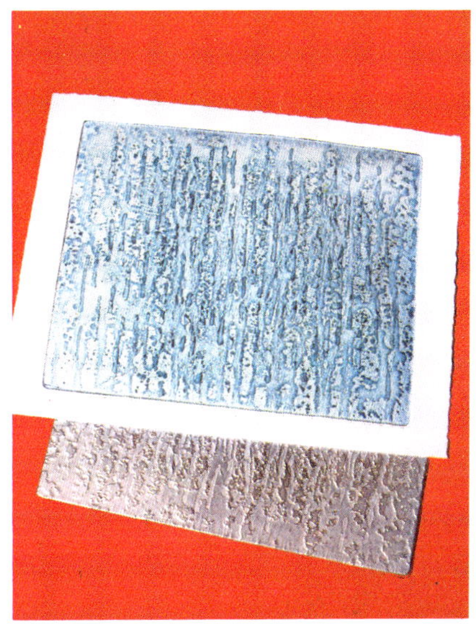

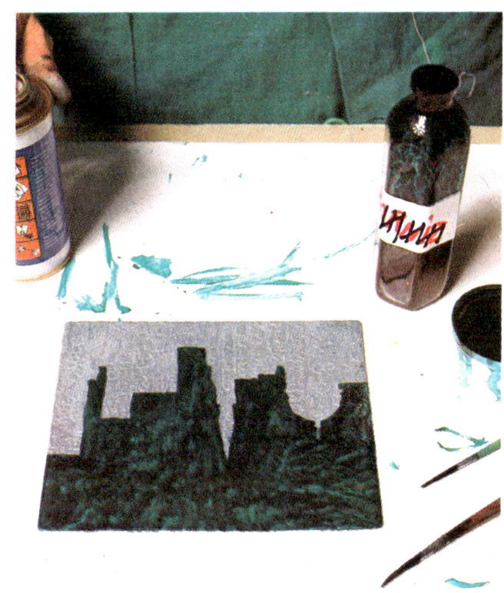

18
Cover the background (sky) with methylated spirit based varnish and make the silhouettes of the buildings dark using car varnish.

19
Spray the paint onto the plate from a distance to obtain the powdered resin effect.

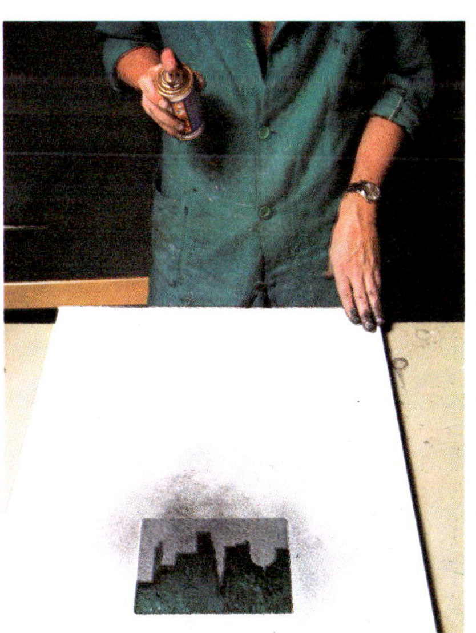

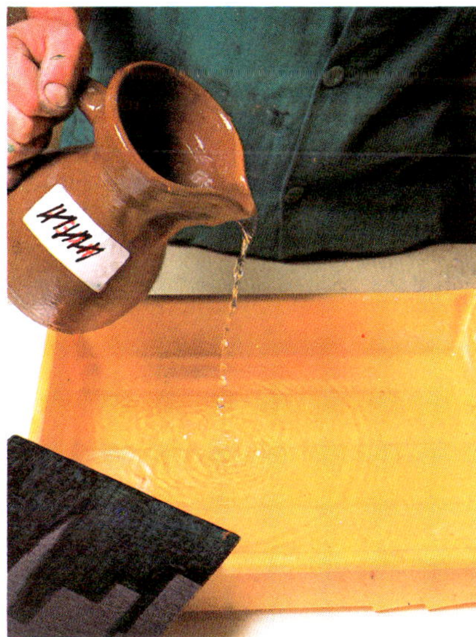

20
Prepare the acid solution with one part of acid to seven or eight parts of water.

21
Leave the zinc plate in the solution for abour an hour.

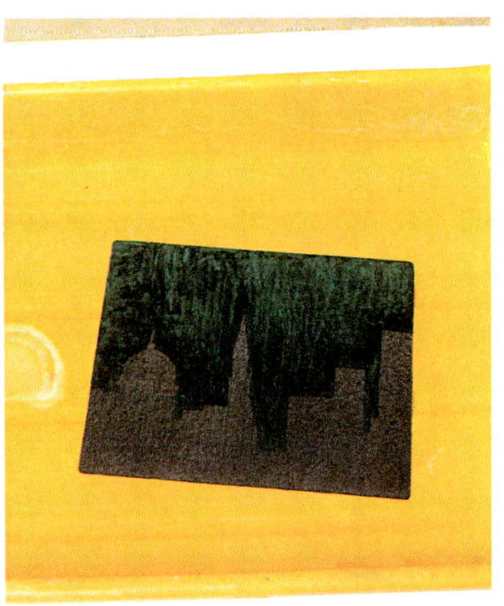

22
Clean the plate using a solvent, and then meths. This also removes all traces of grease.

23
Then cover the plate with ink in the usual way.

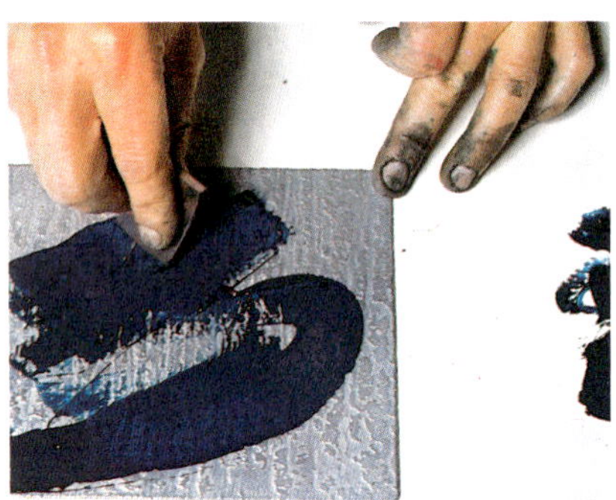

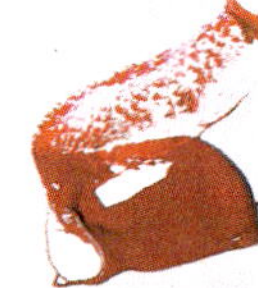

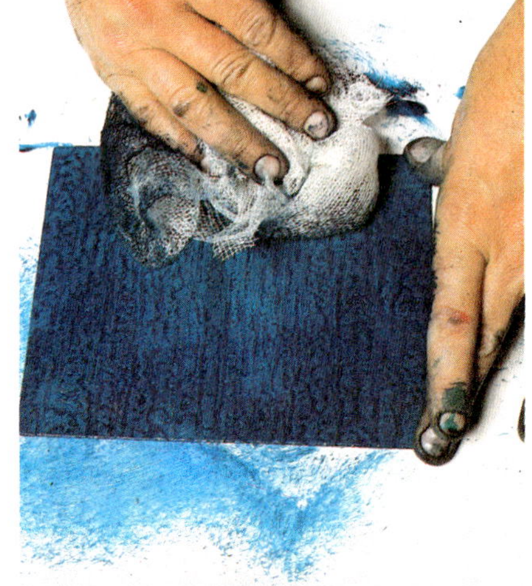

24
Rub the plate with a piece of cheesecloth.

25
Use another colour to highlight the sky by creating a contrast.

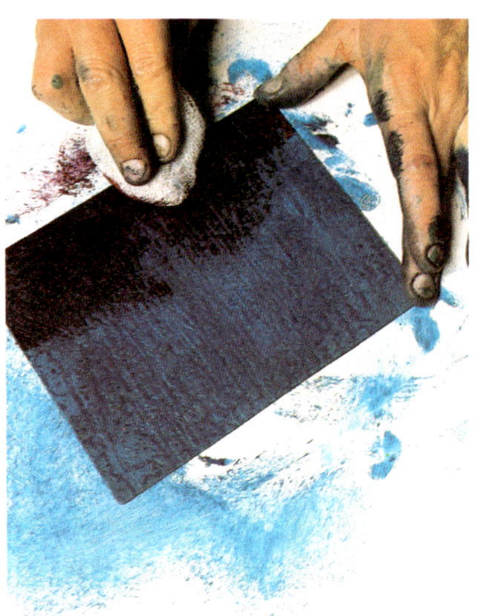

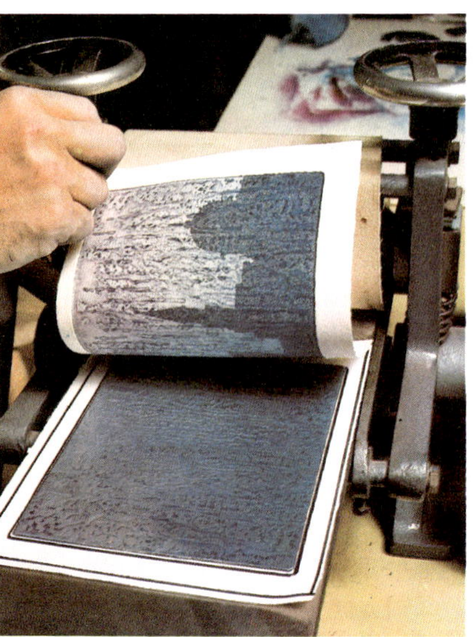

26
Make the final print in the press.

Mou varnish or the soft etching ground technique

The basic principle of mou varnish is that the drawing is transferred directly onto the metal plate. The lines of the drawing that is transferred all have the same intensity and resemble the lines of a pencil or chalk drawing.

In this technique the metal plate is covered with a thin even layer of mou varnish and a sheet of paper with the drawing which is to be printed is laid on top of this. It is also possible to draw directly onto the paper lying on the plate covered in mou varnish.

The mou varnish adheres to the paper only in those places where the pencil has pressed down, exposing the metal so that the acid can have its corrosive effect.

The example described in this section uses a simple drawing. It is laid on the plate and the outlines are gone over with a pencil onto a plate treated with mou varnish.

For this exercise you will need the following tools and materials: a press, a drawing, a printing plate, drawing paper, etching paper, parafin, meths, water, nitric acid, linseed oil, a plastic bowl, sellotape, ink, a spatula, an ink rubber, a pencil or ballpoint, a roller, cheesecloth, a meths burner (an aluminium bowl with water for the meths), mou varnish and methylated spirit based varnish.

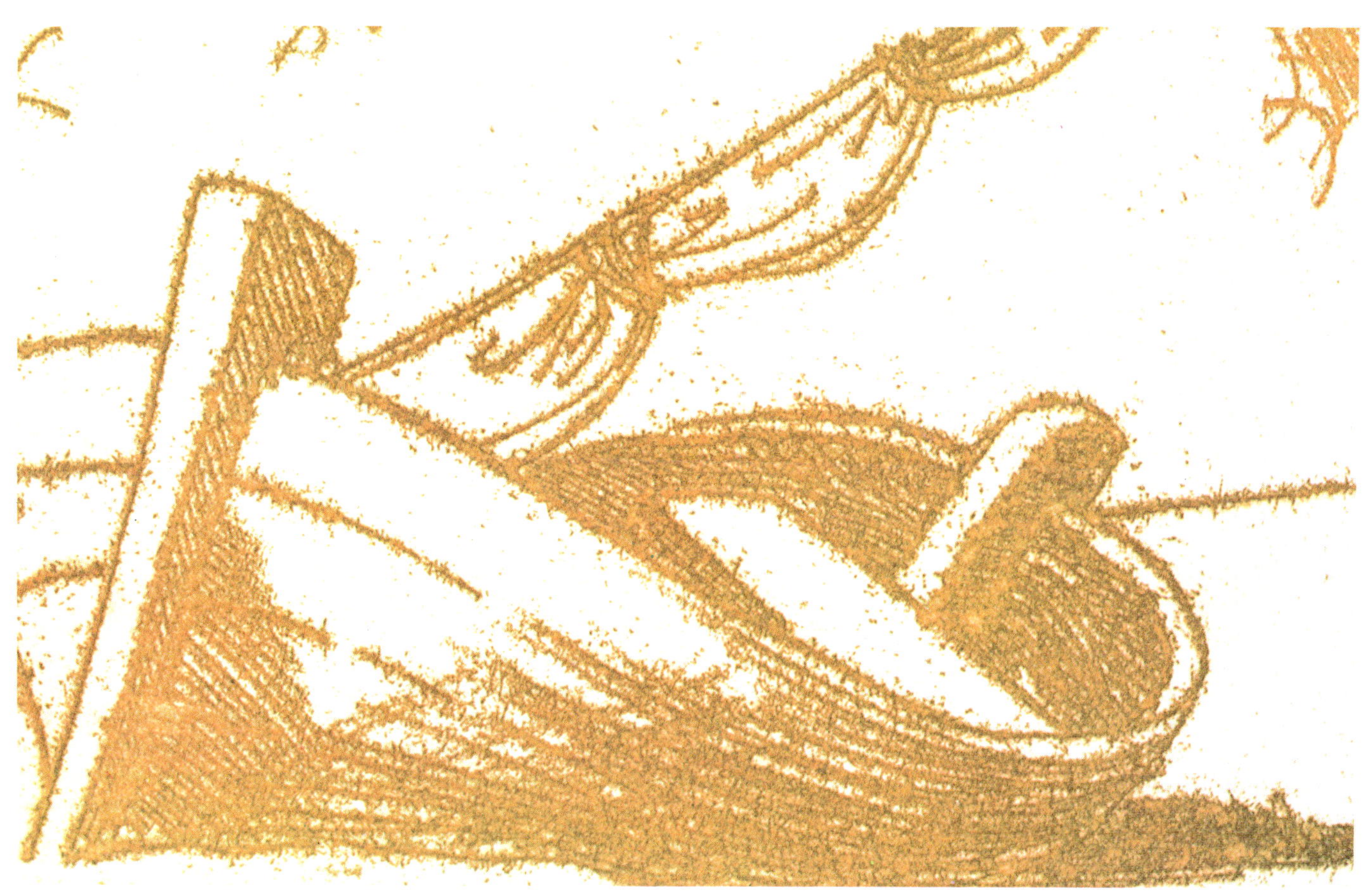

1
The tools and materials required.

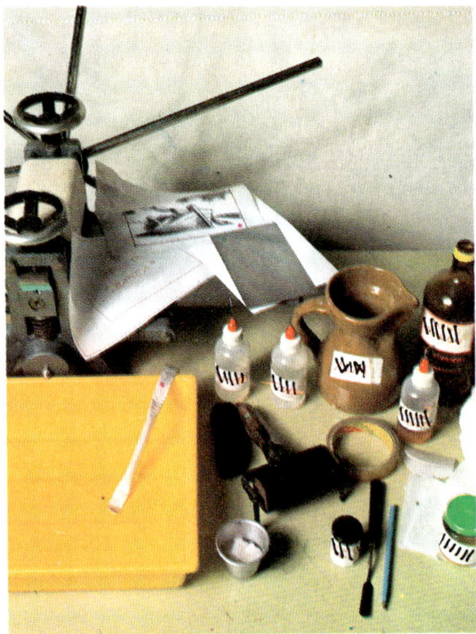

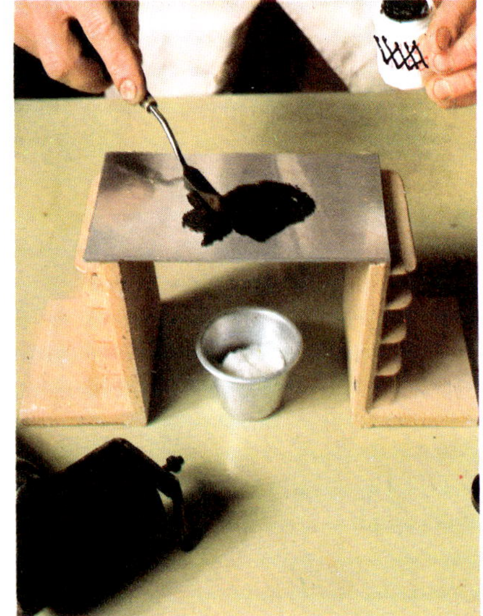

2
Cover the plate with a small amount of mou varnish using a spatula.

3
Spread the mou varnish evenly with a roller, rolling over the plate in every direction while carefully heating it.

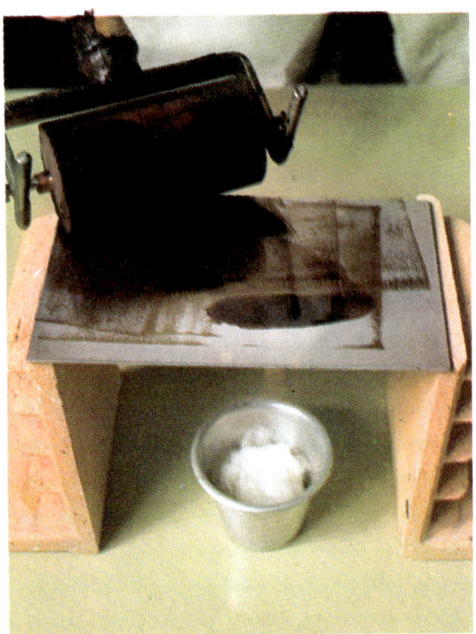

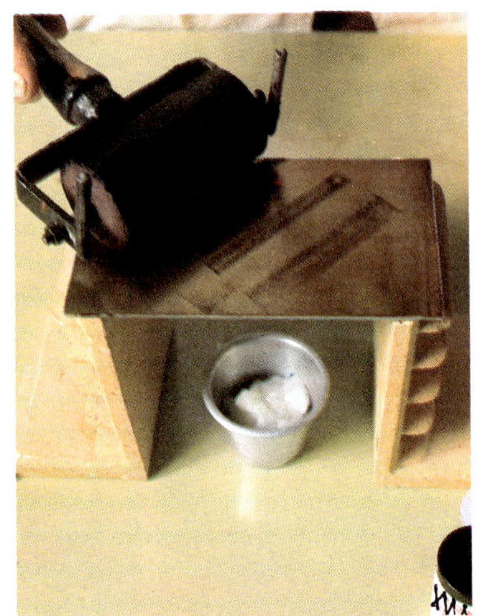

4
Keep rolling until the layer is quite even.

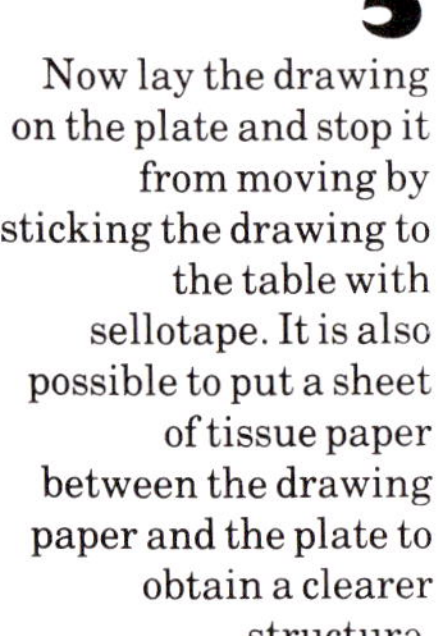

5
Now lay the drawing on the plate and stop it from moving by sticking the drawing to the table with sellotape. It is also possible to put a sheet of tissue paper between the drawing paper and the plate to obtain a clearer structure.

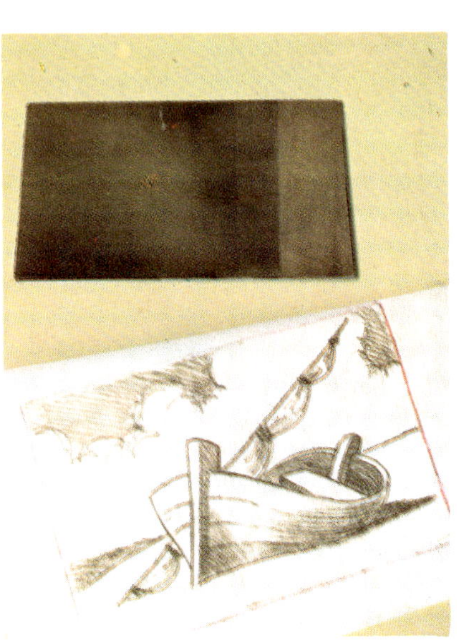

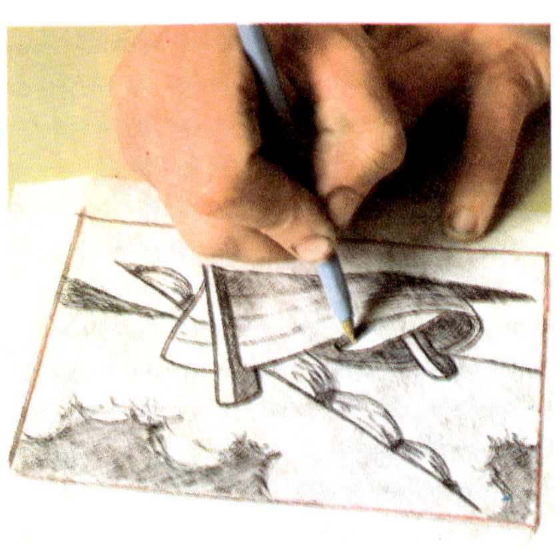

6
Now go over the lines of the drawing with a pencil.

7
The zinc plate is ready for etching.

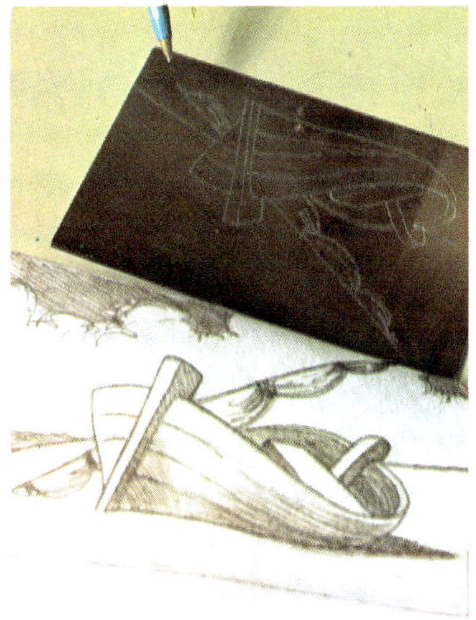

8
Prepare the etching solution.

9
Place the plate in the acid bath.

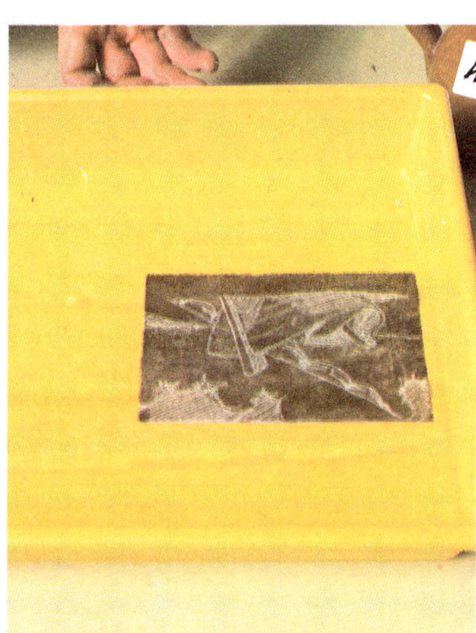

10
Leave the plate in the bath for at least one hour.

11
Take the plate out of the solution and rinse with water.

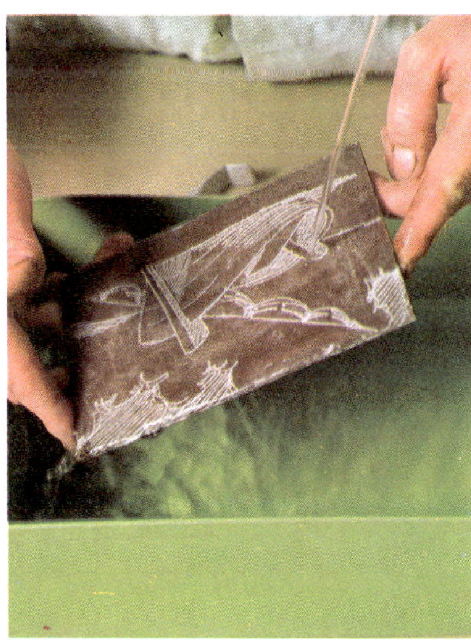

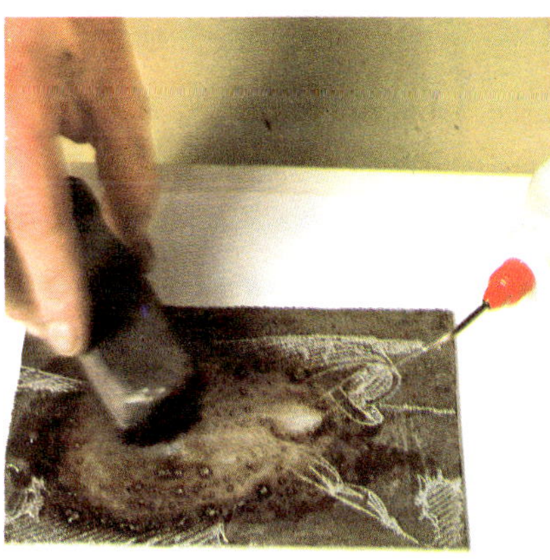

12
Clean the plate thoroughly with parafin.

13
Make sure that the plate is absolutely clean.

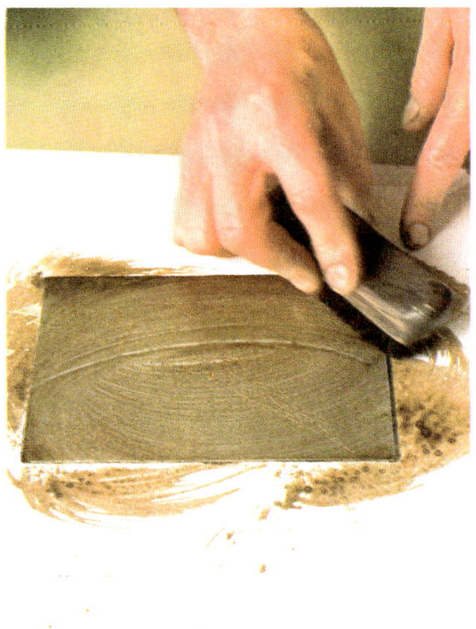

14
Remove all traces of grease with meths.

15
Remove any unevennesses on the edge of the plate with a file.

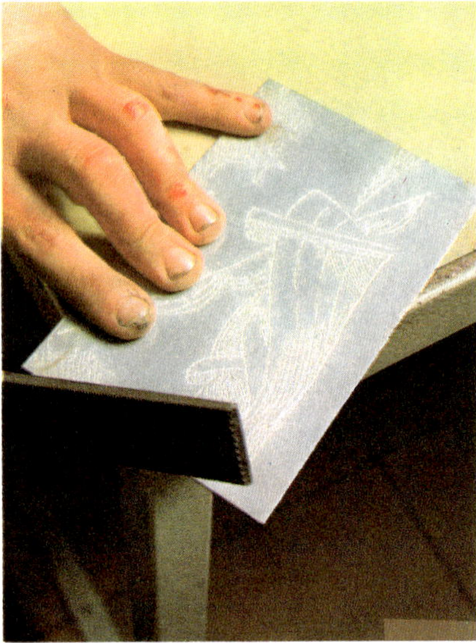

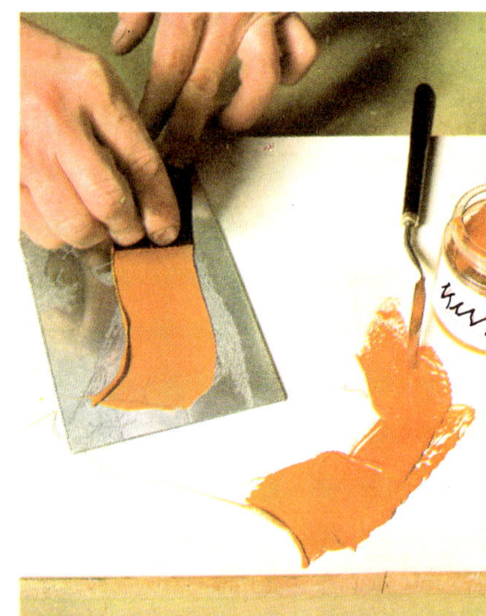

16
Use an ink rubber to cover the plate with ink.

17
Remove excess ink from the plate with a piece of cheesecloth.

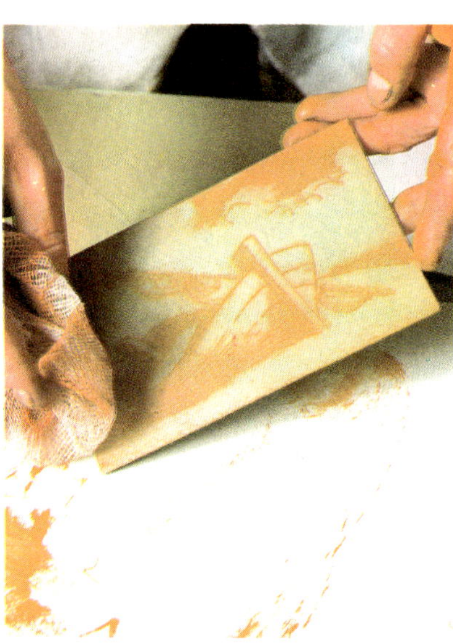

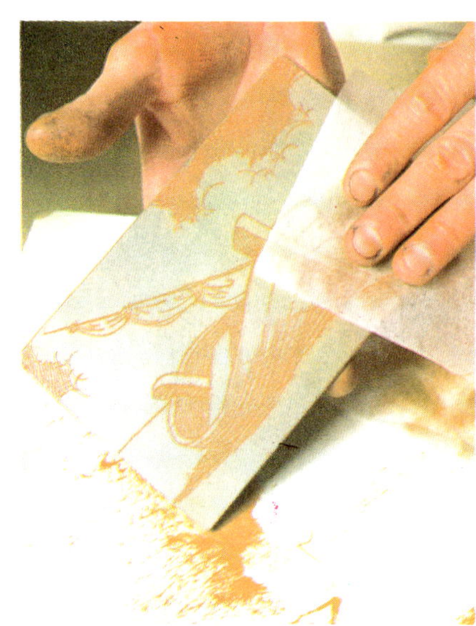

18
Remove the last traces of ink with tissue paper.

19
Put a sheet of paper on the press, showing the exact position of the zinc plate.

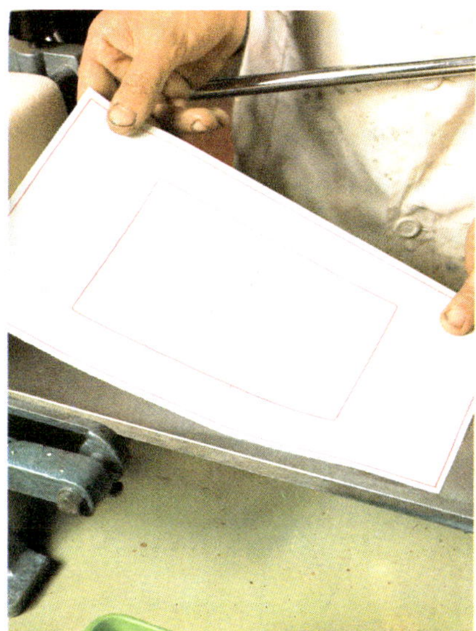

20
Now lay the plate on the press.

21
Take a moistened piece of etching paper.

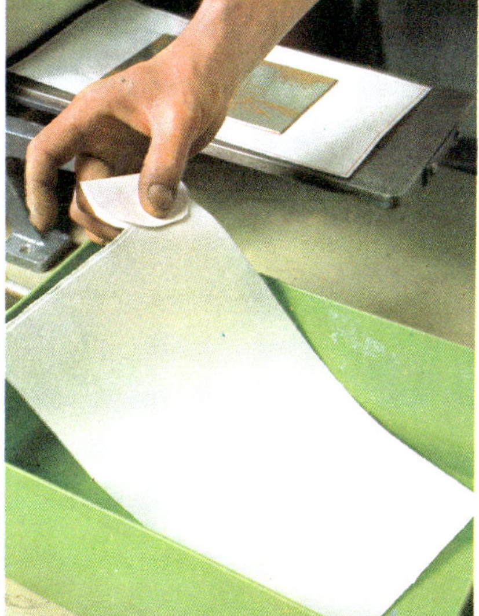

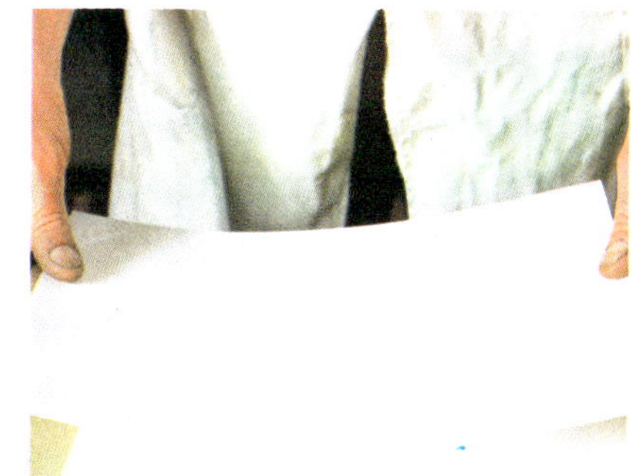

22
Put this wet paper between two sheets of blotting paper to remove excess water.

23
Place the moistened etching paper in the press.

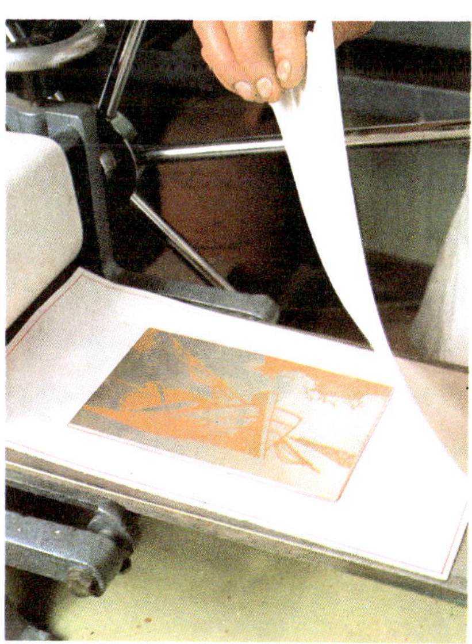

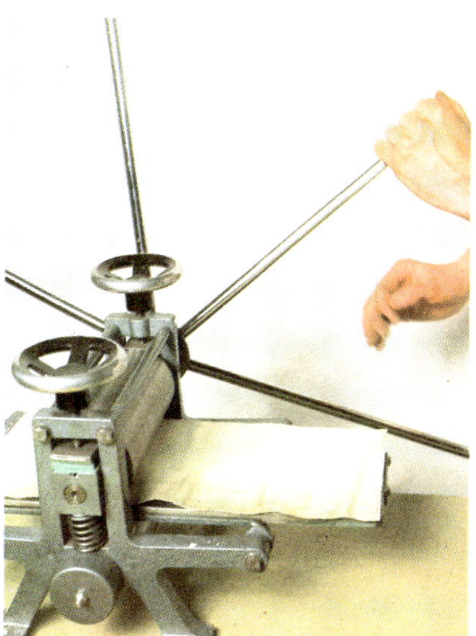

24
Make a print.

Other possibilities using the mou varnish technique

In the last section a drawing was drawn over onto a plate covered with mou varnish. Instead of using a drawing, it is also possible to transfer the patterns in other materials onto a plate, i.e., natural patterns (leaves, feathers etc.) or those found in fabrics.

The example here uses leaves from a tree. Materials required: in addition to the tools listed in the previous section, you will also need some leaves and a piece of cardboard approximately 1.5 mm thick.

1

Tools and materials required.

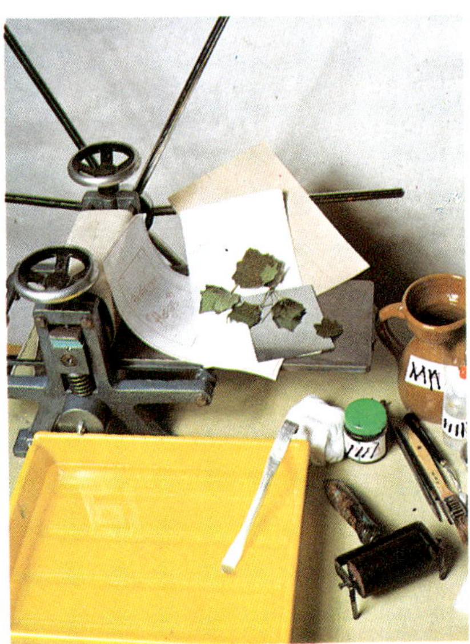

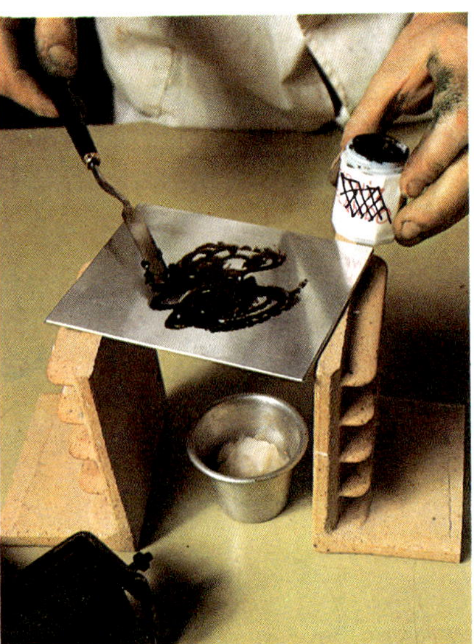

2

Spread a little mou varnish on the plate with a spatula.

3

Spread the mou varnish evenly over the plate, using a roller to roll in every direction; heat the plate at the same time.

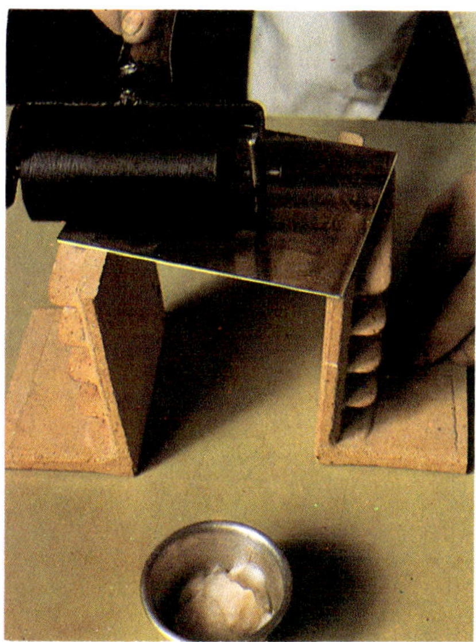

4

Arrange the leaves on the plate.

5

Lay the plate on the press with a piece of cardboard 1.5 mm thick on top of it.

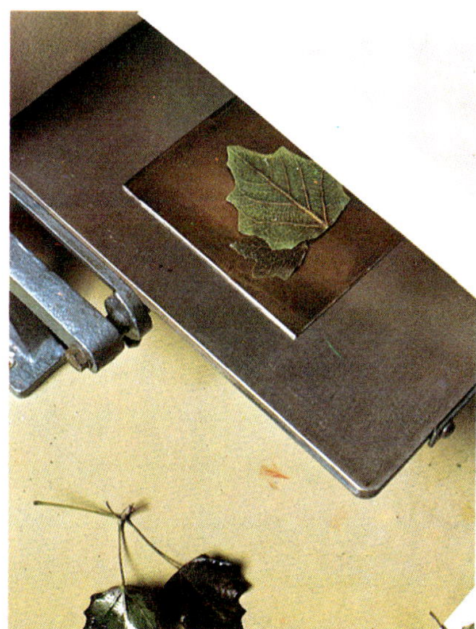

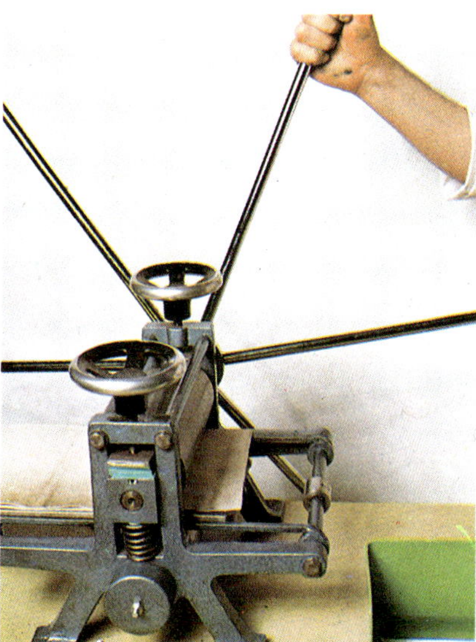

6

Adjust the pressure of the press and pass the plate through it as evenly as possible.

7

Remove the cardboard.

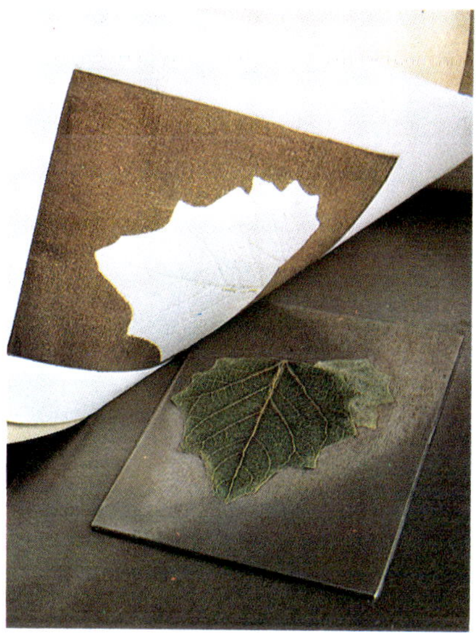

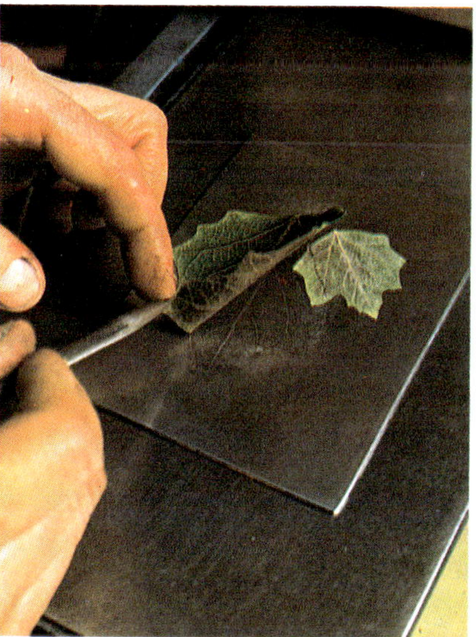

8

Carefully remove the leaves from the plate.

9
Prepare the acid bath with one part of acid to four parts of water.

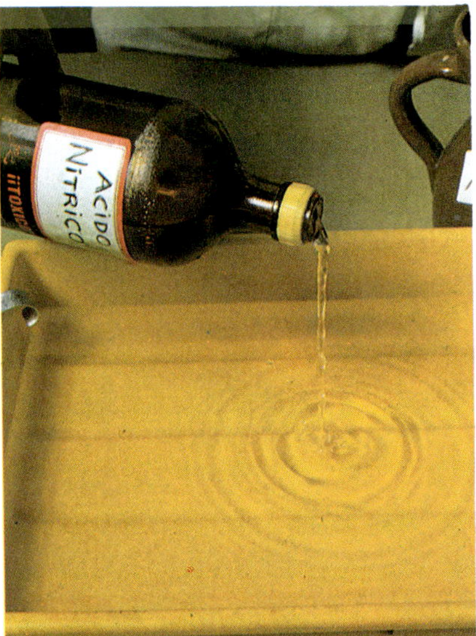

10
Put the plate in the acid bath.

11
Leave the plate in the bath for about 15 minutes.

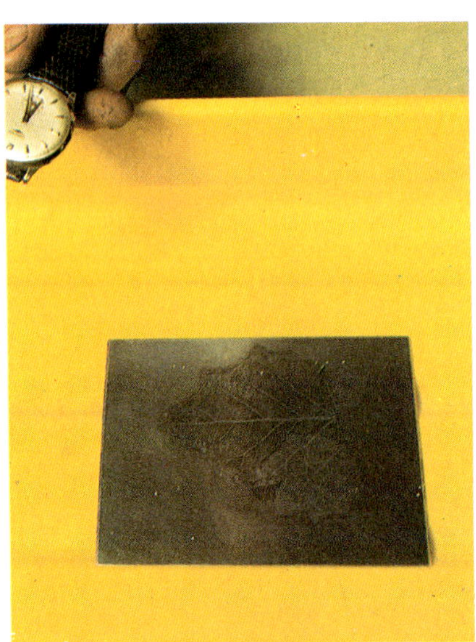

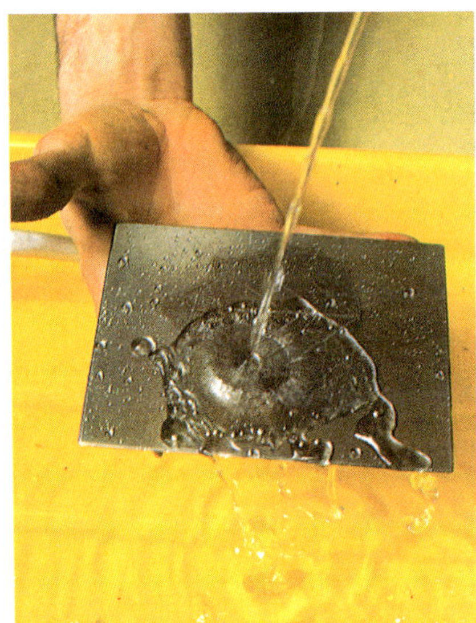

12
Take the plate out of the bath and rinse thoroughly with water.

13
Carefully pat the plate dry.

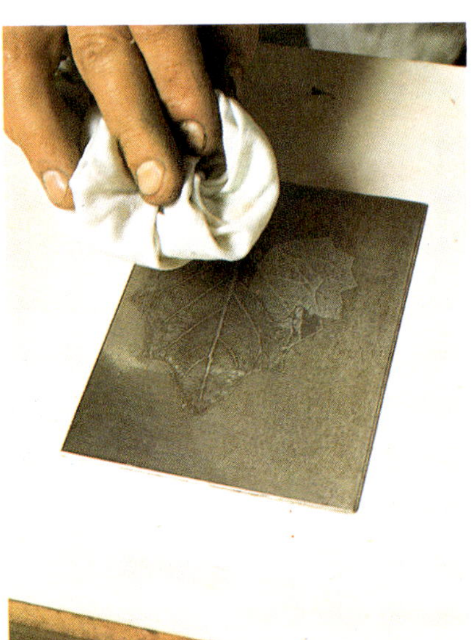

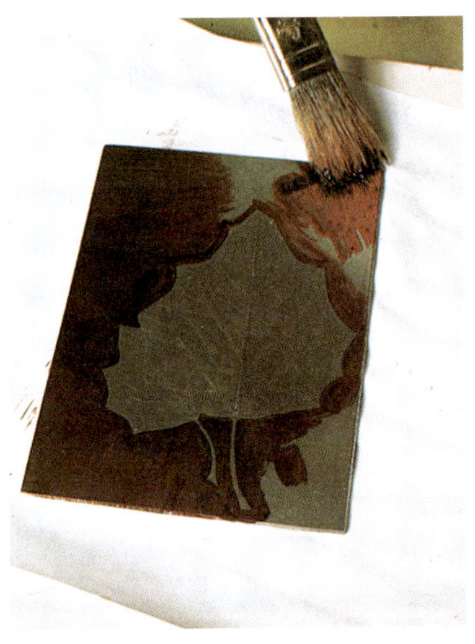

14
Cover the background with methylated spirit based varnish and leave it to dry.

15
Put the plate in the acid bath again for one or two hours.

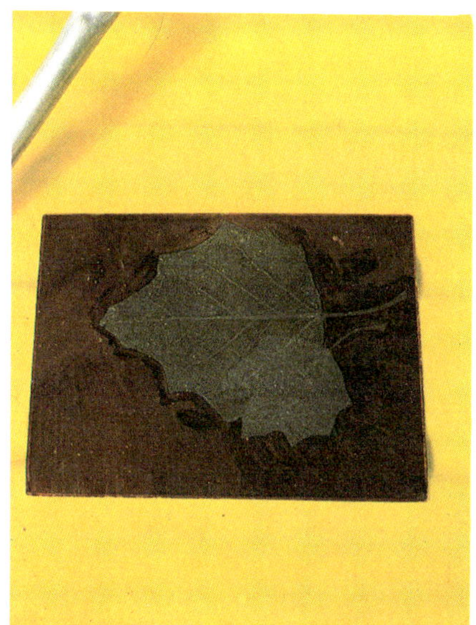

16
Rinse the plate thoroughly.

17
Remove the methylated spirit based varnish with meths and the mou varnish with parafin.

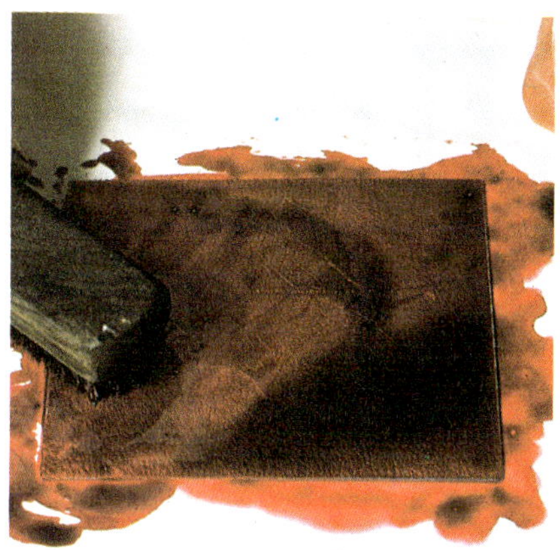

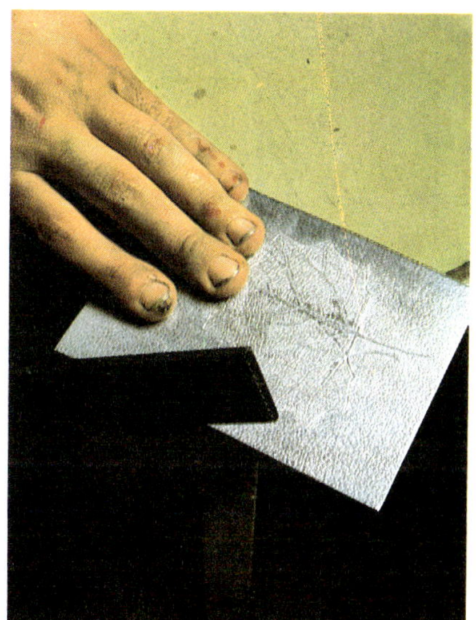

18
File the edges of the plate so that they do not damage the paper in the press.

19
This photograph shows the plate after a lengthy soaking in a strong acid solution.

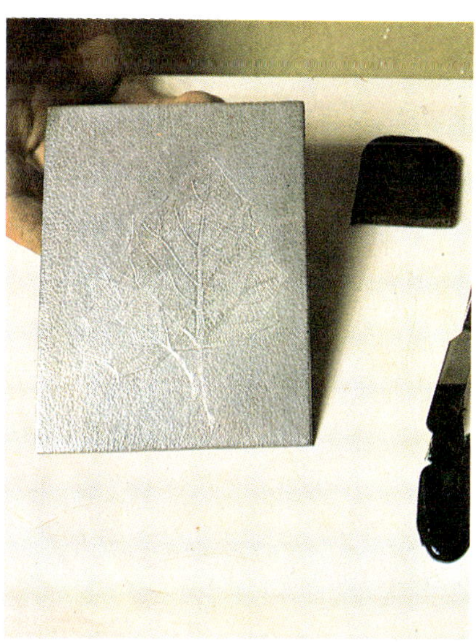

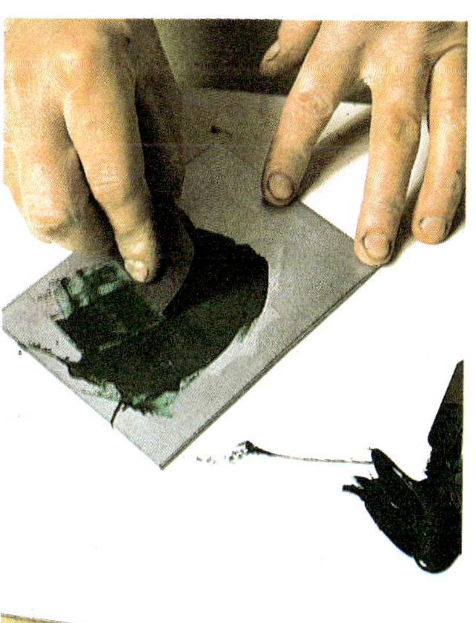

20
Cover the plate with ink, using a rubber block.

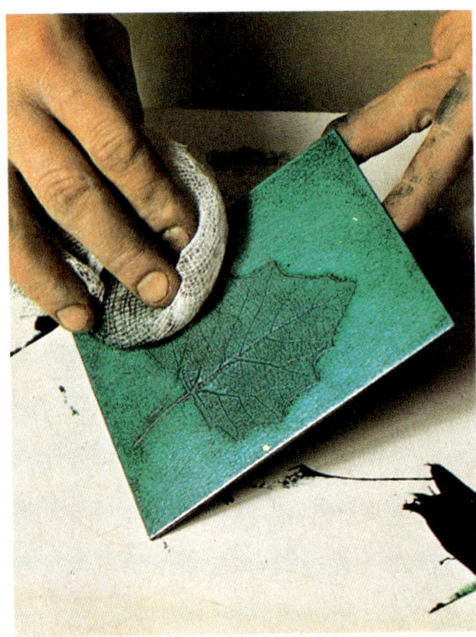

21
Remove excess ink with a piece of cheesecloth.

22
Remove the last traces of ink with some tissue paper.

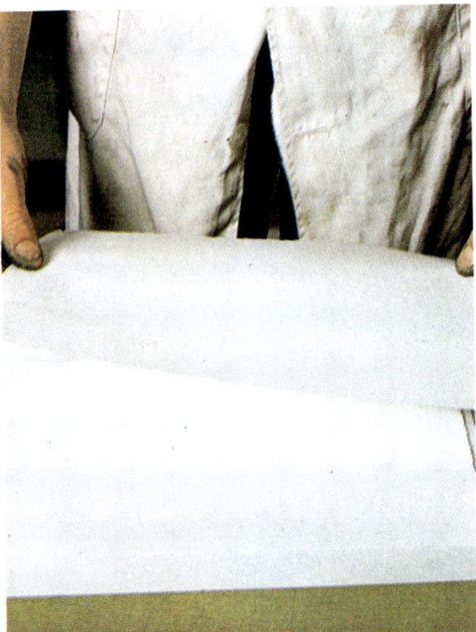

23
Place a wet piece of etching paper between two dry sheets of blotting paper to soak up excess water.

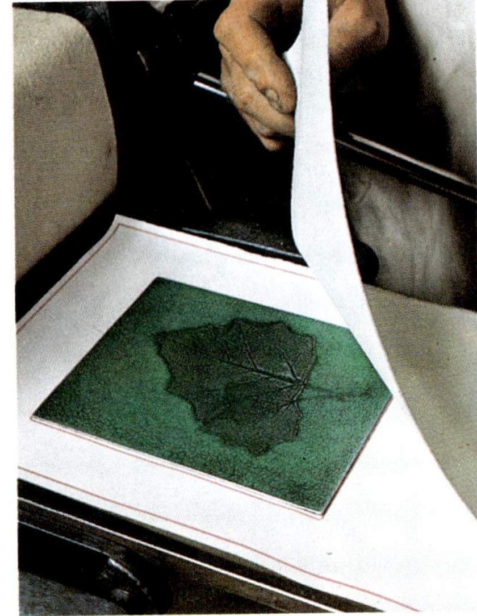

24
Place the moistened etching paper in the press.

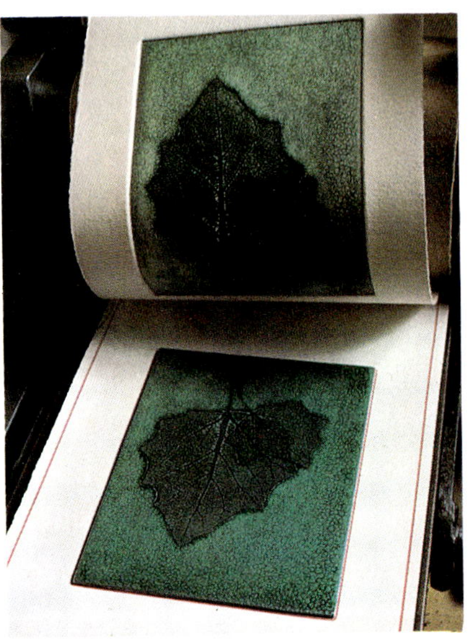

25
Make the print.

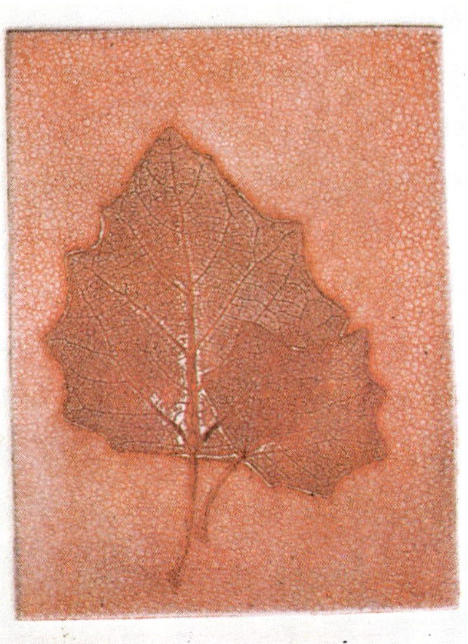

26
This photograph shows a print made with red ink.

Making an etching using carbon paper

Lines which have been transferred onto the metal plate using carbon paper are barely affected by the acid. The carbon paper technique is comparable to the technique using mou varnish because it also works by protecting the plate.
The acid does have an effect on that part of the plate where no lines have been drawn with the carbon paper. This technique was discovered by the etcher, Oscar Manesi; it is often necessary to finish the drawing using an engraving needle so that the lines are better defined.
Before transferring the drawings with carbon paper the plate must be thoroughly cleaned and all traces of grease should be removed, otherwise the carbon lines will not adhere sufficiently to the zinc plate and will only show up partially or will fail to show up at all after the etching.
The plate only has to be immersed in the acid solution for an hour and a half (one part acid to five parts water) to obtain a clear print. If necessary, leave the plate in the solution a little longer.
For this technique the following tools and materials are necessary: a press, a zinc plate, a drawing, carbon paper, cellophane, an engraving needle, a steel scraper, a pencil, printing paper, blotting paper, nitric acid, water, a kitchen timer, a cheesecloth, ink, alcohol, parafin, a small rubber spatula, an ink spatula and a bath for the acid solution.

1
All the tools and materials required.

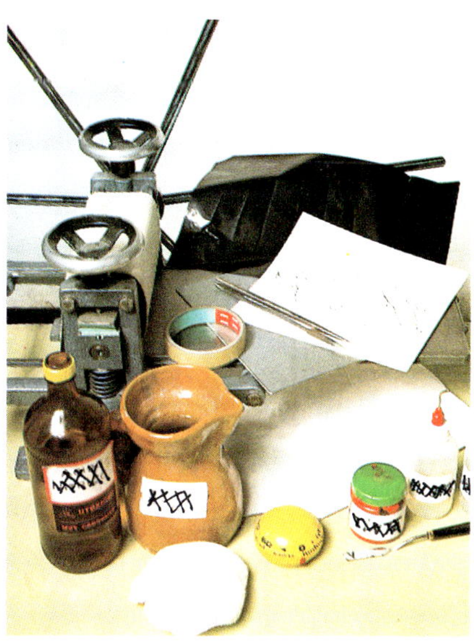

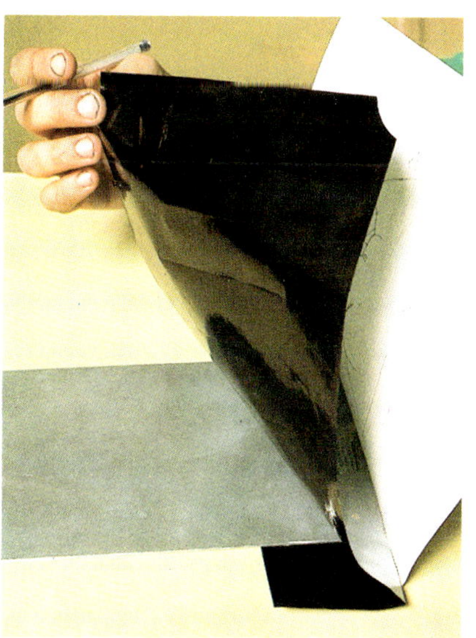

2
Place the zinc plate on the table with the carbon paper and drawing on top of it.

3
Go over the drawing with a ballpoint pen.

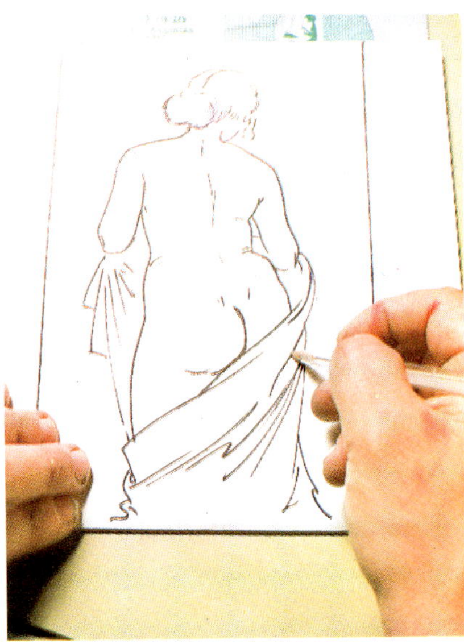

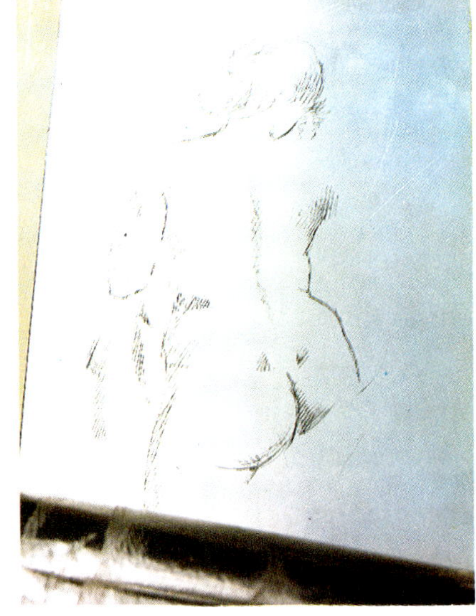

4
Check the plate from time to time while you are transferring the drawing.

5
The whole drawing has now been transferred onto the plate.

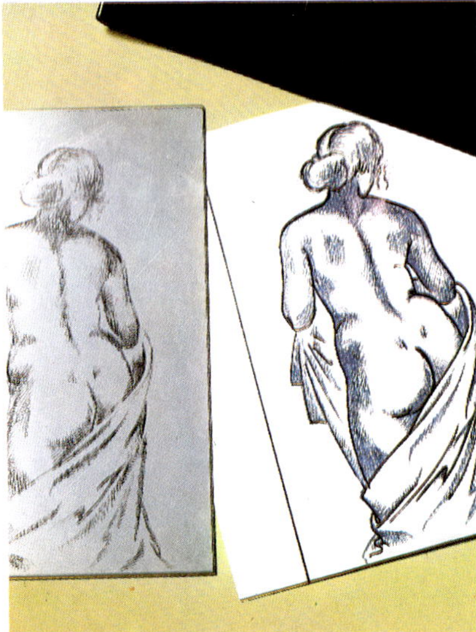

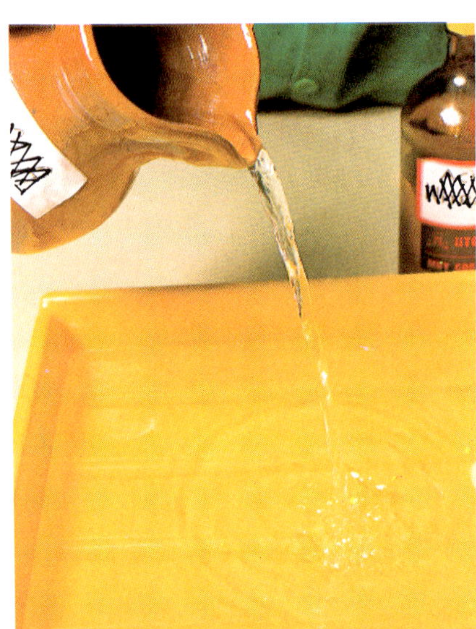

6
Pour water into the bath for the acid solution.

7
Add the nitric acid to the water (one part acid to five parts water).

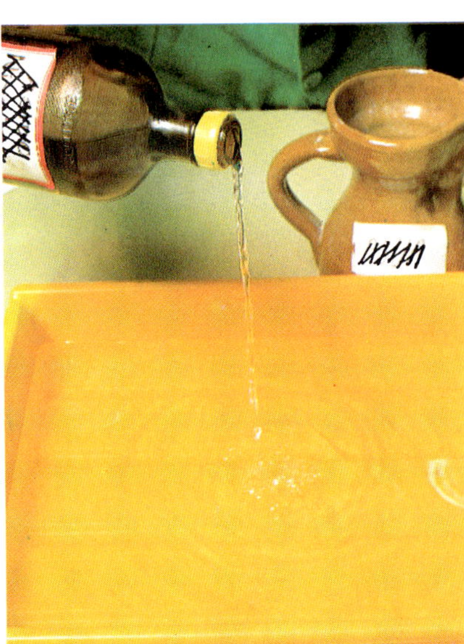

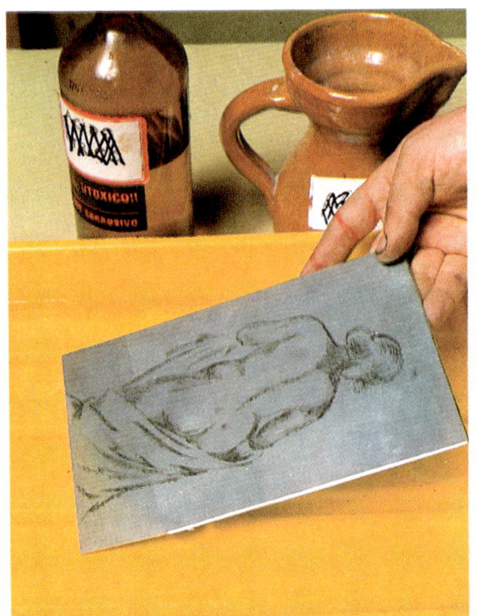

8
Leave the plate in the solution for about one and a half hours. Check the effect of the acid from time to time, and if necessary, leave the plate a little longer.

9

Take the plate out of the bath and rinse thoroughly with water in the usual way.

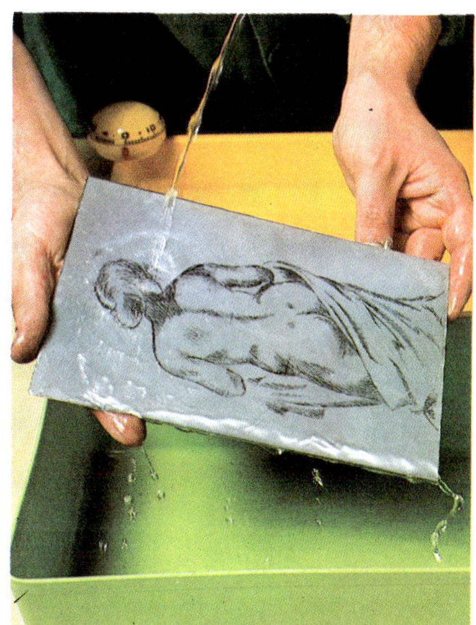

10

Clean the plate by rubbing it with a cloth and some parafin.

11

When the plate is clean, polish it with metal polish (Sidol, Brasso).

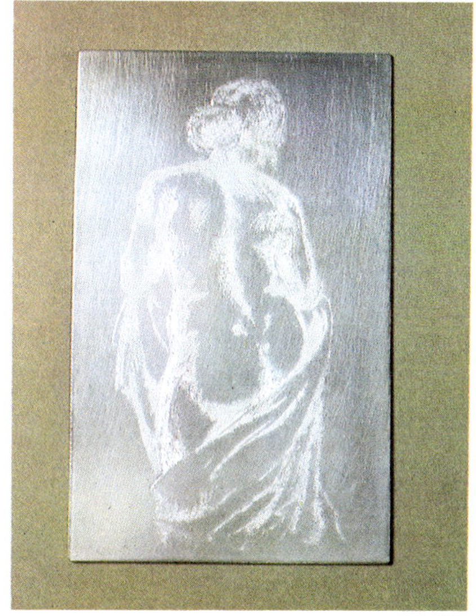

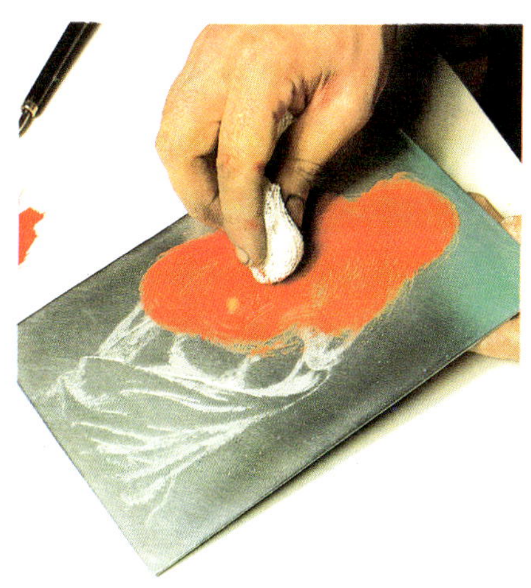

12

Cover the plate with ink using a piece of cheesecloth.

13

By rubbing with the cheesecloth, the ink penetrates the drawing and the rest is removed.

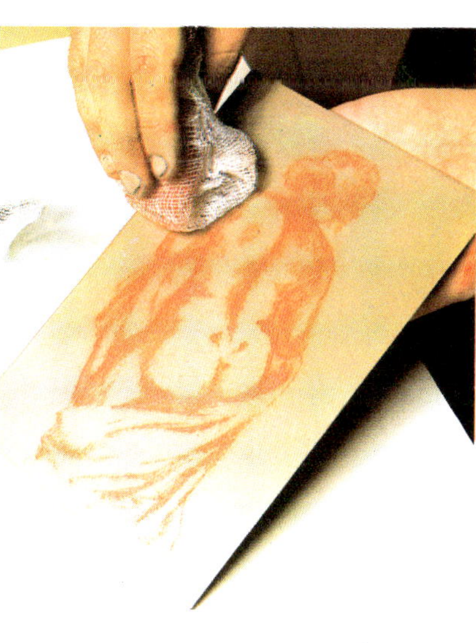

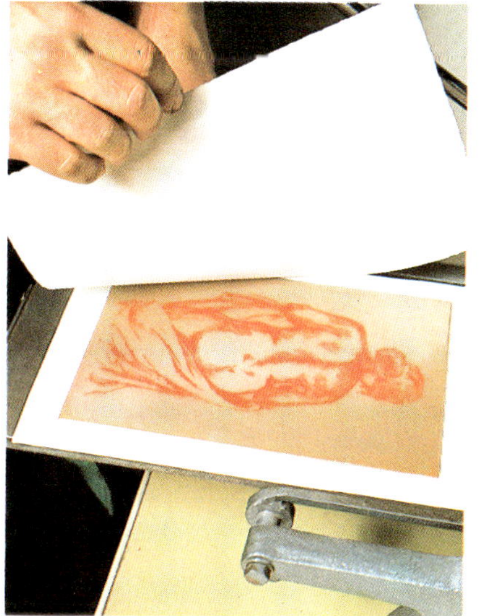

14

Place the plate in the press and cover with a sheet of printing paper. Pass the plate through the press.

15

This produces the first print, which clearly shows which parts have not been sufficiently affected by the acid.

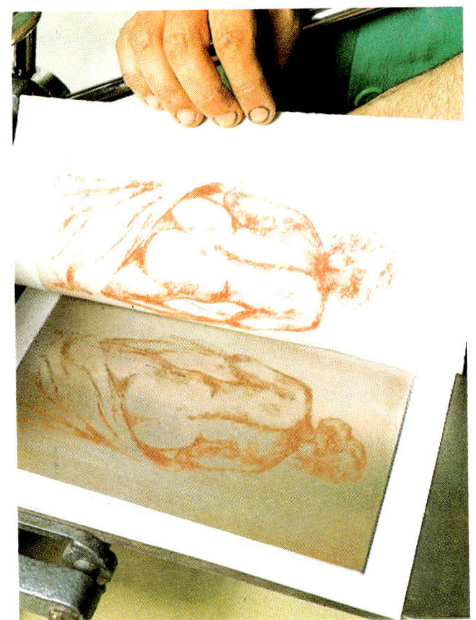

16

Find the parts which have to be corrected on the zinc plate.

17

Accentuate the lines which have not been affected sufficiently by the acid, with an engraving needle.

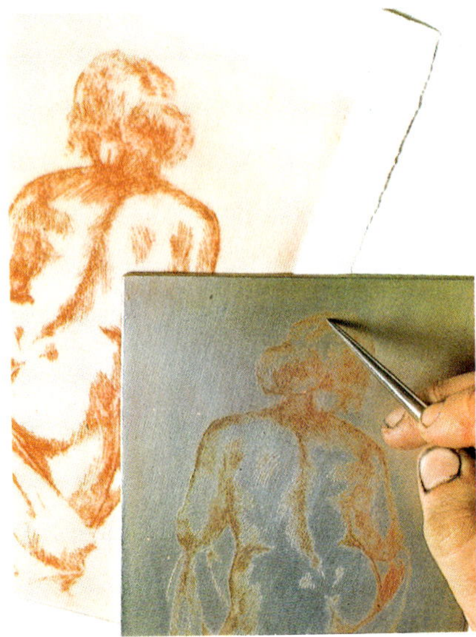

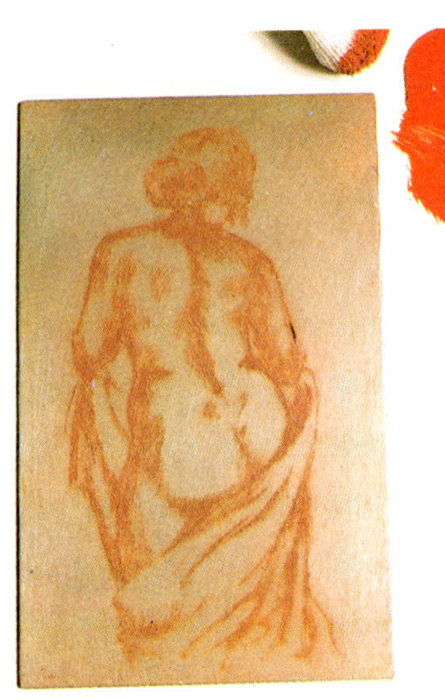

18

Cover the plate with another layer of ink and rub it in with a clean piece of cheesecloth.

19

Put the plate in the press with a sheet of printing paper and make another print. This corrected version is the second print.

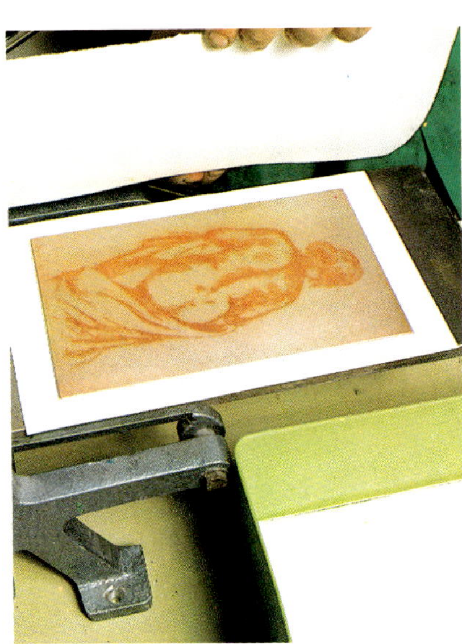

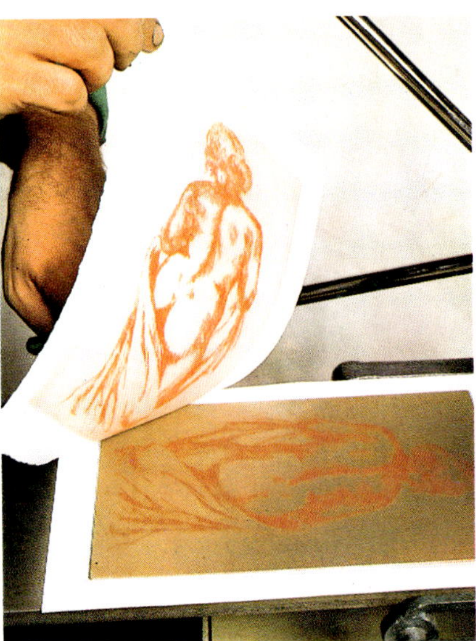

20

Pass the plate evenly through the press.

21
Compare the two prints. Emphasize the lines which have still not been printed clearly, with an engraving needle.

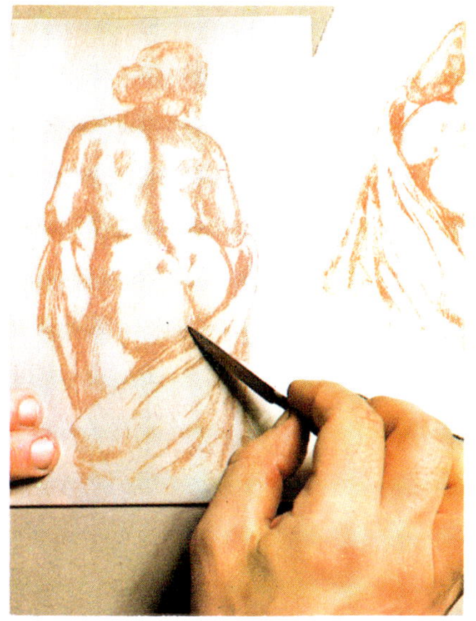

22
Cover the plate with ink again and rub in with a piece of cheesecloth.

23
The final print can now be made. Dry the printing paper between two sheets of blotting paper.

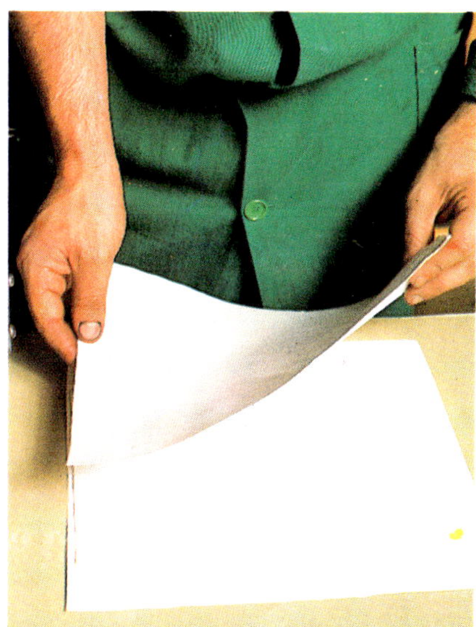

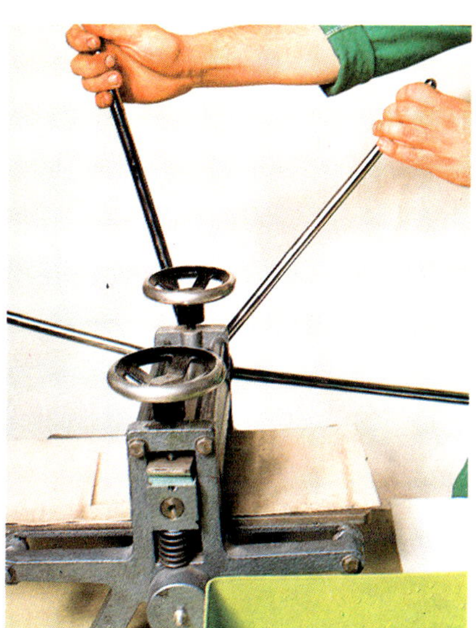

24
Lay the plate in the middle of the press and pass it through evenly.

25
When the plate has been passed through the press, the final print is ready.

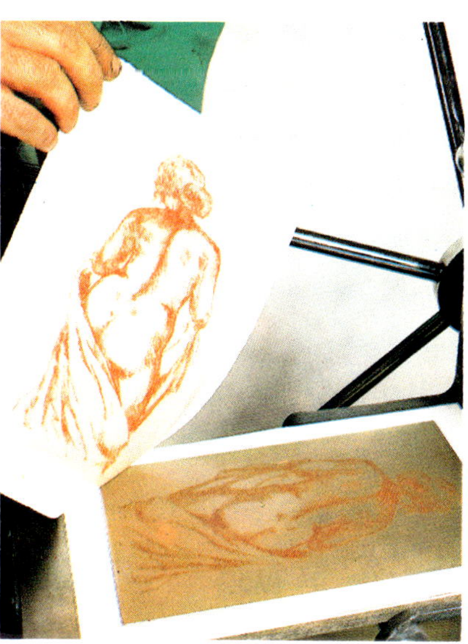

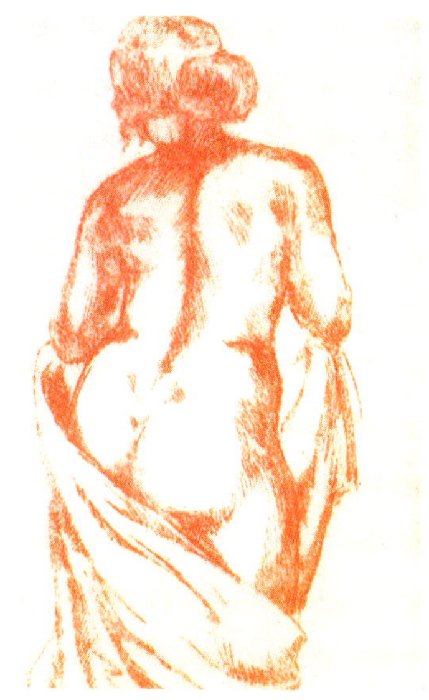

26
The wealth of detail and contrast is the result of using carbon paper.

Black art or mezzotint

The mezzotint technique is very commonly used for etching metal plates. In some cases the method is essential because it can be used to achieve so many different shades of grey.
The mezzotint (= half tone) technique was discovered in 1642 by Ludwig von Siegen, who was living in Utrecht at that time. At the end of the seventeenth century it was adopted by other artists and perfected by English etchers, and is therefore also sometimes known as the 'English method'.
In this technique the surface of the zinc plate is covered with resin and it is then etched in an acid solution. The plate is then worked with steel scrapers, burnishers and polishers, and if necessary, with fine steel wool. The acid solution should be weak (one part acid to seven parts water) and the plate should be immersed three or four times for periods ranging from one to two hours. Each time the plate is taken out of the acid solution it is cleaned with a brush and some alcohol; then it is again covered with resin and put back into the solution. The etching process is contantly repeated until the surface of the zinc plate looks as grainy as fine sandpaper.
Mezzotint plates can also be purchased ready-made from specialist art shops. The structure is then created with a 'rocker'. This is a semi-circular serrated instrument which is rocked backwards and forwards over the plate in all directions.
To make a mezzotint you will need the following tools and materials: a press, a drawing, a zinc plate, blotting paper, printing paper, fine steel wool, a steel scraper, a steel polisher, a ballpoint pen, some cheesecloth, nitric acid, water, ink, meths, parafin, resin, a rubber spatula, an ink spatula, a nylon stocking or a fine sieve for the powdered resin, a bowl with cotton wool, a kitchen timer and an acid bath.

1
All the necessary tools and materials.

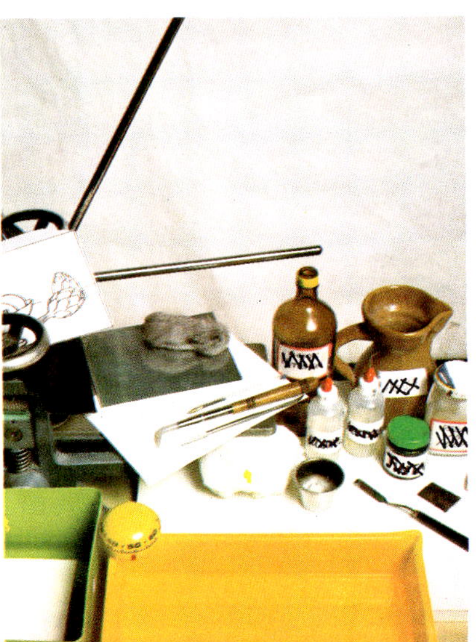

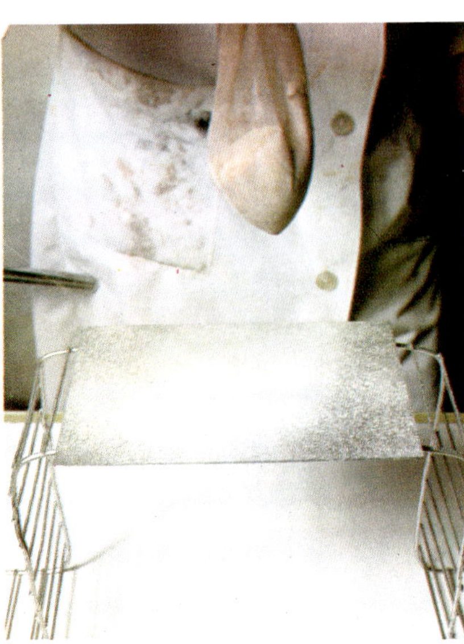

2
Clean the zinc plate and remove all traces of grease with some meths. Then sprinkle the powdered resin evenly over the plate.

3

Heat the zinc plate. The resin starts to melt and adheres to the surface.

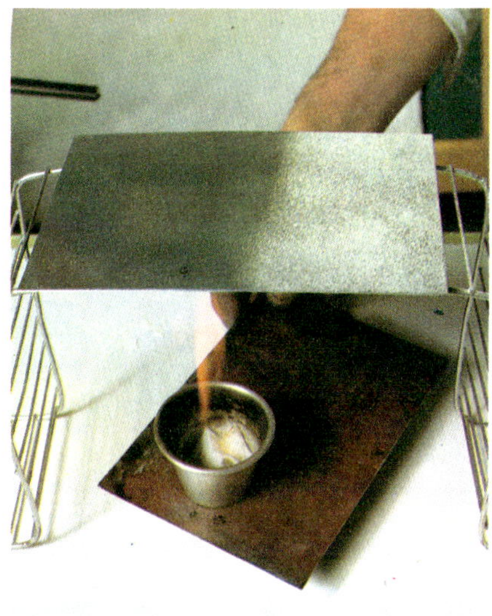

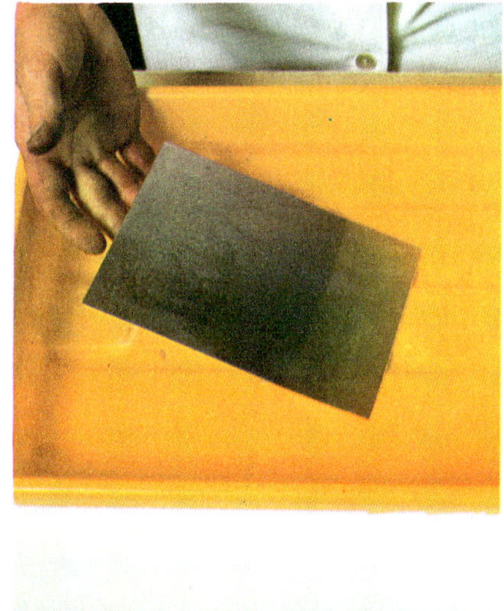

4

Allow the plate to cool and leave in the acid solution for about one hour. The solution should be weak (one part of acid to seven parts of water).

5

Repeat steps 2, 3 and 4 at least three times, then rinse the plate thoroughly in water.

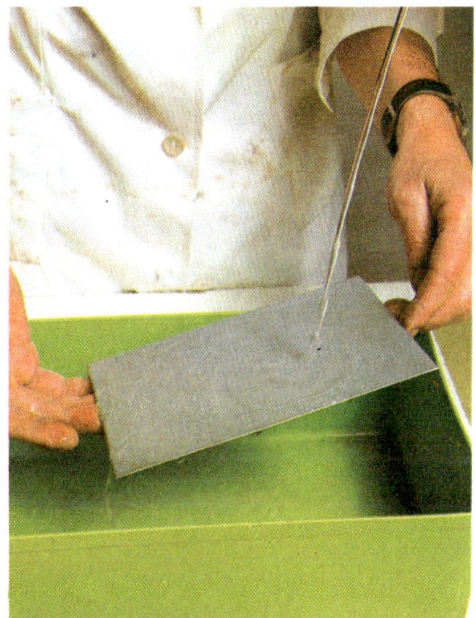

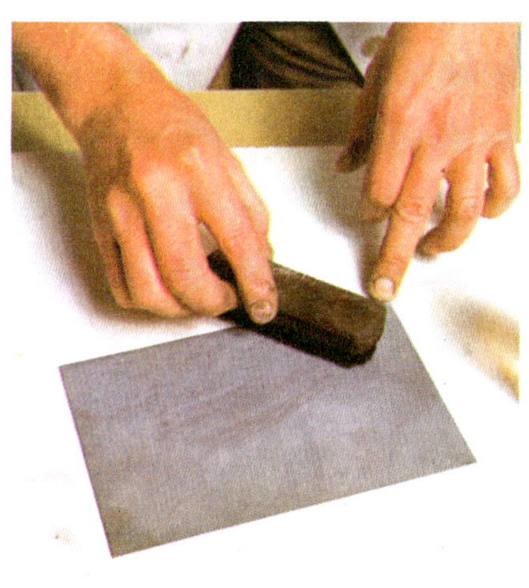

6

Clean the zinc plate with a scrubbing brush and some meths, scrubbing the resin quite hard.

7

Cover the plate with a layer of ink using a rubber spatula to check the state of the plate at this stage.

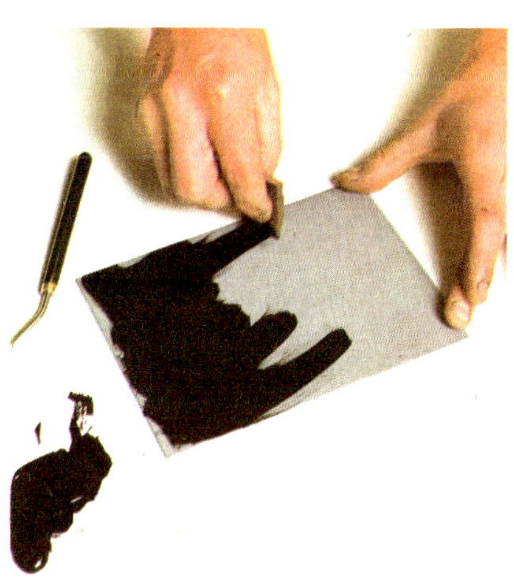

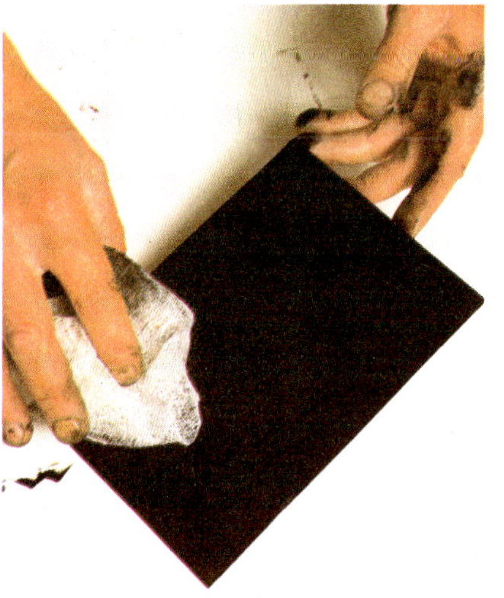

8

Remove the excess ink with a piece of cheesecloth and make a test print.

9
If the plate produces a black print, steps 2, 3 and 4 have been repeated often enough and you are now ready for the next step.

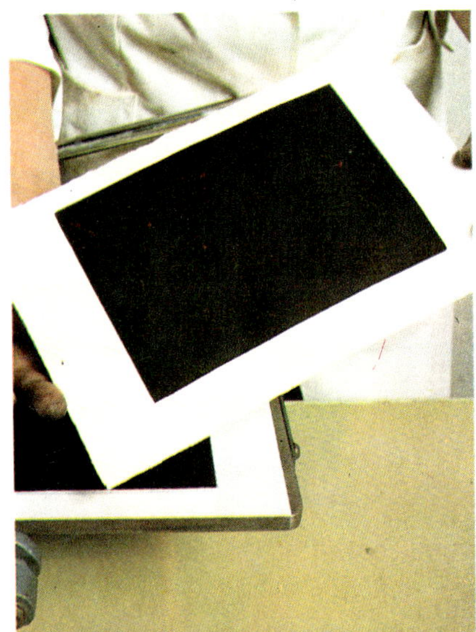

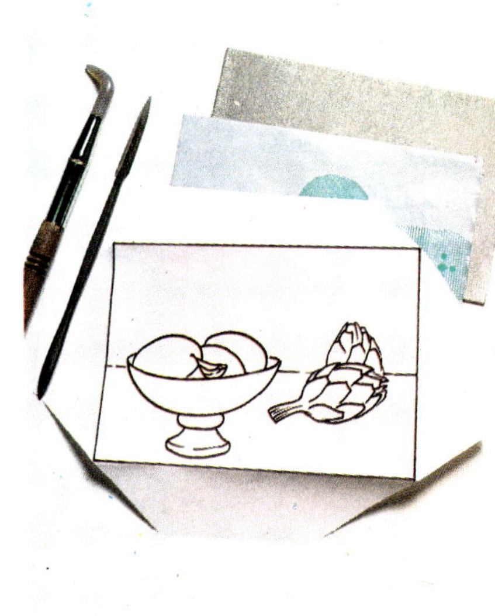

10
Clean the plate thoroughly and put the drawing on the clean plate with a sheet of carbon paper underneath.

11
Go over the drawing so that it is transferred onto the plate.

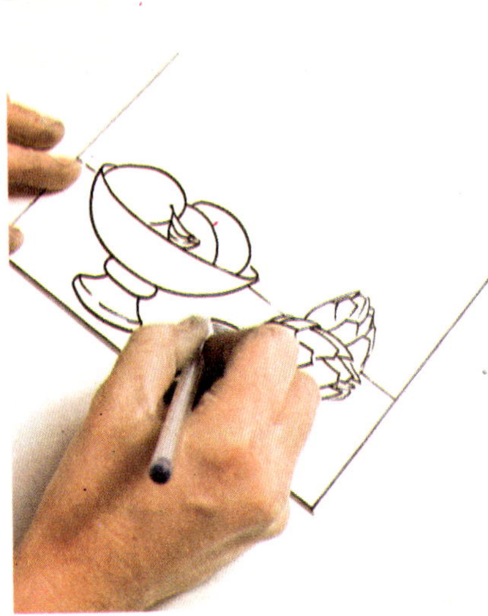

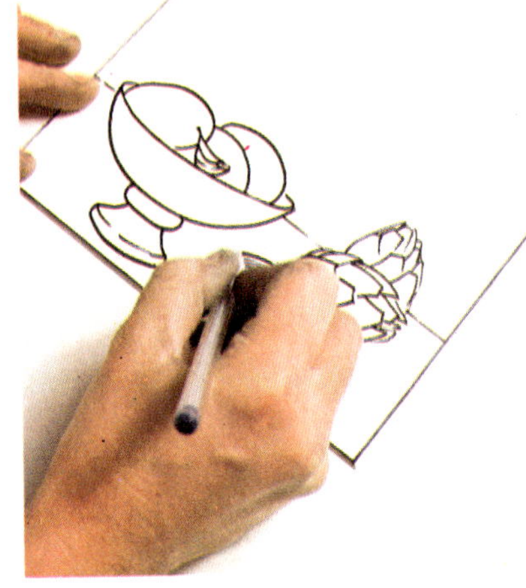

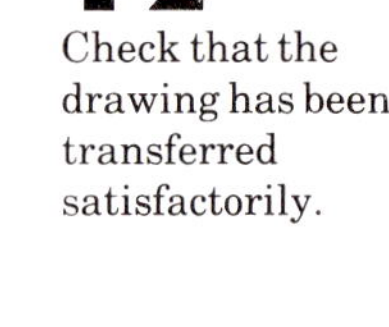

12
Check that the drawing has been transferred satisfactorily.

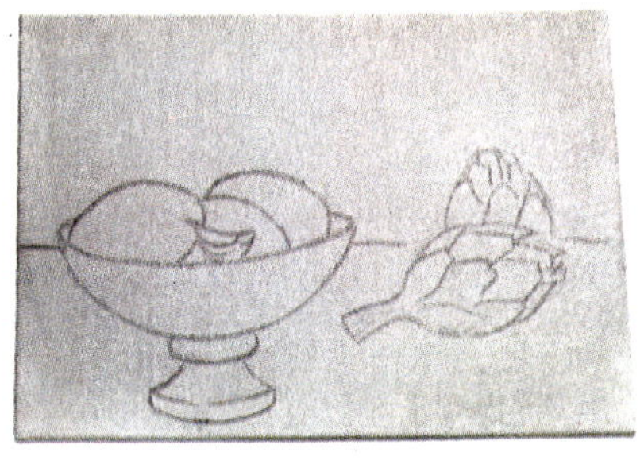

13
With the steel scraper scrape away those parts which will be lightest in the print.

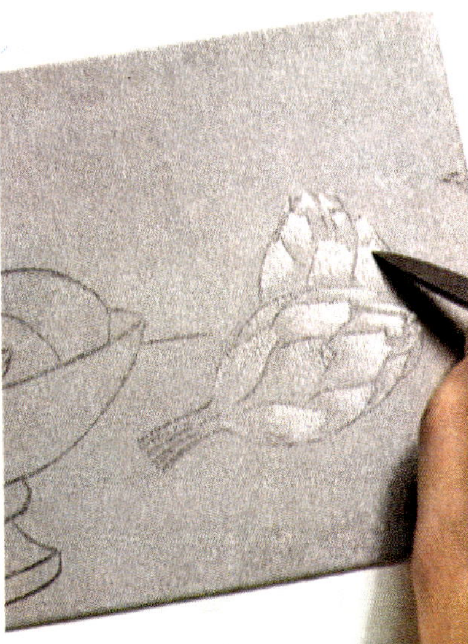

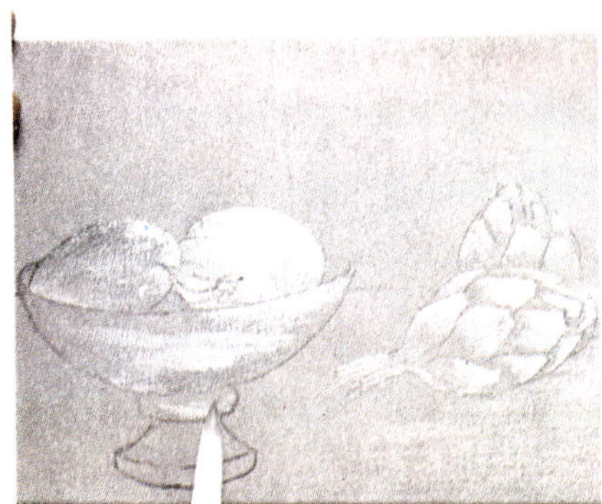

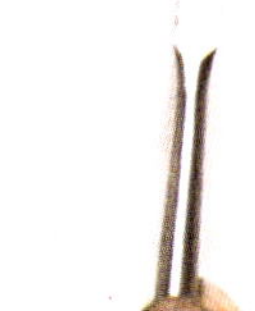

14
The more you scrape away, the lighter the print will be in that area.

15
Finish the whole mezzotint.

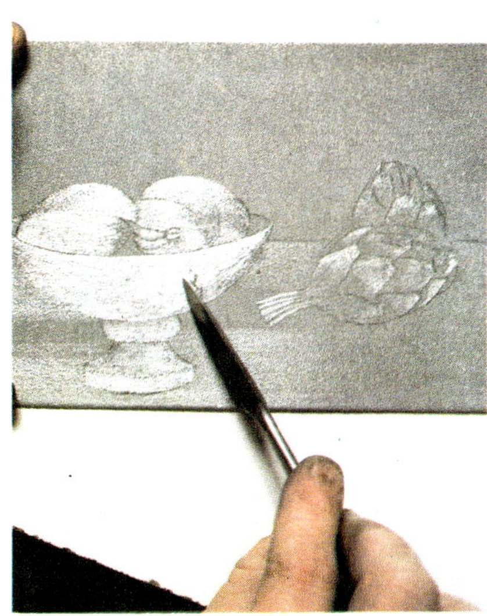

16
Cover the plate with ink and then remove the excess.

17
Make a test print.

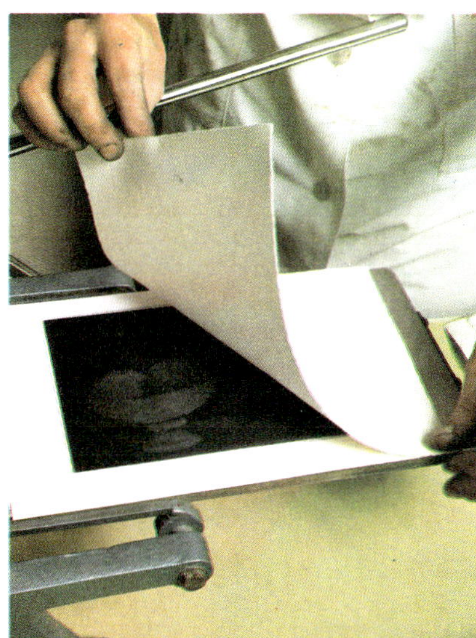

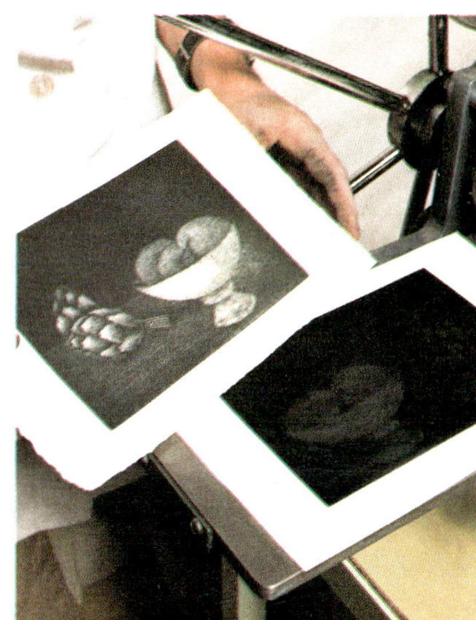

18
See whether any places on the test print need any more work doing to them.

19
Clean the plate with parafin and go over the areas which are not quite perfect.

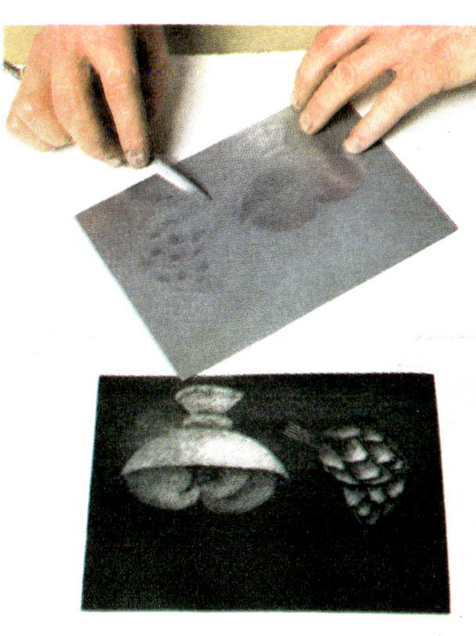

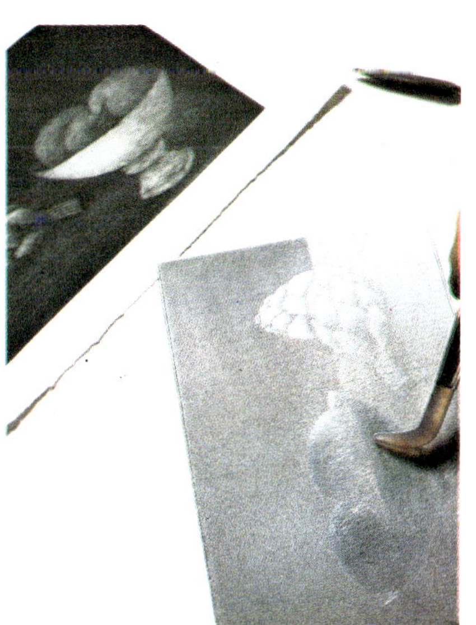

20
The areas which come out lightest can be polished with the burnisher or steel polisher until the structure has disappeared in these places.

21
Larger areas can be carefully rubbed with fine steel wool.

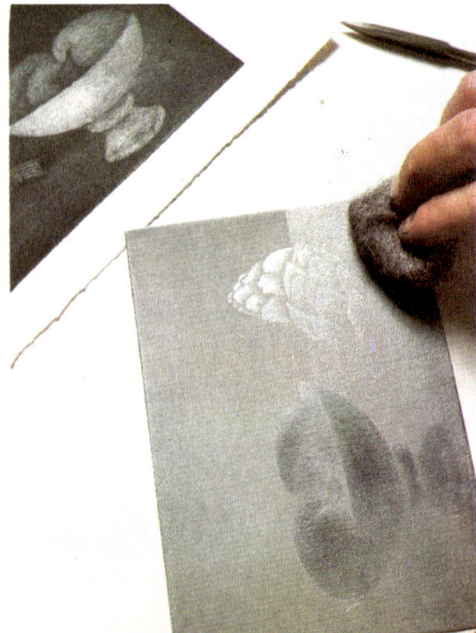

22
Cover the plate with ink.

23
The plate is now ready to be printed when the excess ink has been removed.

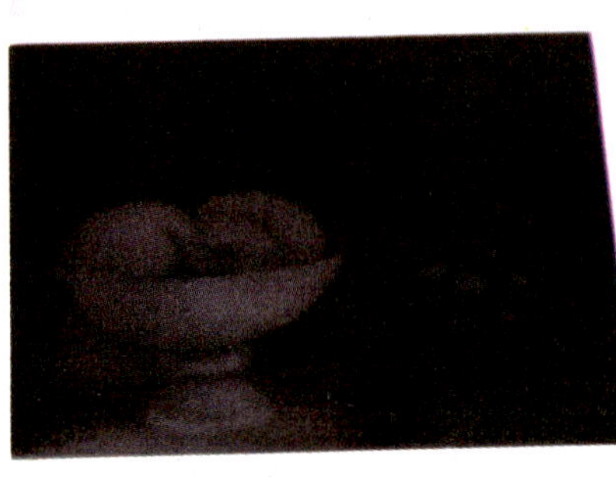

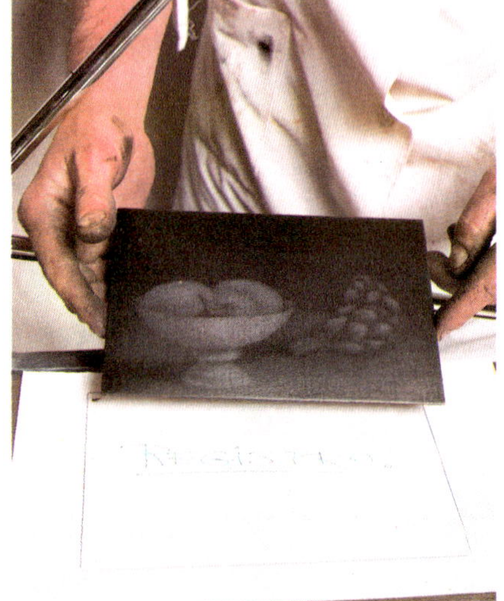

24
Put the plate in the right place on the press.

25
Make the print.

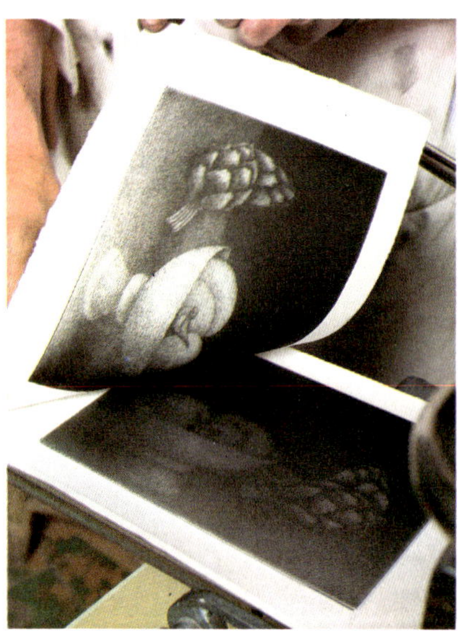

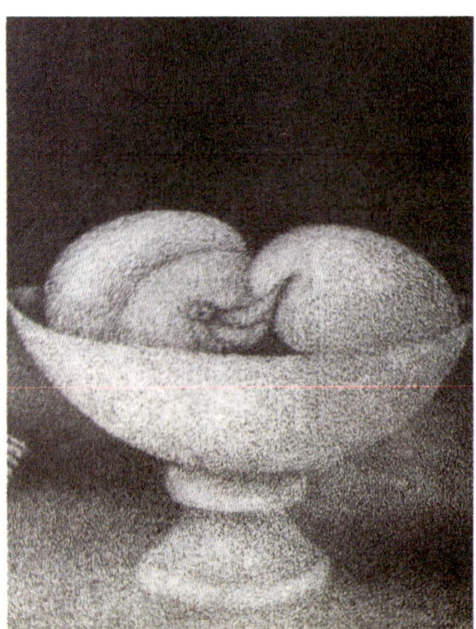

26
Note the contrasts of the shades of grey in the print.

Making an etching using two zinc plates

This series of graphic exercises is expanded with a few examples using printing techniques which have a number of colours. Two zinc plates are used for this technique. The great advantage of using two or more plates to make a print is that this makes it possible to use different colours.

If you wish to use contrasting colours or subtle contrasts of shades of colour, it is advisable to use a number of plates, although this obviously involves a more complicated and lengthy procedure. These qualities are clearly reflected in the following exercises.

Use two zinc plates as a starting point. One has been etched, the other has not. To ensure that the contrast between the colours is clear in the final print, the green and reddish brown of the central motif is printed off the clear blue colour of the sky.

The plates should be exactly the same size so that the colours and lines correspond precisely.

For this technique you need the following tools and materials: an etched zinc plate (plate 1), another plate which has not been etched (plate 2), different coloured inks, nitric acid, a roller, spatulas, a dry needle, newspaper, a press, blotting paper and printing paper.

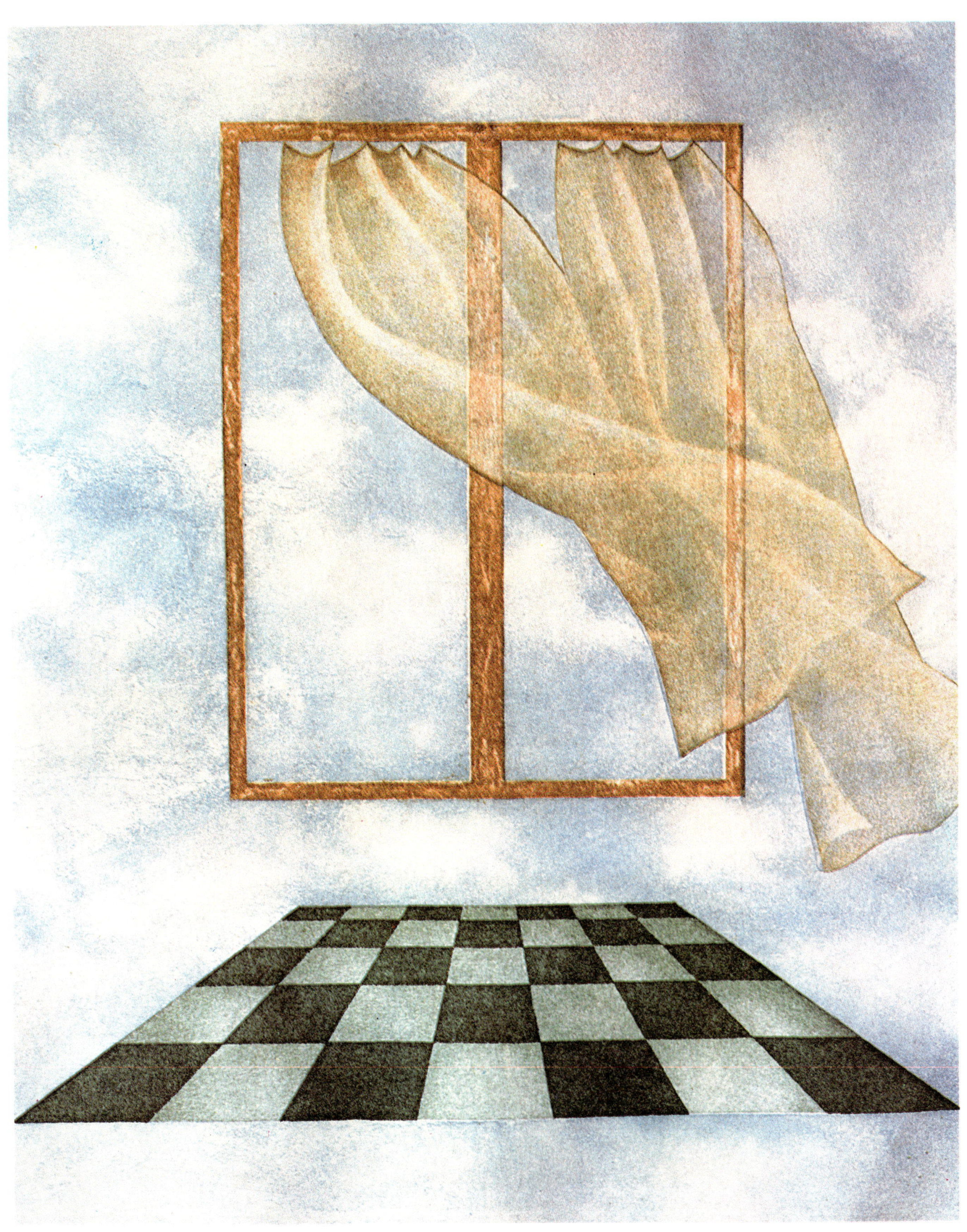

1
All the tools and materials required.

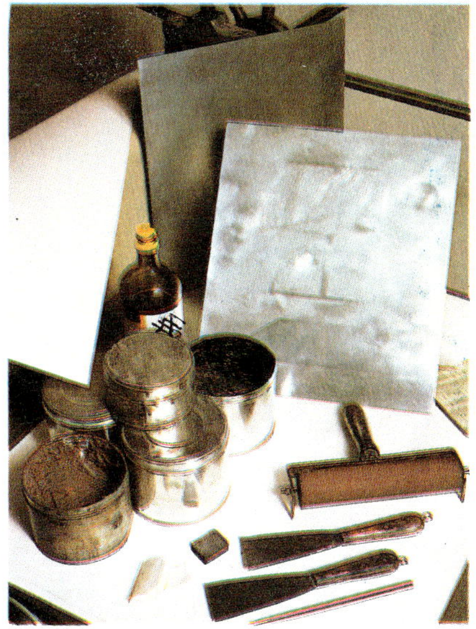

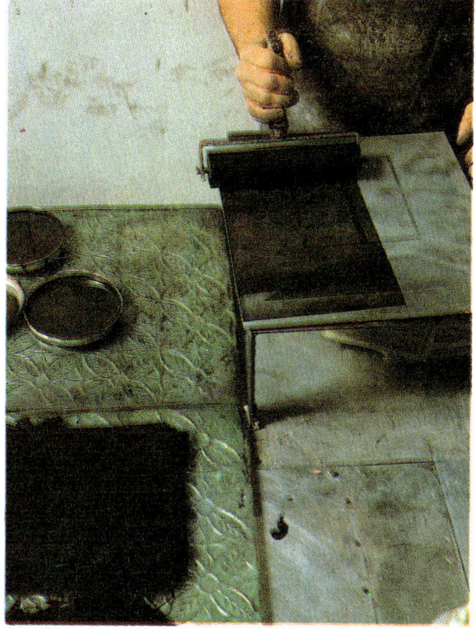

2
Cover the zinc plate which has been etched (plate 1) with a dark coloured ink.

3
Rub the ink into the plate with a piece of cheesecloth and remove the excess ink with a clean cloth. The plate is now ready to be printed.

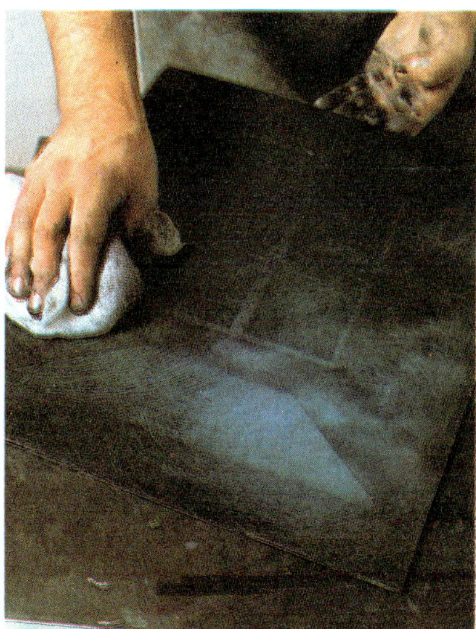

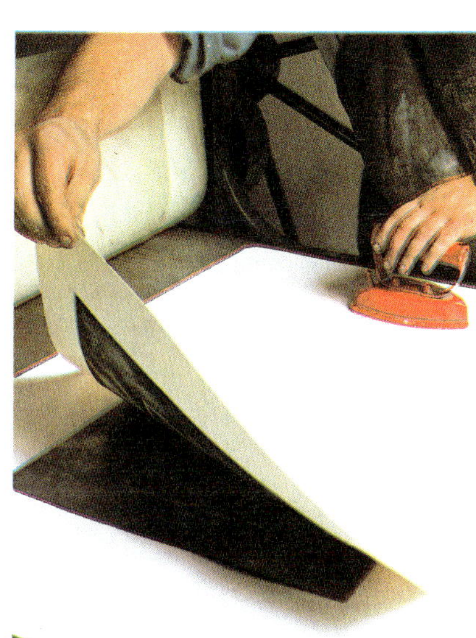

4
When the print has been made, place something heavy on the paper to stop it moving.

5
Lift the print and remove the plate.

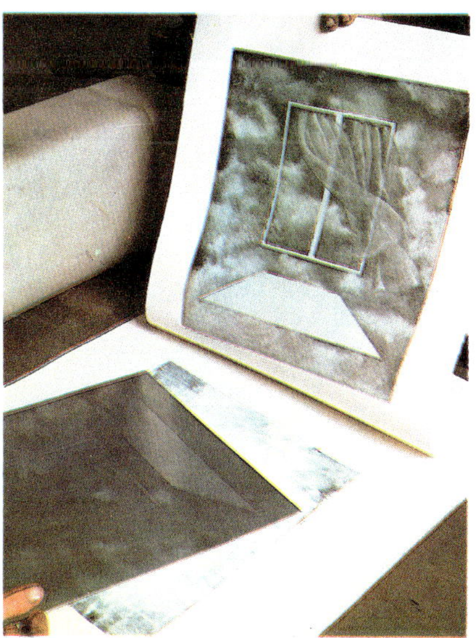

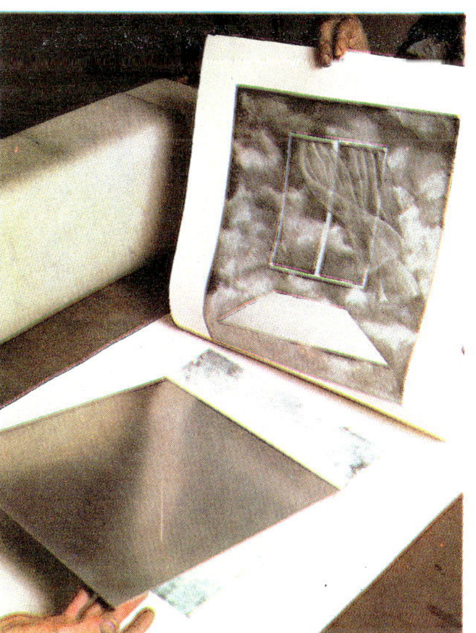

6
Now slide the blank plate (plate 2), which is exactly the same size, under the printing paper.

7

Lay the paper with the print on plate 2 and pass it through the press.

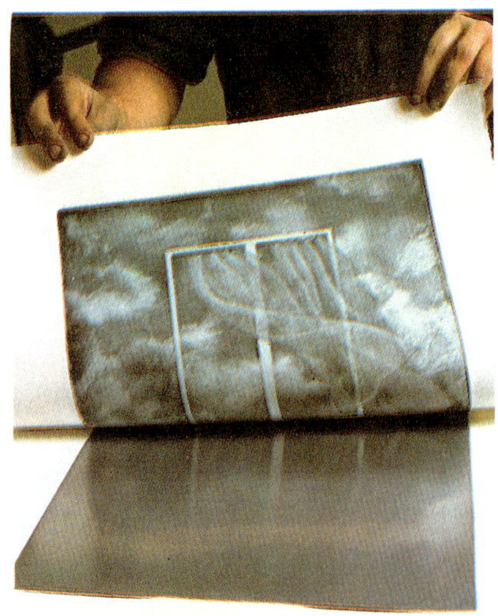

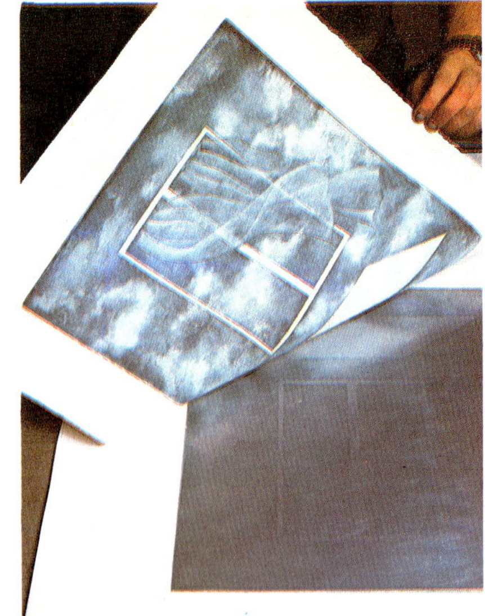

8

The picture is printed from the paper onto plate 2.

9

When the ink on plate 2 is dry, go over the lines of the drawing with a dry needle. Because the ink usually takes a long time to dry, you can add a drop of drying agent to it.

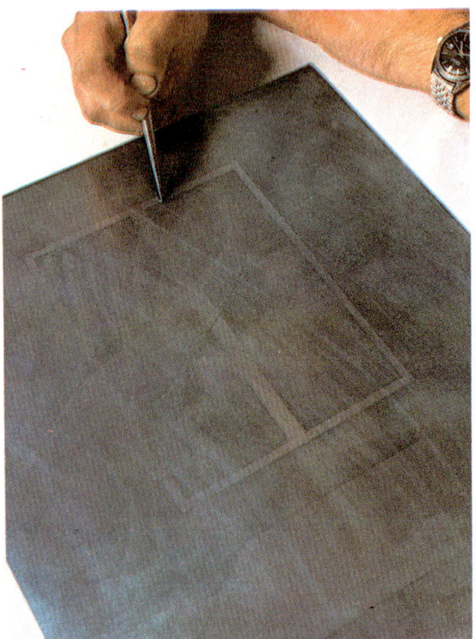

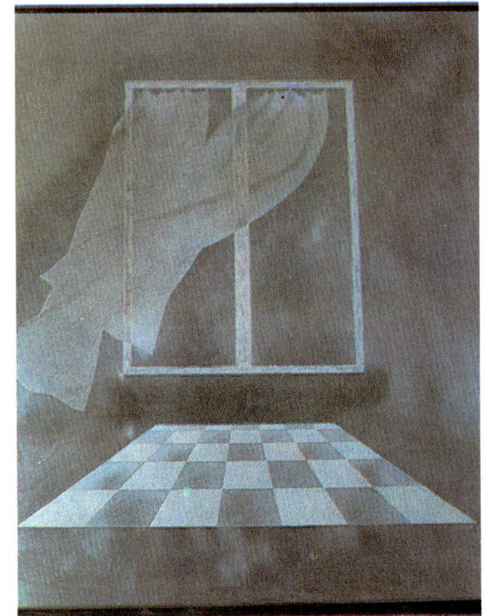

10

This is the etched plate for the second (and possibly third) colour. When the ink is dry, the dry needle and aquatint techniques are applied.

11

Plate 1, which was used first, does not have the objects which were etched onto plate 2.

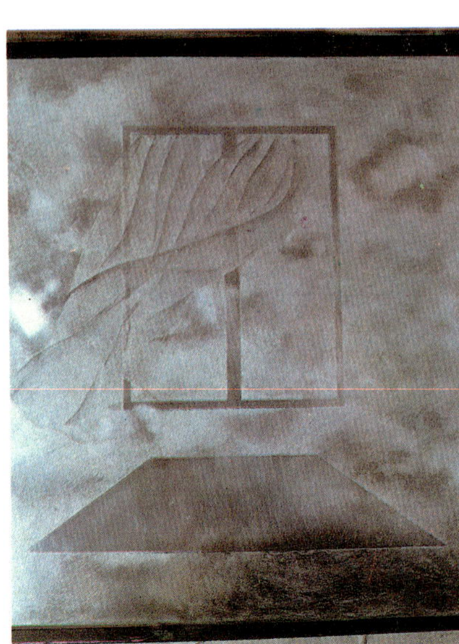

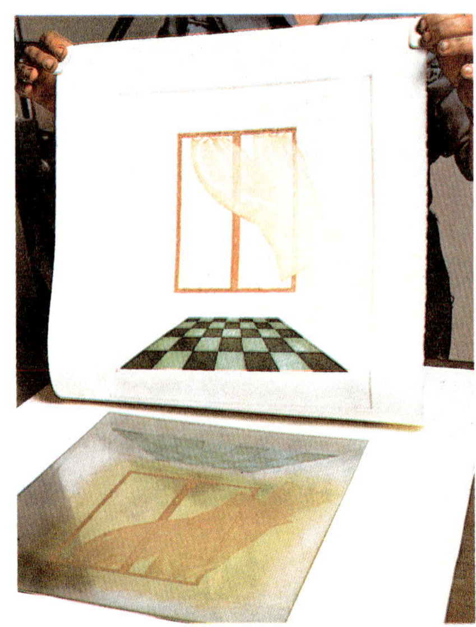

12

Cover plate 2 with ink, in the colours desired, and make a print. This is a test print, and if necessary, any modifications can be carried out.

13

Now cover plate 1 with ink and make another print. This is also a test print.

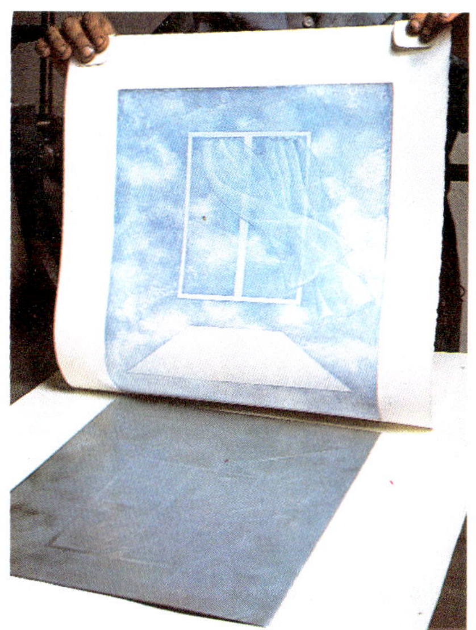

14

Cover plate 1 with another layer of ink. First apply the ink in two places and then use the roller in the usual way.

15

Move the roller over the plate with a thick layer of ink.

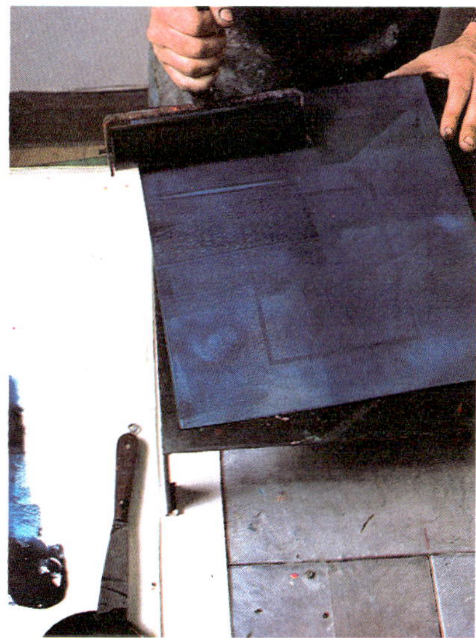

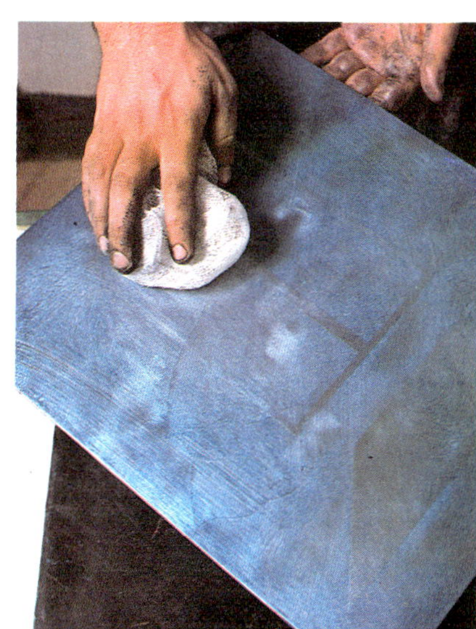

16

Remove excess ink. This plate is used later to print the third colour over the print of plate 2.

17

Cover part of plate 2 with the colour chosen.

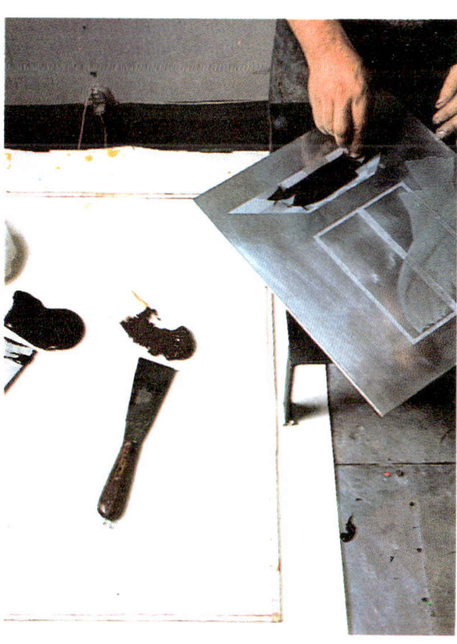

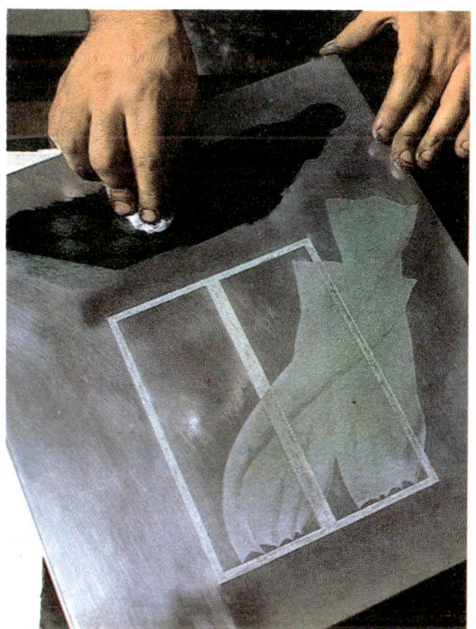

18

Remove excess ink.

19
Remove the last traces of ink with newspaper.

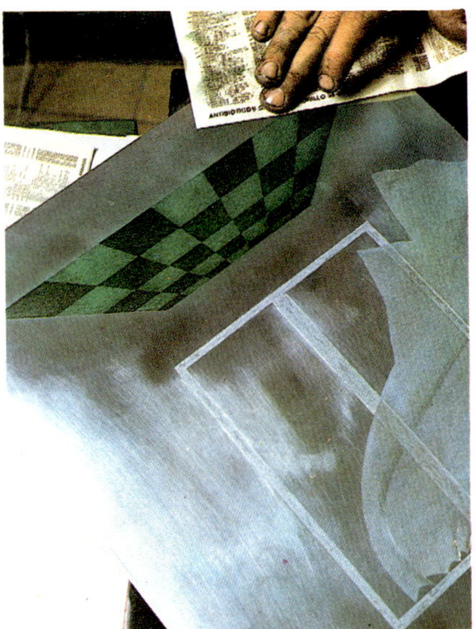

20
Now cover the second part of the plate with a different coloured ink, and remove the excess ink.

21
Remove the last traces of ink.

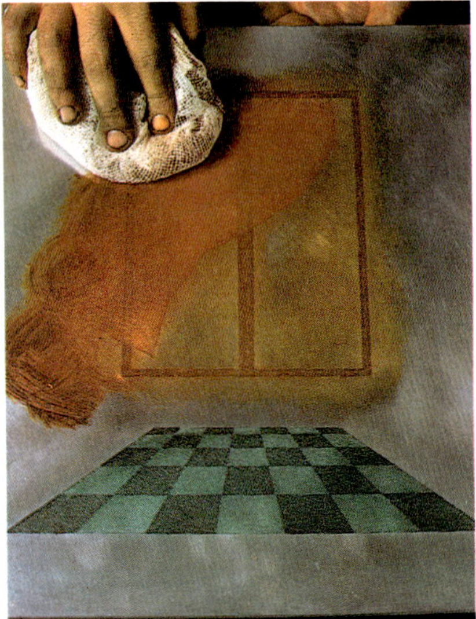

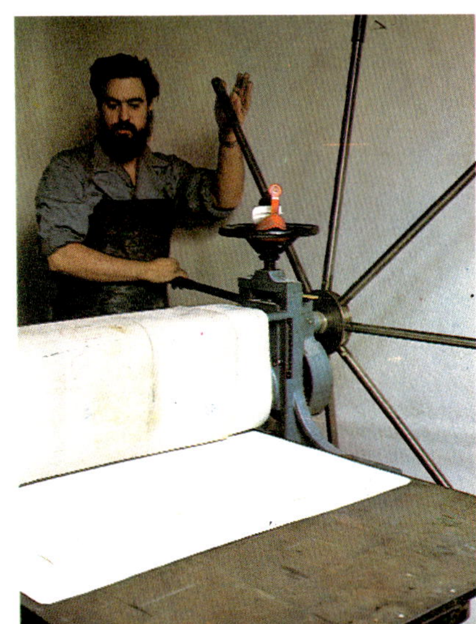

22
Print plate 2.

23
Remove plate 2 without removing the print on the paper.

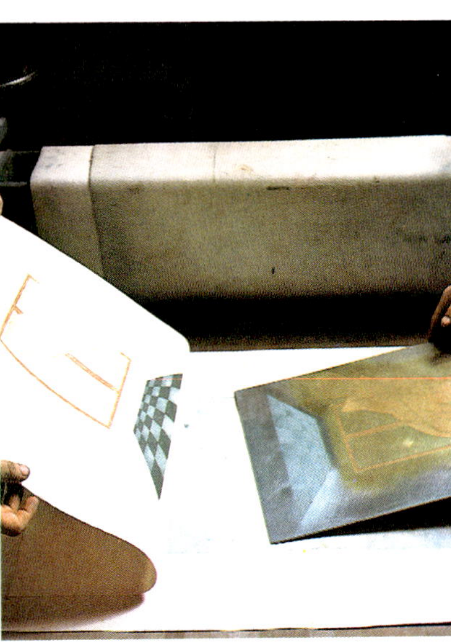

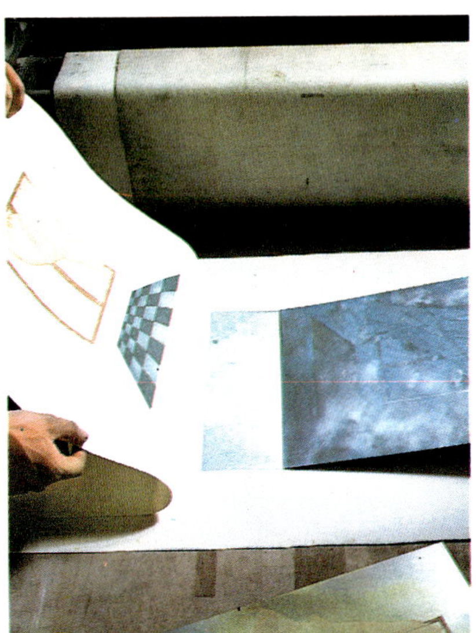

24
Now place plate 1, which has been covered in ink, in the same place as plate 2, and print the third colour.

The Iris print

The use of a number of colours can be applied in innumerable ways in graphic art. It can be used both in figurative designs and in abstract compositions. The results can be achieved in a number of different ways using different techniques and one or more metal plates.

The roller can be used on a single plate or on a number of different ones, and this illustrates the different possible applications of the technique. The printing paper should be as dry as possible; it should be even more thoroughly dried than usual between sheets of blotting paper. If the steps described in the following exercise are followed carefully, the results will certainly be worthwhile.

The tools and materials used in this exercise are: a number of etched plates, paper to use as an underlay in the press, printing paper, blotting paper, an aerosol can of car bodywork varnish, rollers, parafin, meths, different coloured inks, cheesecloth, sellotape, a small rubber spatula, a pair of compasses, a fine brush, a small saw, various spatulas, files, and a bowl of water for soaking the printing paper.

1
All the tools and materials required.

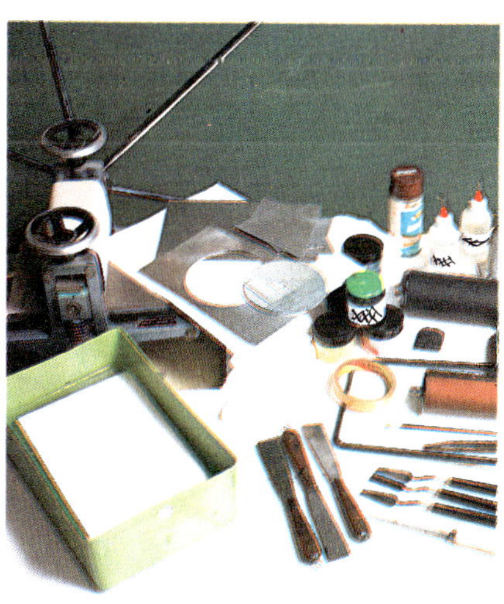

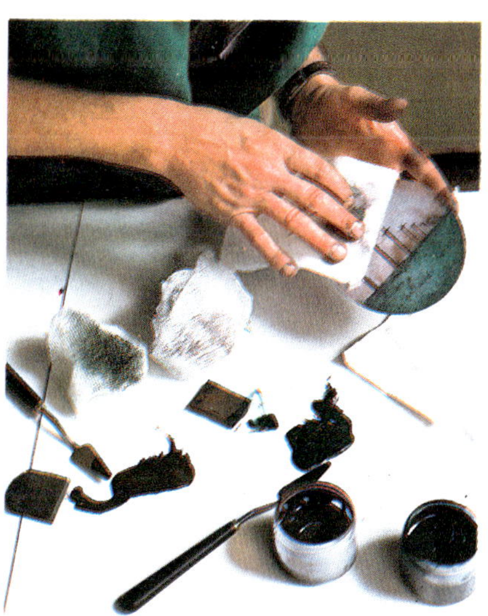

2
A circular etched plate is covered with a layer of ink. The plate in the example depicts a landscape. A number of different colours are used; in this example, green and a dark colour.

3

In this example 'transparents' are used; these are made by mixing one part of coloured ink with three parts of transparent (a colourless ink varnish).

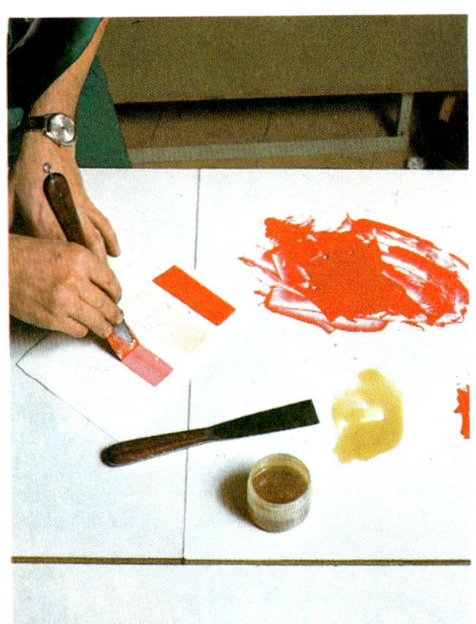

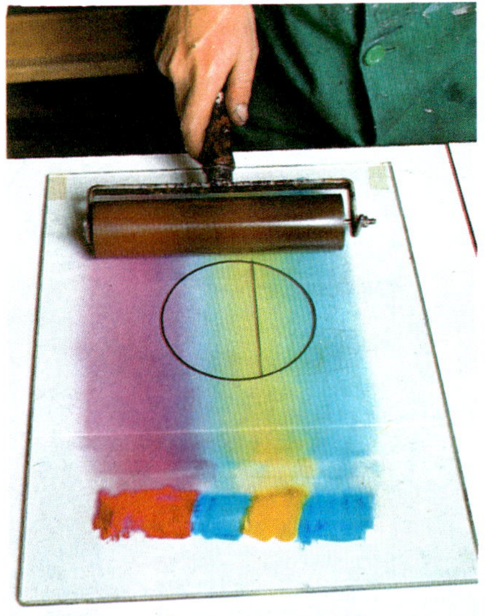

4

The colours are painted onto the glass in parallel lines. Roll out the ink. The circumference and pattern of the plate that is to be covered in ink is shown beneath the glass plate.

5

Determine the position of the colours on the roller vis-à-vis the plate. Then pass the roller over the plate.

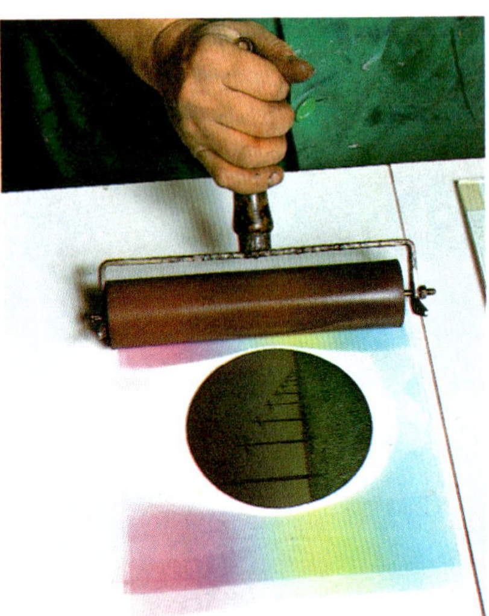

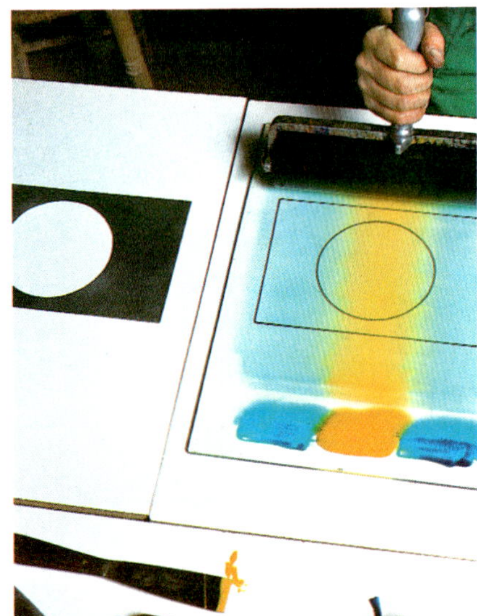

6

Take the colours for the second plate. Pass the roller over the plate.

7

Combine the two parts of the plate on the press.

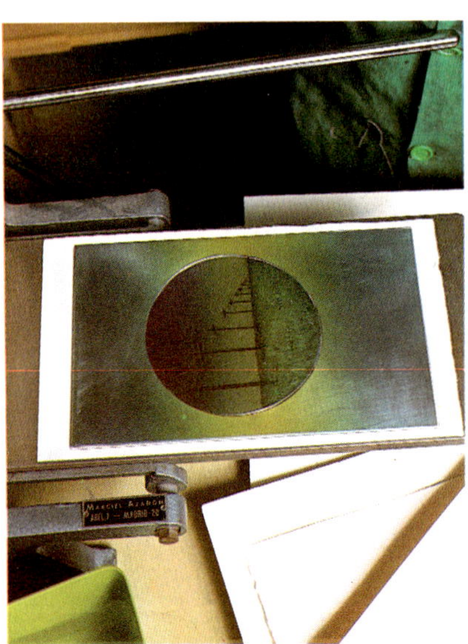

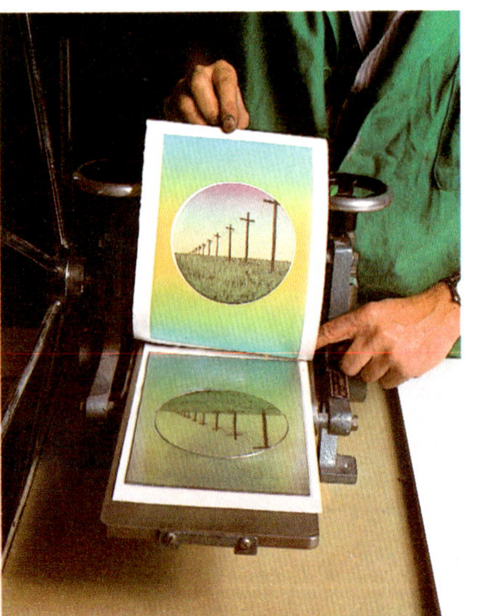

8

Make the print.

Hayter's technique

When Hayter founded his famous 'Atelier 17' in Paris in 1927, his characteristic graphic technique was adopted throughout Europe. This consists of applying various printing techniques with one or more metal plates, and using a number of different colours.
Originally it was described as the method of the hard and soft roller, but now the technique is known by the name of its creator, Hayter. The hard and soft rollers are used to cover the etched plate with a layer of ink at different levels.
This results in an uneven layer of ink and a large number of colour contrasts. To use Hayter's technique you must first etch a metal plate with one or more designs and different depths of relief.
Then one or more coloured inks are applied. The following tools and materials are needed for this technique: a press, a soft roller, a hard roller, small rollers, an etched plate, different coloured inks, vaseline, nitric acid, newspaper, cheesecloth, linseed oil, a number of glass plates, printing paper, blotting paper and a tray.

1
All the tools and materials required.

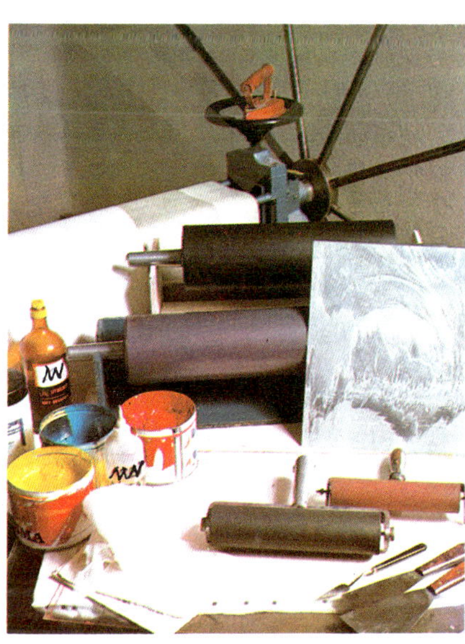

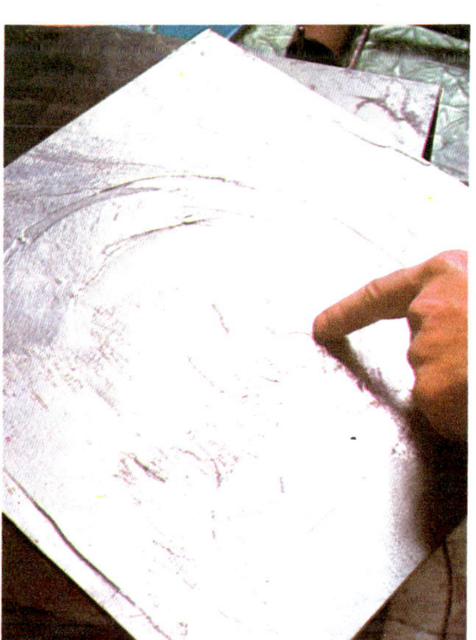

2
The plate, which has been etched (aquatint technique) using different depths of relief so that it can be used for Hayter's technique.

3
With the roller, spread an even layer of ink over the plate.

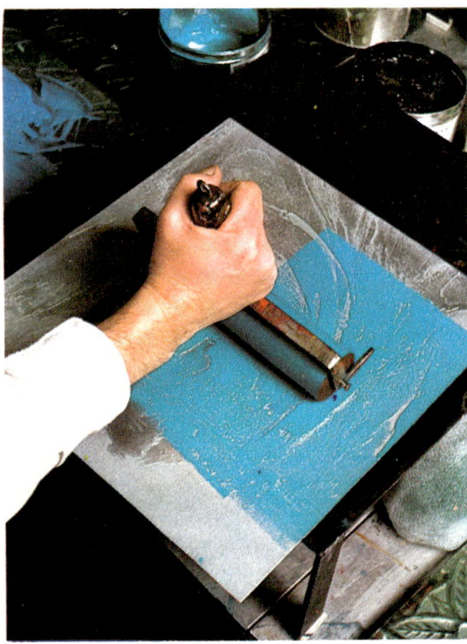

4
Rub the ink into the deepest parts of the plate with a piece of cheesecloth.

5
Remove the excess ink from the plate with a clean piece of cheesecloth.

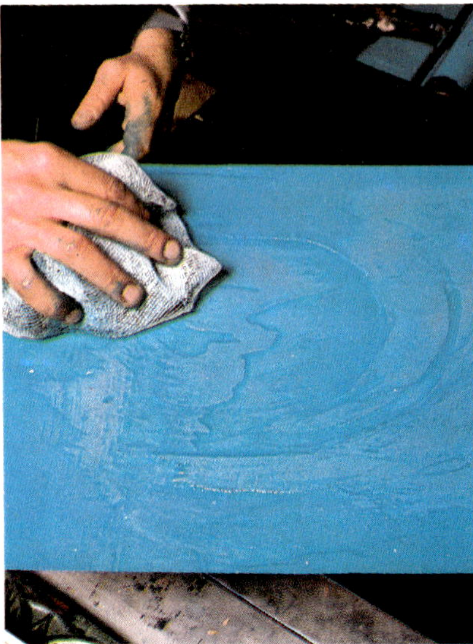

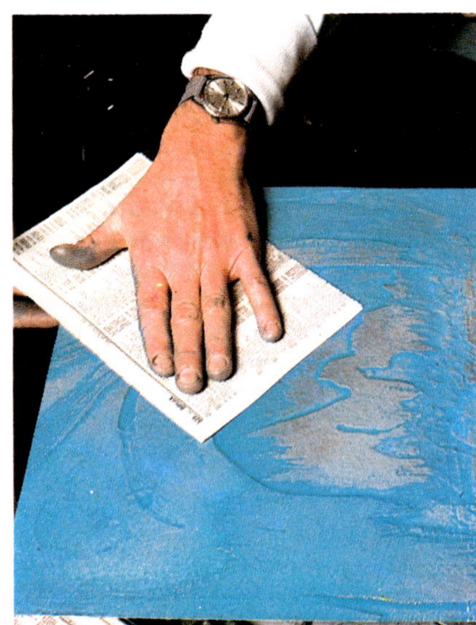

6
Clean the plate again by lightly wiping it with a piece of newspaper.

7
Place the plate in the middle of the press and pass it through the press with a lot of pressure.

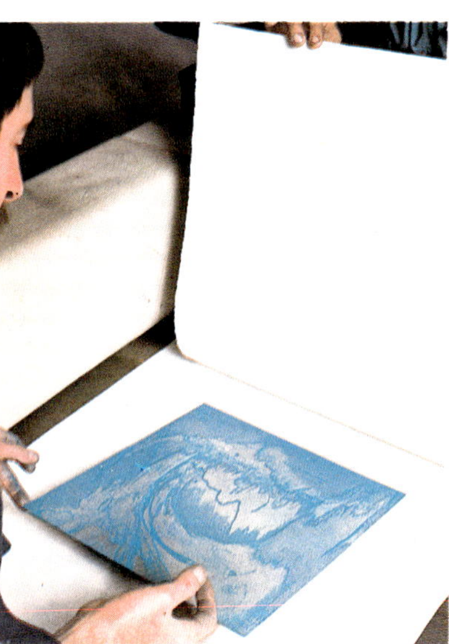

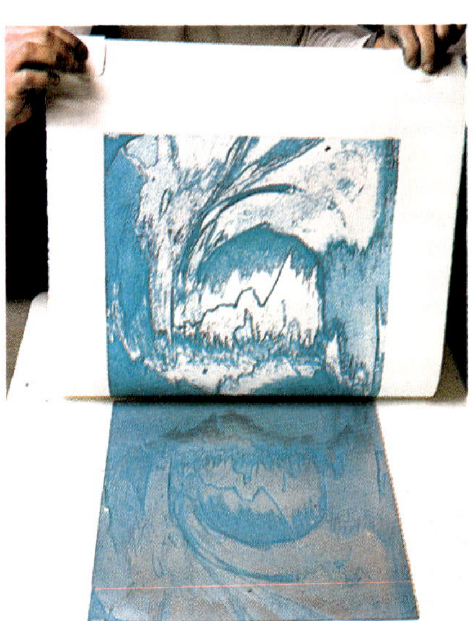

8
Remove the paper and the plate from the press.

9

Cover the plate with another layer of ink and again clean it with a piece of cheesecloth and some newspaper. Now different coloured inks can be applied with a roller.

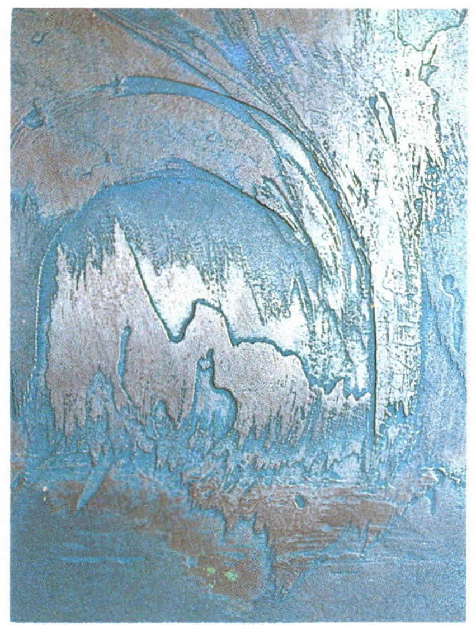

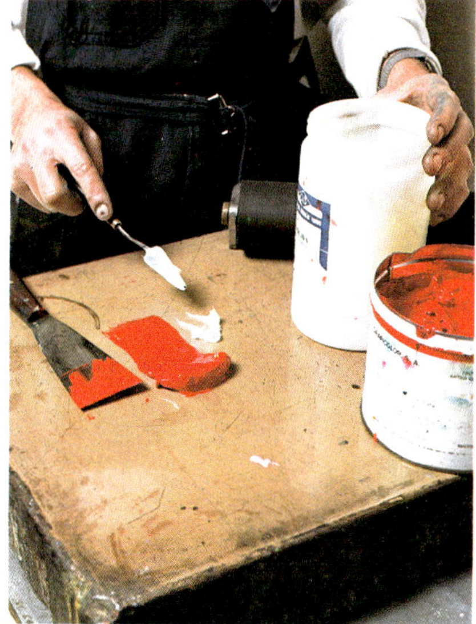

10

Add a little vaseline to the ink to make it more liquid so that it does not dry up.

11

Roll out the ink, which is now thinner, so that the roller is completely covered with ink.

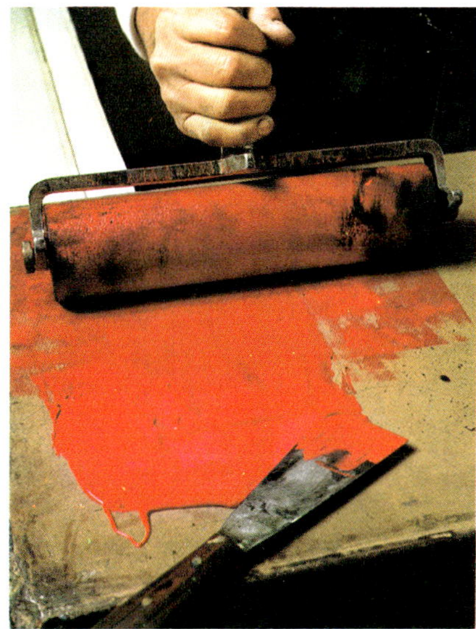

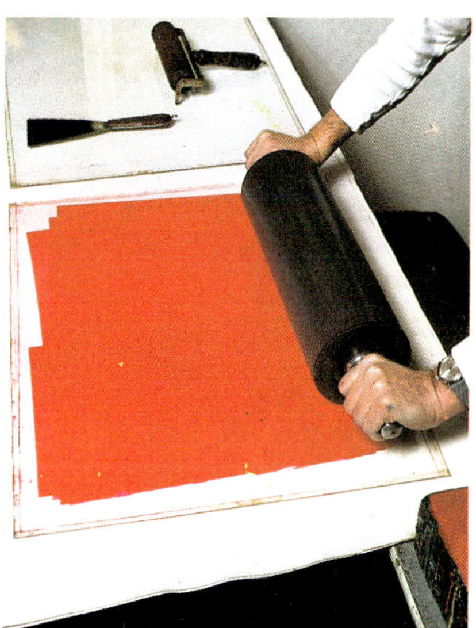

12

Apply a thin layer of ink on the last plate. The soft roller is then passed over the glass plate so that it is evenly covered with ink.

13

Add a small quantity of linseed oil to the ink for the hard roller.

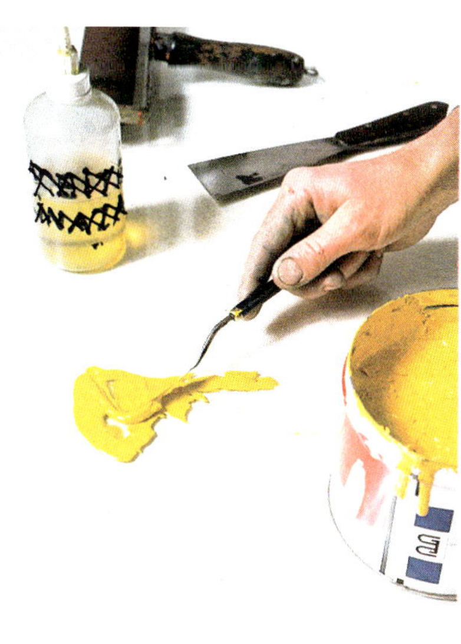

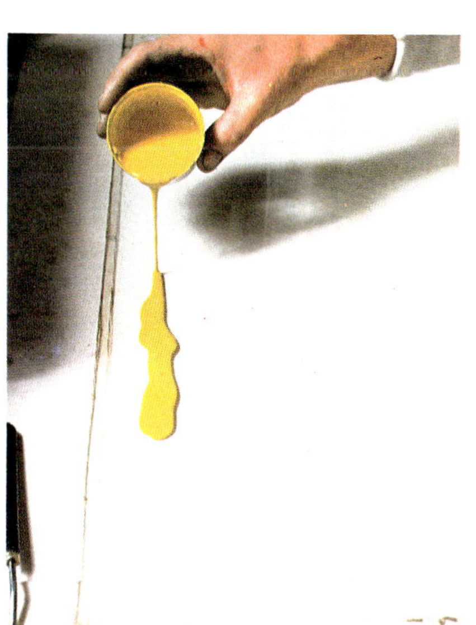

14

Pour the ink, which is now very liquid (see photograph) onto one side of the glass plate.

15

Now apply a thin even layer of ink to the glass plate and then cover the roller with ink. The plate can now be covered with ink, using the yellow first.

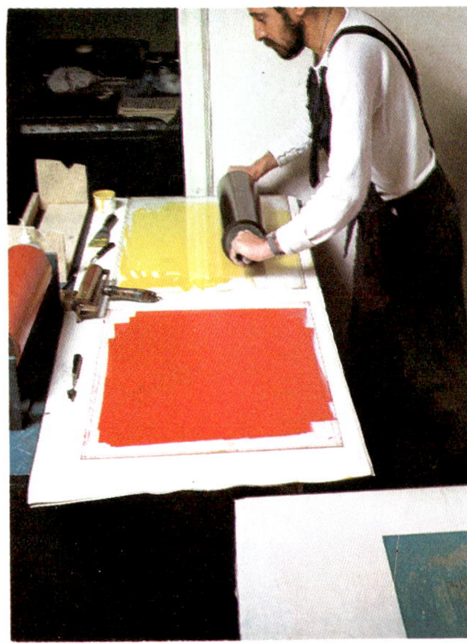

16

The zinc plate is placed on a wooden board covered with a thin layer of rubber. Pass the roller evenly over the plate a number of times.

17

The raised parts of the plate are now covered with ink. Now go over the plate again with a soft roller using more pressure so that the raised and deeper parts are also covered with ink.

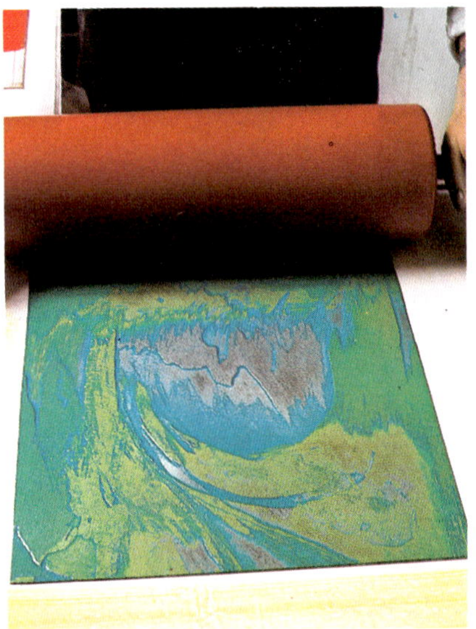

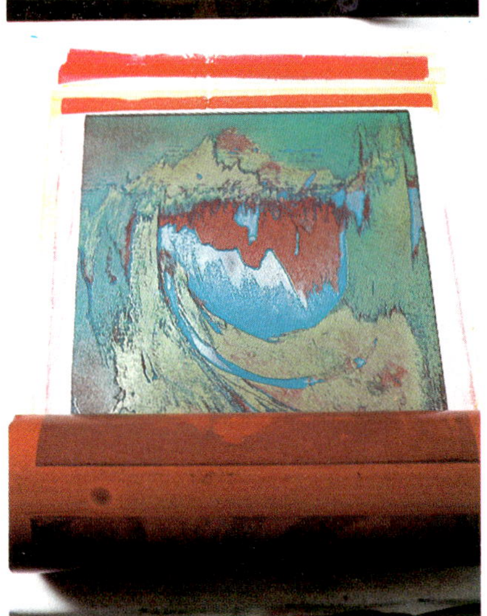

18

The red ink has penetrated the deeper parts of the plate (see photograph).

19

Examine the plate carefully before making a print.

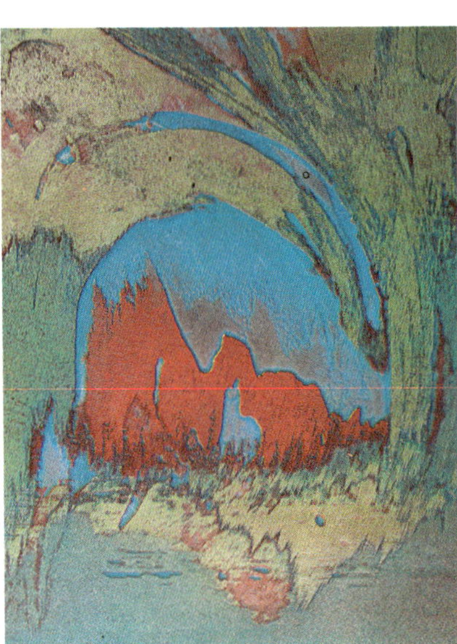

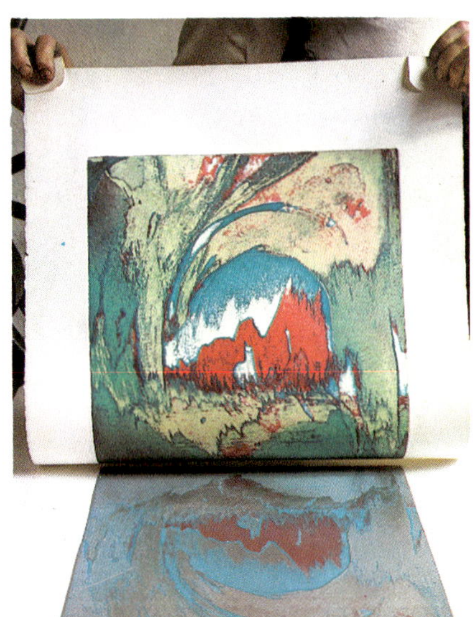

20

Complete the printing process by passing the plate, covered with a sheet of printing paper, through the press.

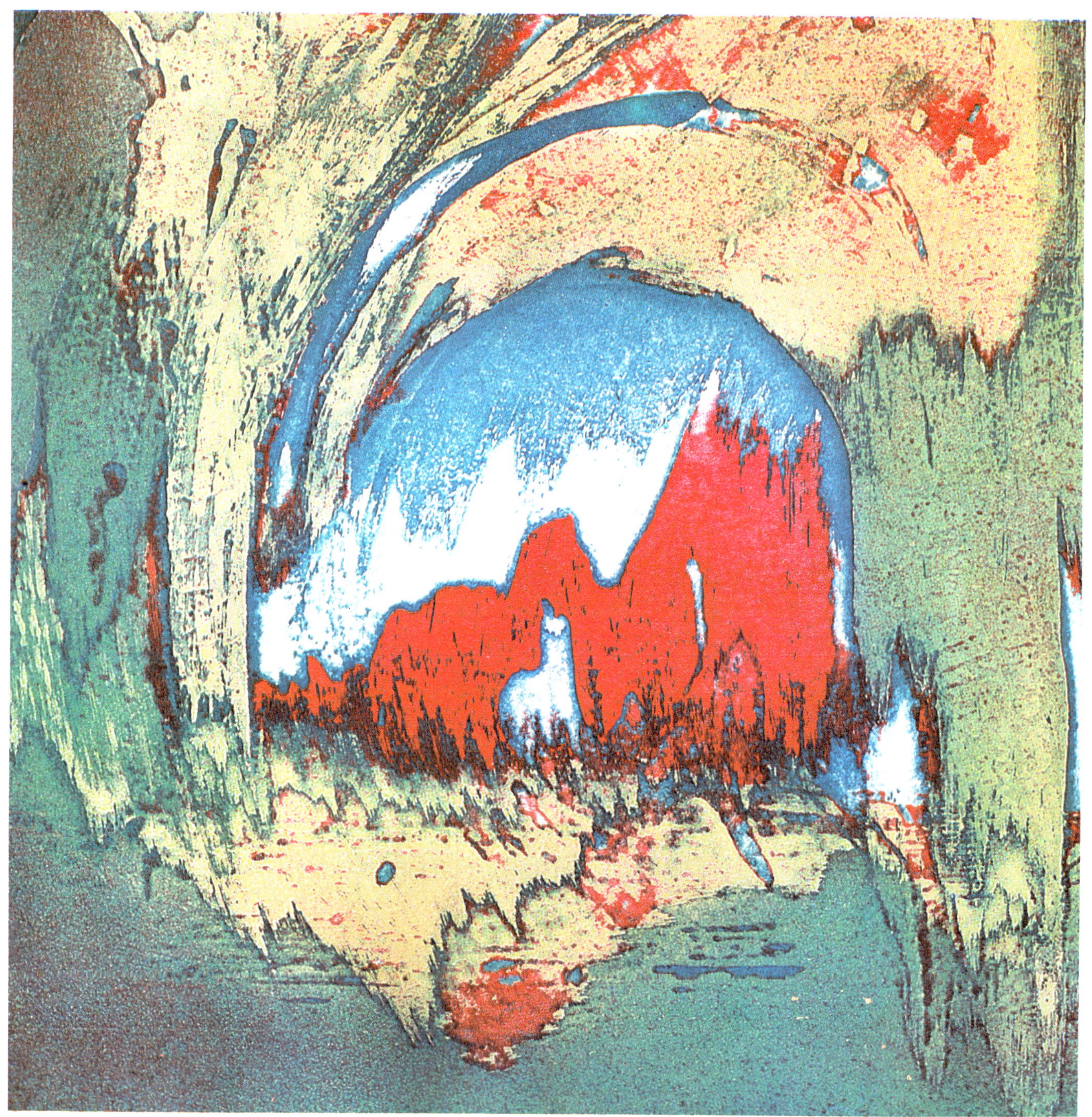

This print, showing many contrasting colours, was made from a zinc plate using Hayter's technique.